CLEMSON HANDBOOK

Stories, Stats and Stuff About Tiger™ Football

By Luther Gaillard

Printed in the United States of America by
Mennonite Press, Inc.

ISBN 1-880652-84-6

PHOTO CREDITS All photographs were supplied
by Clemson University.

ACKNOWLEDGMENTS

What an interesting trip down the historical path of Clemson football, and such a privilege to have been a part of this project. So many people were involved in the completion of *Clemson Handbook: Stories, Stats and Stuff About Tiger Football*. Without their help this book would not have been possible. Our thanks are due to MeLinda Via of Midwest Sports Publications, who glued everything together. Jeff Pulaski, an artist of immense talent, brought this attractive book to life. Jeff designed the cover and his work is woven throughout the pages of this inviting book.

Dr. Harold Vigodsky, a lifelong Clemson fan and Clemson archives expert, cannot be thanked enough. Vigodsky tirelessly pored over the copy, attending to every detail. He also "wrote the book" on the trivia quiz questions and answers, and very well may hold more fingertip information in his head on Clemson football than the best of Clemson trivia experts.

At Clemson University, assistant athletic director/sports information director Tim Bourret opened the doors to his office and staff. Their assistance was invaluable and always cheerful. Associate SIDs Sammy Blackman and Jessica Reo were tremendous in suggesting story possibilities and in providing persons instrumental in the development of stories. Meredith Merritt was tireless in her efforts digging through files. Also, thanks to Athletic Director Bobby Robinson.

No book about Clemson University football, basketball, baseball or any other varsity sport would be complete without the assistance and guidance of the legendary Bob Bradley, SID emeritus. His knowledge of the university's varsity sports programs is extensive. Bradley has provided more off-the-cuff stories and other colorful events over his 50 years in the school's athletic office than any one person. Retired for seven years, he still maintains daily hours at the office answering questions and keeping up with many of the statistics.

— *L.G.*

To my children, Paige, Rhys, Andrew, Julia and Lukas.

And to Coach Howard, whose passing left a void in many Clemson hearts; and to Anna Howard, who joined her husband shortly after his death.

Also to Bob Bradley, who for more than 30 years put up with sportswriters such as myself and other scribes along the way. He is a rock in his own right, and a friend in the truest sense of the word.

And to Dr. Harold Vigodsky, whose eagle-eye proof-reading and trivia expertise elevated the literary level of this project. Thanks, Doc.

— L.G.

INTRODUCTION

Luther Gaillard

Any self-respecting Clemson Tiger fan worth his or her stripes swells with the deepest pride at the strains of "Tiger Rag," the university's athletic anthem. "Tiger Rag" is more than music. For Clemson fans it's their pledge of allegiance; it's a call to arms, a rallying around the flag — the Tiger Paw flag and its precious orange and white colors.

Clemson University is a land grant institution devoted to textiles and the mechanical sciences — and football, which is sopping with tradition from early legends like Walter Riggs, John Heisman, Josh Cody and Jess Neely, on to Frank Howard and Danny Ford.

The genesis of this book is not to dot every "i" or to cross every "t" but rather to bring to you, the reader, some of the color, the splendor, the presence of Clemson football and the men who took it from a curious pastime to a passion of glory, pain and conquest.

Clemson's football crowning glory came in the 1982 Orange Bowl when the No. 1-ranked, but underdog, Tigers stunned Nebraska, 22-15, to complete a clean sweep of the season and win the national championship. That storybook year is chronicled within the pages of this book, but there is more. The stories included here are drawn from many of the figures who carved out places in the hearts of Clemson fans.

Jeff Bostic, who played center in the 1970s for the Tigers and went on to play four Super Bowls and won three Super Bowl rings with the Washington Redskins, said that "no school does a finer job of bringing back former players than Clemson. Over the years, we have come back to share in what this school meant to us, and Clemson works very hard showing us that they haven't forgotten and never will. Many of the players whose names most people recognize come back for more than football games. We come back for Lettermen functions, we come back for reunions and we do what we can to keep the spirit of Clemson alive and healthy."

The idea is that this book, too, will also keep the spirit of Clemson alive and healthy.

TABLE OF CONTENTS

Influences

THE EARLY YEARS

Most seasoned Clemson football fans know that Walter Riggs, not Frank Howard, is the father of Clemson University football. Riggs, an engineering professor brought a keen interest in the sport to the South Carolina school in 1896, when he accepted a teaching post there. At the time, Riggs was highly qualified for the extracurricular activity because he was one of only two people on campus to have ever seen a football game.

Frank Thompkins, who played in the backfield on Riggs' first team, was the other. A modest beginning, to be sure.

And, so it was that on September 30, 1896, a small gathering of curious folks gathered in one of the school's military barracks to hash out the feasibility of organizing a football association. The group appointed a committee of three to seek Riggs' help and make him the coach.

By October 28, the team had a few practices under its belt and the school's first official football game was played in Greenville against Furman. When Clemson's players got their first look at the Furman field, it was a

Action from the Tigers' early days.

In 1896, Clemson's football players practiced on a grassy quadrangle next to Tillman Hall, the first campus building.

first look at an official regulation field for most of them. They had done their practicing on a grassy quadrangle next to Tillman Hall.

Inspired by the onset of history, Clemson earned a 14-6 win that afternoon, then dropped a 12-6 decision to South Carolina in November and closed the "season" with a 16-0 win over Wofford College. Riggs stepped aside after the Tigers' inaugural season, but wasn't entirely removed from the school's athletics because he was handling money matters and engaging contracts with other schools, even though he never was entitled as athletic director.

However, Riggs was responsible for many things that became trademark for the Tigers over the years. When he left Auburn University, Riggs brought the orange and purple colors to Clemson's football program, as well as the nickname Tigers — the same colors and mascot nickname that Auburn had been using.

In the fall of 1899, Riggs answered the call to coach the Tigers once more because the football association was low on money and could not afford to hire a new coach. Riggs coached the Tigers to a 4-2 record, closing the season with three straight wins over South Carolina, N.C. State and Georgia Tech. Clemson also beat Davidson but lost to Georgia and Auburn.

Riggs had distinguished himself at Auburn in athletics and letters, graduating with top honors, and was assistant to the Auburn president until his appointment at Clemson four years later. On March 7, 1911, Riggs assumed the presidency of Clemson College. By 1915, he had helped forge a football stadium and other athletic facilities. Riggs Field, currently home of the school's varsity soccer program, is named after the man who introduced varsity football to the military institution.

Dr. Walter Merritt Riggs brought football to Clemson. He also brought the school's colors and mascot – which he copied from Auburn.

John Heisman, who in 1903 guided the Tigers to their first bowl game, took Clemson from an unknown to a regional power.

TIGERS QUIZ

1. Who was the Clemson assistant football coach who coached the Tiger baseball team to the first ever ACC baseball championship?

JOHN HEISMAN (1900-1903) The man for whom the most treasured trophy in college football is named traces his roots to Clemson football. After W.M. Williams coached the Tigers for a season in 1897, in which Clemson won two games and lost two, the Tigers still found a way to win the state championship, the first of many such titles. In 1898, John Penton came along and guided Clemson to a 3-1 season and another state championship. Penton had played football at Auburn and was coached by Heisman.

Heisman, one of the most recognizable names in football, turned Clemson into a southern powerhouse from a virtual unknown. He earned a law degree from Brown University while playing center on the school's football team. By the fall of 1889, Heisman moved on to the University of Pennsylvania and lettered in football there as well.

Coincidentally, Riggs, while still a professor at Auburn, was in charge of finding a coach. Riggs wrote to a colleague at the University of Pennsylvania asking his friend to suggest a suitable coach. The Penn man recommended J.W. Heisman. Riggs graciously thanked his colleague and sought out this Heisman, whom he found several weeks later raising tomatoes in Texas. Heisman, a serious man, almost smiled when Riggs approached him about returning to Auburn and coaching football. Having dropped virtually all of his money in the tomato venture, Heisman jumped at the chance to coach at Auburn University for the princely sum of $500 annually.

After his stint at Auburn, Heisman coached at Clemson. His career spanned a total of 36 years, including stops at Akron, Auburn, Clemson, Georgia Tech, Penn, Washington & Jefferson and Rice University. Heisman was well ahead of his time, one of the game's principal innovators. He invented the "hidden ball" trick, the double lateral and the "flea flicker."

Heisman also pioneered the forward pass, reasoning that such a ploy would "scatter the mob." He came to football seriously at a time when the game was ripe for change. In the beginning, the center would roll, or more likely, wobble, the football on the ground to the tailback, or quarterback, who would scramble to scoop the ball up and then weigh his options. Finding no rules to the contrary, Heisman ordered his center to "snap" the ball in the air to the tailback, and also had the tailback bark out the word "hike" when he was ready to receive the snap.

It is a little known fact that Heisman guided Clemson to its first "bowl game" in November of 1903, a meeting that pitted the Tigers and Cumberland College for the

Championship of the South at Montgomery, Ala. Cumberland had beaten Auburn, Alabama and Vanderbilt and was a heavy favorite to skin the Tigers. Despite the odds, Clemson dueled Cumberland to an 11-11 tie. Later, in 1916 when he was coaching at Georgia Tech, Heisman issued Cumberland the worst whipping in football ranks, 222-0.

In his short stint at Clemson, Heisman forged a 19-3-2 record and his .833 winning percentage remains the best in Clemson history.

One of the greatest stories in college football belongs to Heisman. In 1902, Georgia Tech was a heavy favorite to beat the Tigers, but Heisman had a plan. He recruited a bunch of students from campus to pose as players and sent them to Atlanta. The impostors showed up at all the lively nightspots, bragging about how they were going to whip Georgia Tech on Saturday.

Word got back to the Tech campus that Clemson was just a bunch of scarecrows and would be fortunate to leave Grant Field in one piece. Meanwhile, Heisman was holed up on the outskirts of Atlanta with the genuine football team. The Tigers stunned the favored Jackets, 44-5, and Tech learned an expensive lesson in the process.

Shack Shealy, the only Clemson player to later coach the Tigers, posted victories against the team's biggest and best opponents.

SHACK SHEALY (1904) Shealy holds the distinction of being the only Clemson player to have coached his alma mater's varsity football team. He lettered four years at Clemson from 1896 through 1899. He also played two years at Iowa State. As a four-year starter at right guard, end and in the backfield, Shealy distinguished himself. In his only year as coach, Shealy posted a 3-3-1 record. His three wins were impressive, over Alabama, Georgia and Tennessee.

ED COCHEMS (1905) Cochems played football at the University of Wisconsin at the turn of the century. He scored four touchdowns against Notre Dame, and had a 100-yard kickoff return against Chicago. As a coach, he logged a 3-2-1 record in his one season at Clemson and went to St. Louis University as football coach and athletic director. Cochems is also credited with perfecting the forward pass, teaching his players to throw a spiral pass, as opposed to the standard end-over-end lob.

Before Ed Cochems coached at Clemson, he played at Wisconsin.

BOB WILLIAMS (1906, 1909, 1913-1915) Williams not only coached at Clemson in three separate stints, he is still likely the only coach in the country to coach at two archrival schools — Clemson and South Carolina. Williams coached first at the University of South Carolina, leading the Gamecocks to a 6-1 record in 1902 and an 8-2 record in 1903. While at USC, Williams shocked a heavily-favored Clemson team coached by John Heisman, 12-6, in 1902 — perhaps one of the principal reasons he was eventually lured to the Clemson campus. He left Clemson in 1915 to practice law in Roanoke, Va., and also served as that city's mayor. He recorded a 21-14-6 record over his five years at Clemson.

FRANK SHAUGHNESSY (1907) Shaughnessy came to Clemson by way of Notre Dame. He spent a year there after graduation, coaching the Irish baseball team. Eventually, Shaughnessy played for Washington and the Philadelphia A's. When he arrived at Clemson, Shaughnessy coached the baseball team for two years, and was head football coach in 1907.

Frank Shaughnessy, a Notre Dame graduate, coached baseball before tackling the football job.

As a player, Shaughnessy scored the only touchdown against Kansas in a 24-5 loss to the Jayhawks, a 107-yard run that set a record that stands at Notre Dame for the longest scoring run. In those days, the football field was 110 yards long and touchdowns accounted for five points.

FRANK DOBSON (1910-12) Dobson was the first Clemson football coach to be offered a contract for more than one year. Riggs, president of Clemson's Athletic Association, felt it unfair to continue shuffling coaches year after year. Dobson coached football, basketball and baseball at Clemson. He became the first basketball coach, leading Clemson to its only undefeated season in school history, 4-0 in the 1911-12 season.

THE MIDDLE YEARS

EDWARD DONAHUE (1917-20) Donahue was reputed to be one of the most organized men in the country. During the 1918-19 school year, he was head coach of the football, basketball, baseball and track teams.

E.J. STEWART (1921-22) Stewart only spent a couple of years at Clemson, but has a long legacy of coaching. In addition to football, he also coached baseball and track between spring football practice sessions. After a mediocre first season (1-6-2) in football, Stewart improved to 5-4 in '22, but turned to coaching track the next two years.

Before moving to Clemson, Stewart coached at Nebraska and the University of Texas. At Nebraska, Stewart's combined record with the Cornhuskers was 11-4, and the Huskers won the Missouri Valley Conference title both seasons After leaving Nebraska, Stewart entered the automobile business as president and treasurer of the Stewart Motor Company. After a short stint in the auto industry, and for purely economic reasons, Stewart ducked back into coaching.

Besides coaching at Clemson, E.J. "Doc" Stewart spent time at Nebraska and Texas.

BUD SAUNDERS (1923-26) Saunders received a law degree from Missouri, excelling in football and basketball as well. He was restricted to only two varsity sports at Missouri because of a rule forbidding an athlete from participating in more than two sports.

Before landing at Clemson, Saunders coached at Knox College. He coached the Tigers for four seasons. He also coached the basketball team in 1924 and 1925. His best football season was a 5-2-1 record in 1923, a year in which the Tigers beat South Carolina, but tied Auburn in the season opener.

JOSH CODY (1927-30) Cody was known as "Big Man" because he was, and always will be, a favorite of lifelong Clemson fans. He stood 6-2 and weighed 220 pounds. He led Clemson to four straight victories over South Carolina, and that is exactly the type of achievement that will endear Clemson fans to almost any football coach.

Even though his stay was short, Josh Cody was one of the more popular coaches among players and fans.

Cody indeed was one of Clemson's more popular football coaches. During his tenure, Cody was so highly received by Clemson faithful that he was presented a new automobile, an unheard of gift at the time. But his popularity was widespread, for he enchanted Clemson fans wherever he traveled. Cody simply was known as a "square shooter," from his players to his peers.

In his final season at the Clemson helm, the Tigers finished 8-2. Cody also coached the basketball team for five years, finishing with a 16-9 mark in 1930.

JESS NEELY (1931-39) Neely is another Clemson legend. Clemson went to its first bowl game under Neely,

The 1931 coaching staff got together in 1980 when Rice played at Clemson. From left to right are Bob Jones, Frank Howard, Joe Davis and Jess Neely. Neely, the Tigers' coach for nine years, was Rice's coach for 27 years. Davis served as his assistant at Rice, too. Howard became head coach at Clemson, a post he held for 30 years, and had Jones as an assistant all that time.

Jess Neely is a member of the College Football Hall of Fame.

beating heavily-favored Boston College in the 1940 Cotton Bowl, 6-3. Neely came to Clemson in 1931 and later recruited Banks McFadden. McFadden, an All-American in football and basketball, took Clemson to another level of competition. By 1938, Neely, with McFadden, took Clemson to a second place finish in the Southern Conference (forerunner of the ACC). In 1939, Clemson won a trip to Dallas and the Cotton Bowl and Neely left the next spring to coach at Rice University. He later was inducted in the College Football Hall of Fame.

FRANK HOWARD (1940-69) See Chapter 2.

THE MODERN YEARS

HOOTIE INGRAM (1970-72) Hootie Ingram didn't discover the Blowfish and was never a member of the world renown rock group that attended the University of South Carolina. However, Ingram is best remembered for two things in his short stint as Clemson football boss — the three-yards-and-a-cloud-of-dust offense and the Tiger Paw emblem that distinguishes the Tigers today, 26 years hence. Just before Ingram came to Clemson's football program from the University of Alabama, Clemson unveiled the Tiger Paw on its uniforms.

There are two lasting contributions from Ingram's short stint with the Tigers: the three-yards-and-a-cloud-of-dust offense and the Tiger Paw emblem.

Ingram's best year at Clemson was hardly scintillating. He got off to a 3-8 start in '70 after inheriting the shoes that virtually no one could fill. His best season, 1971, was 5-6 and good for second place in the ACC. But a season of 4-7 gave Ingram an opportunity to resign quietly. Ingram served as athletic director at Alabama until his retirement in the mid-1990s.

JIMMY "RED" PARKER (1973-76)
When Parker left The Citadel to take the football job at Clemson, he said that coaching the Tigers was like "dying and going to heaven." Why anybody would want to go anywhere else to coach was beyond Parker's reasoning, and he might have stayed a lifetime at Clemson had things not turned sour.

Parker's task was plain and simple: bring Clemson football back to the heights it enjoyed under Howard and others before him. He certainly had turned Citadel's Bulldogs into a powerhouse at a time when attending military institutions was hardly the popular thing to do.

Parker lured Steve Fuller of Spartanburg into signing with Clemson, and indeed, Fuller's presence made all the difference in the world for Clemson football. The Tigers were 7-4 in 1974, including an undefeated mark at home.

The program was certainly on a sharp rise, but in 1976, with coaches out on recruiting assignments, the tide turned for Parker. He was abruptly fired after seasons of 2-9 and 3-6-2 in 1975 and 1976. Parker claimed that he was "knifed in the back" and made a bitter retreat.

CHARLEY PELL (1977-78) Pell was Red Parker's top assistant, and landed the head coaching job shortly after Parker was dismissed. The Tigers came out of their swoon in 1977, propelled by an 8-2-1 record that landed the Tigers a berth in the Gator Bowl, where Pittsburgh administered a thorough 34-3 whipping. Still, Clemson found itself 19th nationally in the final rankings.

Pell's initial season at Clemson was labeled as college football's "Cinderella" story. That being the case, Pell's '78 season might well be tagged as college football's "Bizarre" story. After guiding the Tigers to a 10-1 regular season finish (losing only to Georgia, 12-0), Pell stunned football fans by announcing that he was leaving Clemson to coach the University of Florida football program. The news of his departure was especially shocking to Clemson fans, for newspaper and television/radio accounts in the weeks leading up to the speculation that he was rumored to be leaving were brushed aside by Pell as false and media hype.

Nevertheless, Pell was off to Florida, leaving behind an 18-4-1 record, to coach at a university that he said would give him a shot at "winning the national championship."

The sting was tremendous for Clemson fans, but they got over it. Pell not only never won a national championship, he got in some really hot water with the NCAA and was forced out at Florida.

DANNY FORD (1979-89) Ford isn't linked genetically to Frank Howard, as far as we know. But, if ever a college had a successful father-son act in its coaching ranks, Clemson has had at least one. When Charley Pell went south, Ford, a slender, virtually unknown offensive line coach who had followed Pell to Clemson several years earlier, was singled out to take Pell's place as head coach.

The irony was thick. The school had settled on a young Frank Howard to lead its football program. Howard was a lineman at the University of Alabama; Ford was a lineman at the University of Alabama. Howard found himself a home at Clemson and stayed; Ford found a way to Clemson and stayed 11 years.

Red Parker is credited with bringing Steve Fuller to Clemson, but Parker left the Tiger program with bad feelings.

In his first season as head coach, Charley Pell took Clemson to the Gator Bowl and a No. 19 finish in the national polls. He shocked Tiger fans when he left Clemson for Florida after just two seasons at the helm. Those fans felt a little better when Pell ran into NCAA trouble with the Gators.

Danny Ford, who moved on to the head coaching job at Arkansas, left Clemson after taking the Tigers to eight bowl games, six of which they won.

2. Who are the only two players to captain the Tiger football team three different seasons?

Howard talked country and was a great speechmaker; Ford talked country and was a master speechmaker, too.

Howard won; Ford won.

When Howard retired, fans mourned; when Ford announced he was leaving Clemson (under fire), fans rebelled against the school's administration.

Clemson's love affair with Ford began when he was named head coach and tabbed to lead Clemson against Ohio State in the Gator Bowl. In tribute to Ford being named head coach, and in defiance of Pell leaving the school, Clemson backers presented their new coach with a new Jaguar. Ford motivated the Tigers to a 17-15 win in a game that also brought the Woody Hayes' era to an abrupt, controversial end. Hayes punched a Clemson player who had been forced out-of-bounds after intercepting a pass that sealed the Buckeyes' fate.

Ford kept the Tigers on the winning track in his initial season as football boss, finishing 8-4. In 1980 Ford's team had to beat South Carolina to avoid a losing season. Ford had been under considerable fire by fans, media and even some university personnel. He considering quitting before the USC game, but was talked out of it by close associates. The 27-6 win over South Carolina that year became landmark for Clemson fans, for Ford was embittered by the assaults from inside the university community as well as from longtime fans who also turned on him.

A year later, Ford propelled the Tigers to a 12-0 season, and a 22-15 upset of No. 3-ranked Nebraska in the Orange Bowl for the national championship. Clemson posted consecutive 9-1-1 seasons after that national title, finishing in the Top 12 both seasons.

The Tigers won three straight ACC championships between 1986-88, and closed his career at Clemson with a 27-7 win over West Virginia in the Gator Bowl, his sixth bowl win in eight appearances, and his fourth bowl appearance in succession — all wins.

Ford still ranks as the youngest coach to win the national championship, at the age of 33. He coached 26 first-team All-Americans. Forty-two of his players were drafted by the NFL. In addition, eight of his former players won Super Bowl Championship rings.

Ford left Clemson in 1989 after battling school administrators on several issues. He left coaching for two years but returned to the profession, and in 1996 he was still the head football coach at the University of Arkansas. Although Ford will not talk publicly about the specifics surrounding his resignation, he visits the Clemson area frequently.

KEN HATFIELD (1990-93) By historical accounts, Hatfield's reign as Clemson football coach was successful. He led

Ken Hatfield, posing here with racing legend Richard Petty, took the Tigers to three Top 25 finishes in his four seasons.

the Tigers to a 32-13-1 record in his four years at the helm, and took the Tigers to three bowl games. The problem was chemistry.

It was the fans, perhaps not enough of them to call a majority, who had the problem. They were sick of Hatfield before he ever set foot on Clemson property. Looking back, it might have been anybody that Clemson fans would have lashed out at. They wanted Danny Ford at the helm, and students as well as other orange faithful, led a more-or-less peaceful, but loud, demonstration outside the university president's campus home on the day of Hatfield's presentation as head coach.

Earlier in the day, Frank Howard waved his cane at a small, angry mob of people who attempted to prevent Hatfield from entering the stadium where the press conference announcing his arrival was about to begin.

To say that Hatfield was never accepted by Clemson's faithful is true, by and large. The stadium, although rarely filled to capacity during that era, was replete with ticket holders biding their time until they could stand up and yell their objections to the coach they loved to loathe.

It didn't matter that Hatfield was just the eighth coach in the previous 13 years to take a Clemson team to a Top 10 finish. He also led the 1991 and 1993 teams to Top 25 rankings.

It also didn't matter that Hatfield had led the Arkansas Razorbacks to back-to-back Southwest Conference championships, but he wasn't appreciated there, either.

After continually battling criticism from media and fans, Hatfield waved the white flag and resigned shortly after the 1993 season.

In 1996, Hatfield was the head coach at Rice University.

Ken Hatfield led Clemson to a 32-13-1 record in four years as the head coach. Clemson fans were so upset about the departure of Danny Ford that they gave Ken Hatfield a very cold welcome

The Howard Legacy

Frank Howard got off to a quick start, winning the Southern Conference championship in his first season at the helm. He finished his career with eight conference titles.

FRANK JAMES HOWARD (1909-1996) Frank Howard, who coached the Tigers from 1940 through 1969, will be forever known in Clemson circles as the man who brought Clemson football to the pinnacle, to national prominence, to respect; commanding pride despite its rural (and military) roots. Had the tobacco-spitting Howard not had all the confidence in himself, he might have been forced to look for coaching work elsewhere, for the school's athletic council was in session looking for a successor to the highly-regarded Jess Neely, who packed his bags to coach at Rice University.

Howard was at the nomination meeting, sitting in the back of the room where the council met, and when his name was submitted as the 16th successor to the head football job, Howard most surely became the only coach in history to second his own nomination. A brilliant move, for Clemson had itself a football coach for the next 29 years. You might as well say that those three decades marked the most colorful and poignant years of the school's love affair with the pigskin. Howard's wit was widespread and Clemson University reaped plenty of ink from his ability to seize the moment. Clemson fans became accustomed to reading about their Tigers on the front page of the sports section more often than not.

Howard's lines were funny, well-timed and often searing. They always made a point, and occasionally the Baron from Barlow Bend, Ala., would catch himself in a trap he had set. Once, when Clemson was in Atlanta to play Georgia Tech, a sportswriter from the *Atlanta Constitution* was assigned to do a story on Howard. Howard talked to the scribe at length and the next morning, at breakfast, turned to the sports page, instantly appalled.

What Howard read shocked him. The sports scribe had quoted Howard verbatim at a time when journalists were accustomed to cleaning up the speech of those they interviewed. Howard may not have been incensed, but he strode to a telephone, woke the newspaper's sports editor and said, "The next time you send somebody out to interview me, make sure you tell them to quote me in plain English." And then he hung up the telephone.

Howard had nothing in common with "plain English." To some university officials and fans, Howard came across as a hayseed. They felt he demeaned the Queen's English to the point that he compromised the school's integrity. Disturbed by this slight, Howard went to see a retired English professor who lived in town, and explained his dilemma with the school's high brass.

The retired professor listened to his plight, then asked how many speeches he gave a year on the university's behalf. Howard guessed that he spoke in front of assemblies on 200 to 300 occasions. The retired professor smiled, then said, "Well, coach, we've got six English professors over there who could deliver a message using correct English. But, if you want to keep going, you'd better stick with what you've been doing. Those six professors aren't asked to give a total of six talks a year among them."

Howard smiled, bowed and thanked the man, and banked check after check, flawed speech and all. Wherever he went to deliver a speech, Howard had audiences eating out of his hand. They loved him, and his southern Alabama twang.

As good as he was on stage, Howard was equally keen on the football field. When he took the football reins from Neely, Howard opened his career by winning the Southern Conference championship, the first of eight conference

General Bob Jones was assistant coach throughout Howard's tenure as head coach.

Howard, ACC Coach of the Year, proudly displays the ball symbolizing his 150th victory as head coach at Clemson during the 1966 season.

3. Who did Clemson play in its first game in history?

titles Howard brought to the school in his career.

His most successful season came in 1948 when the Tigers ran up an 11-0 record, the first perfect season since 1900 when John Heisman's team breezed to a 6-0 record. The Tigers were Southern Conference champs and beat Missouri, 24-23, in the Gator Bowl. Clemson finished the season ranked 11th nationally.

In 1950, Howard guided the Tigers to a 9-0-1 record and whipped Miami (Fla.), 15-14, in the Orange Bowl. That win gave Clemson 10th place in the final national rankings.

By the time he retired in 1969, Howard was the fifth winningest coach in the nation with 165 victories. He logged 96 wins as an ACC coach, which still stands as the third most in the conference, and he won six ACC titles (five outright and one co-championship), more than any other coach in the league, then or now. Howard took his teams to six bowl games, and 63 of his players were NFL draft picks.

Howard was a two-time ACC Coach of the Year. He coached 25 Academic All-Americans. He was inducted into the College Football Hall of Fame in 1989.

When Howard resigned, there were mixed feelings among Clemson's stalwart fans. Some felt they had betrayed the man, others felt his time had run out.

Howard even put his own retirement in perspective. He told audiences for years afterward that he retired for

Action from the 1952 game against Villanova. Howard's Tigers lost, 14-7.

health reasons: "The alumni got sick of me."

But Howard's memory is everlasting.

As long as there is a Clemson University, as long as the world spins on axis, Howard will live in the hearts and minds of Clemson's family, just as surely as footballs fly in the autumn of the year.

Frank Howard is Clemson football. He was the "rock" upon which the Tigers were solidified. There will never be a time when a Clemson football player doesn't run down the Memorial Stadium hill without swiping his hand over the Death Valley Rock that signifies sacred commitment to achievement, from Saturday to Saturday, from season to season. It's tradition. It's Howard.

In the nearly 60 years that Howard was a presence at Clemson University, he commanded attention though he seldom sought it. Over the years, the "boys" he turned into men most always made a point of seeking out their hard-driving coach, reliving a few memories and seeking his blessing, which was mostly a two-edged sword. But they loved it, and they loved him.

So, this is not so much a chronicle of a legend gone as it is a celebration of life as only he could have lived it. It is a tobacco-spitting, side-splitting, sometimes melancholy, warm and delightful look back at one of the giants of his day — a celebration of his life.

On a sunny, chilling day in January of 1996, Howard went to join the Clemson legends who made the trip before him. He died on Friday, January 26, at 86 years of age. The members of the unbeaten 1948 team that squeezed by Missouri in the Gator Bowl escorted Howard's body to its resting place. Some folks wept, some didn't. All who showed up mourned his passing.

TIGERS QUIZ

4. Who scored the first points for Clemson in a bowl game?

Howard in his later days.

All who attended the funeral service knew this: Howard was at peace. He was with colleagues in that tiny cemetery, prepared to take charge once more. Furthermore, he had warned them all before their passing.

"They put that cemetery in for me and just a few other people," he said. "When I go, I want to be up there so I can hear all them people cheering my Tigers. Then, I won't have to go to heaven. I'll already be there."

Howard left a treasure of stories behind. The following are a sample of the collection, some that passed from mouth-to-mouth, others that were chronicled elsewhere. They're about life as Howard saw it. They are outrageous, funny, melancholy, unique — as was he.

THE ROCK About the famed rock from Death Valley, the desert. Many years ago when Presbyterian College coach Lonnie McMillian used to take the annual obligatory

The most lasting tradition left by Howard is his rock.

Frank Howard poses with several players from one of his early teams.

beating from Howard's teams, generally to kick off the season, McMillian once told reporters that "going up to play Clemson is just like playing in Death Valley."

A year or so later, a Clemson graduate traveling out west stopped in the desert, picked up a Death Valley rock and laid it on Howard's desk, thinking he had done a mystical thing. Howard thanked him, and after the man, S.C. Jones, left his office, Howard tossed the rock aside, not knowing what to do with it.

Several years passed, and Howard was tidying up his office. He came upon the rock, picked up the phone and had Gene Willimon, executive director of IPTAY(the fund-raising group, I Pay Ten A Year) at the time, take the rock, and "throw it over in the valley. I thought he was just going to pitch it over the fence. Instead, he made a stand for it and put the rock up on the top of it."

Sheer genius. The accidental birth of a tradition.

Back in those days of the 1960s, Clemson's football players had to walk a couple hundred yards to the field, then run down onto the field between two long lines of students.

Before one game in 1967, Howard was inspired by the rock sitting on a pedestal atop the hill.

"All of you who are going to give me 100 percent when you go into the Valley today, you can rub my rock. It will give you good luck. Any of you who isn't going to give 100 percent, keep your filthy hands off my rock. Don't touch it!

"A woman wrote me after that and said that if I believed more in God and less in that rock, I'd be a lot better football coach. But, they've been rubbing that rock ever since that day, and now whenever the band strikes up "Tiger Rag" and they shoot off that cannon and the players come running down that hill onto the field, well, we figure that's the most exciting 25 seconds in college football."

NOTHING TO BRAG ABOUT In his book, *Howard, The Clemson Legend*, Howard recalls wearing out three of the school's presidents. The first one, Dr. Enoch Sikes, the man who hired Howard, encouraged Howard to refrain from talking to people about his paycheck.

Howard looked at Enoch, and said, "Heck, Doc, I ain't

Frank Howard coached the Tigers for 29 seasons. His most successful campaign was in 1948, when Clemson beat Missouri, 24-23, in the Gator Bowl to finish with an 11-0 record.

going to tell anybody because I'm as much ashamed about it as you are."

JACK OF ALL TRADES Money was a problem for Howard when he was at Alabama, as it was for many students. As a sophomore, Howard landed a job as the bouncer at school dances. He was hired by a school administrator and followed a bouncer who let some of the male students off easy. The job paid $75 a month and Howard pocketed $25 and sent his mother $50 each month.

As it turned out, Howard was tested his first night on the job. A man came bobbing through the door, and Howard stopped him and ordered him off the premises. The man said he wasn't going to leave, but challenged Howard to meet him after the dance. Howard declined in only a way Howard could, saying, "No, I'm not going to meet you after the dance ... We're going outside right now!"

Howard escorted the young man outside and claimed to have blackened both the fellow's eyes.

Word got around.

Everything went smoothly at the dances until the administrator who hired Howard wandered in "a little drunk" one evening. Howard turned him out, too.

The next morning Howard was summoned to the man's office. Howard made his way to the office knowing that he had shot himself in the foot. Howard expected the worse, that the job was over and the $50 he was sending his mother every month would be cut off. He had a speech lined up but the man cut him off.

"Frank," he said, "I would appreciate it immensely if you wouldn't make a report on my conduct last night to the university president."

Howard wagged his index finger in front of the man's face, "I won't report it this time, but don't you ever let it happen again!" The quickest trip he ever made from the outhouse to the penthouse, Howard chuckled.

FLIGHT LESSONS The first airplane flight Clemson's football team ever took was to Boston in 1948, the year that the Tigers went 11-0 and won the Gator Bowl. Howard was a little lukewarm about flying the distance to New England, but some of his coaching colleagues were booking charters, so Howard joined the ranks.

He remembers having his son, Jimmy, at the Anderson airport waving good-bye, when Jimmy was just a tike. Howard said he remembered feeling a touch awkward leaving the boy standing there with his mother, and the plane disappearing into the sky.

Howard's Tigers beat Boston College, 26-19, and the flight to and from Massachusetts was by and large

TIGERS QUIZ

5. *Who was the first player ever signed by the New England Patriots?*

TIGERS QUIZ

6. *Who were the two Tigers who played in the 1972 American Bowl Game?*

uneventful. The flight was a first-time experience for most of his players, Howard noted, adding that "only one or two of them threw up."

What Howard remembered most, though, was Jimmy standing just outside the steps leading down to the concrete ramp when the plane's doors swung open. "I scooped him up," Howard said, "and the first thing the little breadwaster asked me was, 'Daddy, when you were way high up in the sky in that plane, were you high enough to see God?' I didn't know rightly how to answer a question like that, so I said, 'Son, you know, He didn't say hello to us or anything, but God is everywhere and I know He must have been flying right along beside us.' "

Coach Howard gets ready to come down the hill in the east end of Memorial Stadium. He had just rubbed Howard's Rock (hidden behind him now) for good luck.

Flying became routine for the Tigers, but the flights weren't all as smooth as glass. On a night flight back to Anderson after a win in Alabama, the flight attendants distributed food trays and drinks to all the players, coaches and other members of the party. According to Howard, the pilot's voice came over the intercom asking passengers to check their seat belts, for they were

expecting some turbulence ahead.

"A little turbulence," Howard said. "We had all turned our attention back to eating what was in front of us, and the next thing you know, the plane felt like it dropped a couple of hundred feet, and then shot back up three or four hundred feet. It was a pretty scary thing for a little while there. I think most everybody lost their supper one way or the other. I know that there were mashed potatoes stuck to the ceiling and green peas everywhere. We got past the storm after a while, but nobody had the stomach to eat after that."

THE PAPER TO PROVE IT Howard graduated from the University of Alabama in 1931, but didn't have the $10 to pay for his diploma. After 25 years had passed, and Howard was firmly entrenched at Clemson, he sent the registrar's office $10 for his long overdue diploma. Several weeks later, someone handed Howard a tube and said, "Coach, somebody sent you a calendar or pin-up girl."

"Better than that," Howard said. "It's my diploma."

Several heads spun around, eyes round as headlights. Howard chuckled, and disappeared into his office.

ASK FOR DIRECTIONS One of Howard's favorite stories involves the South Carolina series and Big Thursday. For years and years and years, Clemson made the trip to Columbia in November for Big Thursday, where the two archrivals would play before a full house. The trip rankled Howard and Clemson supporters because they were denied the home field advantage year after year.

The series finally became a home-and-home affair in 1960, and Howard recalled the first time South Carolina fans had to come to Clemson they were greeted by a sign in Greenville that proclaimed, "Clemson, left."

Howard was used to finishing the story. "Did you know that every one of those dumb devils turned around and went back home?"

That inspired Carolina fans to come up with their own geographical chart. "To get to Clemson, they would say," Howard smiled, "you go west until you smell it and then go north until you step in it."

SPREADING THE GOOD WORD Howard was proud of his boys who made something of themselves after their football days. Often, he would muse about how many generals, doctors, CEOs, lawyers, university presidents, even preachers — you name it — sprang from Howard's wing. "Lord knows," Howard would drawl, "how any of them boys became preachers after being around me four years. All those boys who made something of themselves

7. What is the only Big Ten team to defeat Clemson?

8. What is the only current Southeastern Conference school that has not played Clemson in football?

TIGERS QUIZ

9. How many times
have Tiger football
teams won 10 or
more games in a
season?

are the ones I'm most proud of. To me it means that I put
something in those breadwaster heads that stuck with
them and made something out of them. I'm sure that
some of their mommas and daddies had something to do
with it, too."

One morning at the Holiday Inn bordering Lake
Hartwell, Howard was holding "coffee court" as usual,
when one of his former players, Joe Bowen, was in town
visiting home folks and stopped by the inn to say hello to
his former coach.

Spying him, Howard called the preacher over and
said, "Reverend Bowen, did you ever play football for
me?" Bowen said, "I sure did. And I heard the Lord's
name used more often on the football field than I ever
did in the seminary."

A JOKER In his book, *Howard,The Clemson Legend*,
Howard also recalls a tale he often told about his good
buddy, Peahead Walker, who coached the Wake Forest
University football team. With Wake Forest headed to
Clemson for a date with the Tigers, Howard had some of
his highway patrol buddies "play a trick on Peahead."

On the day of the game, as the Wake Forest contingent
pulled onto Clemson's campus, Howard had his pals
handcuff the Wake coach to a telephone pole near the
fieldhouse dressing room. The troopers claimed that
Walker resembled an escaped fugitive masquerading as a
bus driver, and they needed to check out his identity.

Eventually, the troopers took the cuffs off Walker and
he got his team dressed and assembled for the game. The
'fun' however, wasn't over. As Walker stood at the
players' entrance gate as his team passed through, an
officer stopped the Wake coach from entering the field
because he wasn't wearing a sideline pass, which
presumably was misplaced when the "arrest" was made
several hours before.

TIGERS QUIZ

10. Who are the only
two Clemson
quarterbacks to have
thrown at least 200
passes in a season
twice?

By that time, Walker was fuming. He called for his
team captain to identify him to the officer manning the
gate. Walker told his captain to tell the officer who he
was, to which the team captain said, "Officer, I've never
seen that man before in my life."

After Walker returned home, he picked up the phone
and told Howard that he ran his team captain, Pat
Preston, around the practice field until he remembered
"who I was."

Payback is hell, Howard learned. On a trip to Canada
to visit Walker, who was coaching in the Canadian
Football League, Howard stepped off the plane, head
swiveling to spot Walker, who was supposed to meet
him there. Walker was nowhere to be found.

An immigration officer approached Howard and

asked if he spoke French. Howard replied that indeed he did not.

The officer told him that in order for him to gain entrance to Quebec, Howard would have to have a working knowledge of the language, otherwise the government wouldn't take responsibility. Sorry, Monsieur Howard, and all that rot.

What Howard didn't know was that Walker was hiding behind a curtain, baiting the situation, savoring the sweetness overdue revenge brings.

The officer asked Howard his profession.

"I'm a football coach," Howard replied.

"You don't look like a coach to me," the uniformed man said.

Howard knew he was in a pinch — in Canada, being detained, and where the hell was Peahead Walker anyway?

Moments later, Walker stumbled out from behind the curtain, holding his belly, laughing so hard that tears streamed down his cheeks.

Walker circulated the story among his buddies, but, naturally, Howard had the last word.

"Why don't you tell folks the truth about the story. When I told the man I was a football coach, he said, 'Welcome to Canada. That fella we got up here sure ain't one!' "

A SMART MOVE One of the smartest things Howard said he ever did was to pass on hiring Bear Bryant as an assistant when he became head coach at Clemson. Howard had known Bryant during his playing days at Alabama and Bryant was some years younger than Howard.

Howard passed on picking up Bear Bryant as an assistant for fear of losing his own job.

The two were fast friends, but Howard said if he had added Bryant, who at the time was an assistant at Vanderbilt, to his staff, within "six months he would have cut my throat, drank my blood, had my job and had Clemson on probation for life."

LEAVING A MARK Chewing tobacco was one of Howard's favorite habits. When workers were pouring the foundations for Memorial Stadium, Howard tossed a chew in each of them as the fresh concrete was being poured. Howard dropped his favorite plugs in the holes so that he could say, with conviction, that his love for chewing tobacco would be around longer than he would.

When he retired in 1974 as athletic director, the stadium's field was named Frank Howard Field. Memorial Stadium was named in honor of all the former Clemson students killed on all the battlefields involving the United States.

ON THE ROAD For the most part, Howard enjoyed

recruiting. Jess Neely once sent Howard, then an assistant coach, to Charleston to recruit a 240-pounder, at a time when there were few of those beefeaters around. When he finally found the house where this heavyweight lived, Howard called out the boy's name and a 150-pound squirt showed up at the door.

Howard asked the boy's name, and the kid said, "That's me."

Howard changed gears, and said, "Well, son, I'm selling subscriptions to *Saturday Evening Post*. Would you like to buy one?" And he turned on his heel, and drove back to Clemson.

On another trip, along the back roads of Georgia, Howard was caught in a speed trap designed to snare out-of-town drivers. He was fined three dollars. Howard handed the cop six dollars, and said, "Officer, I'm in kinda a hurry, so don't stop me when I come back through here in about an hour."

WHAT DID YOU SAY? IPTAY doesn't mean "I Plow Twenty Acres A Year," as South Carolina fans claim, Howard would chuckle. IPTAY, perennially one of the top fund-raising programs in the nation was formed originally to raise $10,000 for Jess Neely's plan to expand recruiting.

A Dr. Rupert Fike, a cancer specialist, was credited with coming up with the slogan, "I Pay Ten A Year," which was reduced to IPTAY. Once, a week before Clemson traveled to Columbia to face South Carolina on Big Thursday, USC coach Warren Giese took a swipe at Howard, saying that only Howard and God know what goes on with IPTAY funds.

When the Clemson party arrived in Columbia, a sportswriter asked Howard to respond to Giese's remark. Howard scratched his head for a moment or two, then said, "Well, buddy, since we have shut them out for two straight years, I guess Giese knows about as much about IPTAY as he does about scoring or crossing our goal-line."

Howard's punchline backfired. The Gamecocks upset Clemson, 26-6. After the game, Howard invited attending sports scribes to come into the dressing room "and claim the body."

The next year, 1959, was the last Big Thursday game, and Clemson avenged the loss. The Tigers blanked the Gamecocks, 27-0, to close the door on that unbalanced era in one of the biggest rivalries in the college ranks.

MONEY DOESN'T ALWAYS HELP Referees weren't Howard's favorite folks. But he had an unusual encounter with one "zebra" one year at the Gator Bowl. Howard was having breakfast in the hotel, his bags packed and waiting in his room. Just as he was about to check out, smoke began

TIGERS QUIZ

11. Which team has scored the most points against the Tigers in a single game?

TIGERS QUIZ

12. What two bowl games did Clemson play during the calendar year of 1959?

pouring throughout the restaurant. Howard dashed to his room on the second floor, grabbed his belongings and watched the building burn from across the street.

"The prettiest sight I ever saw came when a helicopter hovered over the roof of the hotel, let down a ladder and flew them people to safety," Howard said.

A referee named Bobby Sandell and his wife were staying on the 11th floor and came out of the hotel with just the clothes on their backs. Howard gave the ref $200 and told him to get a room in another hotel and buy some clothes if he needed them.

Some time later, Sandell sent Howard his $200 back. As fate would have it, Sandell worked one of Clemson's football games the following fall. Sandell called Clemson for clipping on a play that nullified a touchdown.

After the game, Howard was chatting with Sandell's wife and said, "Did you see that doggoned husband of yours call that touchdown back? The next time I catch him in a fire, he'll roast for sure."

Howard gave Clemson fans lots of laughs over the years. He always had a good joke or story to share.

WHERE THE SUN DON'T SHINE Lou Bello was one of the most colorful referees in football, and he used to give Howard (and other coaches as well) fits. In many ways, Bello was the show when he was on the football field or the basketball court.

Once, when Bello was officiating a Clemson game, he was running out of gas toward the end of the game. Winded, he blew his whistle, walked over to Howard, grimacing on the sidelines, and asked, "Coach, who should I give the ball to after the game is over?" Howard scowled, and barked, "Bello, if you haven't got any more sense than to ask me a fool question like that, give the ball to us if we win, and give it to them if they win. If it's a tie, you can take that football and stick it up your butt."

Retreating back onto the field, Bello turned back to face Howard and said, "Coach, would it be all right with you if I let the air out first."

Virginia Tech beat the Tigers that day, and Bello dodged a painful bullet.

FOND MEMORIES Howard was a self-made man, pulling himself up by his own bootstraps. His life was consumed by his passion — football. Howard dined on football and the characters who fueled it. He stood by every Clemson coach the school hired after he retired. Howard wasn't all that chummy with every coach who has directed Clemson's football program, but he cared about them and pulled for them to succeed. Some did, others didn't.

Former basketball coach Bill Foster, now head coach at VPI, said he appreciated Howard's concern.

"In all those years, when we would have a tough loss,

Bill Foster, now coaching at Virginia Tech, appreciated Howard's help when Foster was coaching the Tiger basketball team.

Former Clemson coach Danny Ford, now coaching at Arkansas, had a special relationship with Howard.

Coach Howard would come by the office, and I appreciated it," Foster said, following Howard's death. "He had been through those things, and saw it from a coach's standpoint. Coach Howard never bothered with the good times, when most others came by, but he was always there when times got tough."

When Rick Barnes signed on as basketball coach in 1994, Howard was there. In fact, their first meeting was typical Howard, at his best.

"When I reached out to shake his hand," Barnes recalled, "he said, 'Are you worth a damn?' I said, 'Why do you ask?' He said, 'Well, I see how much money they're paying you. The damn football stadium is named after me, and they're not paying me that much.' "

Barnes was touched.

Danny Ford was Howard's favorite. Both of them were from Alabama, both played at Alabama and both of them coached the offensive line. Howard's passing touched Ford deeply.

"I was like a son to him," Ford said. "He took me under his wing, and I'll never forget what he did for me. When I got the head coaching job here, Coach Howard told me everything I had done wrong at the press conference. I kind of hem-and-hawed into the microphone, and afterward, he told me that I was the one in charge and that I had to act like I was in charge.

"Coach Howard said he would help me through the things I needed help on, and I'm not sure I could have done it all without his help. Every Sunday he would come by and tell me what he thought went wrong, and his guidance helped me. I learned a lot from Coach Howard."

"Coach Howard put the word 'toughness' into Clemson football," Tommy West said. "That was his trademark. He was tough, but inside that tough individual was a heart that was enormous."

Now, another football season is upon us. Frank Howard's remains rest in the tiny cemetery behind the South grandstand. Howard is at peace. He lived a full life, as at home before royalty as he was among common, everyday people. He enjoyed a presence few people are blessed with.

Bob Bradley, Sports Information Director Emeritus at Clemson, closed out Howard's eulogy on January 26 with an emotional farewell. His voice cracked as he bid good-bye to his boss, a man larger that life.

"I could stand up here all day long telling Coach Howard stories and never tell the same one twice," Bradley said. "But I'd like to say, because of you, Coach Howard, I became maybe one person in a thousand who got up every morning and looked forward to going to work.

The entire Clemson family had respect for Howard, including current coach Tommy West.

Frank Howard's love for Clemson was obvious throughout his long career with the university.

"But now, it's time for you to discard all those old stale football jokes you've been telling all these years and find some new ones. I'll catch up with you one day, and we'll find some more people to tell them to.

"Thanks for everything, Coach.

"Good-bye."

Personalities

O.K. PRESSLEY (1926-28) O.K. Pressley was destined to become a Clemson College student. Had to be destiny, for his brother Tom Pressley had himself a deal to play football at Wofford College. Tom had seen his brother in action in sandlot pickup games. They would have made a great duo at Wofford College in Spartanburg, S.C.

O.K. left his brother standing at the steps of the rail coach as it slowly chugged away from the downtown depot. He left Tom standing there alone to follow his heart. Yet, 15 miles out of Spartanburg and headed to Tiger Town, young O.K. Pressley considered jumping off the train like those daring train robbers he'd heard about.

The picture of his brother standing at the train station, watching the train disappear from sight really got to O.K. by the time the train whistled its way through Greer, S.C. and bore down on Greenville.

It took every ounce of his willpower for Pressley to stay in his seat as the train rumbled on down the track. An hour later O.K. Pressley was dumped out at his field of dreams with no promises of playing football, for no one knew, save Pressley and his brother Tom, the talent that was bursting to let go.

O.K. Pressley was Clemson's first athlete to be made an All-America selection.

"O.K. was a great player and a great person," said running back Bob McCarley, a teammate and friend. "He gave it his all. He was an inspiration to all of us. He played clean and was a good sportsman who represented Clemson well. We all admired him. He was a great leader and was our team captain."

When O.K. Pressley stepped off the train, he did the logical thing. He signed up to play on the Clemson YMCA team. It made sense because O.K. was just another student in a small college town that took its football as seriously as it took its barbecue.

The curious thing about Pressley playing for the Y team was also the obvious. He wanted to become a Tiger. The Y squad often scrimmaged the Clemson varsity on Bowman Field, below Tillman Hall, the first building built on the school campus. Although Pressley distinguished himself at center, he became an instant star at defensive tackle for the YMCA.

TIGERS QUIZ

13. Name the only Clemson head football coach who was also a captain of a Clemson football team?

In his debut against Clemson's varsity, it didn't take long for the Tigers to line up their best blocker over Pressley. That strategy foiled, so Clemson double- and triple-teamed this Tiger in a YMCA uniform. The situation became so distressing to Clemson players that they began charging Pressley with having somehow stolen their signals.

Pressley smiled, and suggested that the Tigers take their huddle inside Tillman Hall. The Y'ers would wait.

It isn't exactly prophetic to report that a star was born that day. Head coach Josh Cody fairly bounded over to O.K.'s side and fulfilled the young man's lifelong dream. Just like that, he had become a full-fledged Clemson Tiger.

It is also safe to make the claim that O.K. Pressley, Clemson University's first ever All-American at anything, was overshadowed by history. Clemson's trophy cases are full of lore involving dozens of All-Americans in football and others in various sports. But, O.K.'s career came at a time when there was little hype and barely any fanfare over All-America status.

Eventually, in 1983, some 50 years after his blaze of glory in Clemson orange, Pressley was inducted into the Clemson Hall of Fame. A year later, he died.

There are some ardent Clemson supporters who feel the man and his legend should be emblazoned in bronze in Memorial Stadium's Ring of Honor, the ultimate honor for a Clemson athlete. That isn't likely to happen, even though Pressley left behind more that his blocking skills and fierce obsession for the game of football, Clemson's signature sport.

Coach Josh Cody made O.K. Pressley's dream come true by asking the player to join Clemson's football team.

For starters, Pressley filled in as the team's trainer, publicist and motivator — anything that helped spell winning. As trainer, Pressley assisted team doctor Lee Milford. Pressley was often pressed into action with his bag of bandages, iodine and smelling salts.

In a 1983 interview, he remembered a particularly nasty incident in a 1928 game when two Clemson players banged heads and suffered severe cuts over their eyes.

"They could barely see out of them," he said. "Dr. Milford wanted to take the two boys out of the game, but those were the days when you couldn't substitute. If you left the game you were finished for the day. We didn't have anybody else to put in the game. I worked on one of the boys and he worked on the other one. We patched them up so they could see. They remained in the game."

On another occasion, the day before the Tigers were in Alabama to play Auburn, Pressley paid 25 cents for a banana split and requested 12 spoons so that his teammates could share in the rare treat. The next day, Clemson cashed in on that special moment the afternoon before, and upset Auburn, 6-0.

There was a price to pay, however. Pressley suffered a severe hand injury. He sat out the North Carolina State game the following week and was on the sidelines against South Carolina, Clemson's archrival.

Pressley pleaded with Cody to play, but Cody steadfastly refused his star player. The Tigers were losing ground. South Carolina had pressed to the Tigers'

TIGERS QUIZ

14. Who is the only Clemson player to lead the ACC in both passing and total offense?

TIGERS QUIZ

15. Who was the first Clemson player to rush for 1,000 yards in a season?

10-yard line. Cody tilted his head toward the field. Pressley disappeared into the knot of players. He swung the momentum of the game in Clemson's direction in one swift and decisive move, dropping South Carolina's ball-carrier for an 8-yard loss. On the next play, Pressley cut down a USC runner seven yards behind the line of scrimmage, and on the next two plays made two more tackles that cost South Carolina another 12 yards.

Although both teams brought identical 5-0 records into the game, the Tigers hammered USC, 32-0, inspired by Pressley's performance despite a not-yet-healed hand wrapped heavily in gauze. That autumn afternoon in Columbia, SC, may well rank as one of the most amazing performances in Clemson football history. It certainly solidified Pressley's mark as an All-American football player.

"Back then, we wore patches on patches when we got banged up," Pressley once said. "But those were the good times. We often tossed those leather skullcap helmets to the sidelines and played without them. We had one player who shunned any pads or protective equipment because it slowed him down."

Pressley's training at Clemson served him admirably in the Marine Corps. He took his football skills into the service, and played and coached that team for seven years.

Before retiring from the Corps after 20 years, Pressley became a highly decorated officer. When he returned to his native Chester, SC, he taught in public schools, then retired to his farm to live out the rest of his days.

"A better center than Captain O.K. Pressley of Clemson would be hard to find," former South Carolina football coach Billy Laval once reflected.

"O.K. Pressley was like his initials," former teammate Henry Asbill said, "He was OK!"

"My father was a great father and an All-American in every aspect of his life," said his son, Kirk Pressley.

TIGERS QUIZ

16. Who is the only Clemson player to lead the ACC in scoring twice?

BANKS McFADDEN (1937-39) Clemson University has had its share of football All-Americans. Banks McFadden, 78 years old at the writing of this book, a two-sport All-American stands as the greatest of the great.

The romantically bold name, the legacy he left at the school are woven into an incredibly indelible mark that will never be duplicated, much less surpassed. You can almost see McFadden as a young lad scoring touchdown after touchdown in his front yard, making game-winning field goals and racing with the wind as he dreamed of being a Clemson Tiger one day when he finally would pack his bags and leave home for the first time.

McFadden's is a dream fulfilled and then some, but Clemson is fortunate to have formed a lifetime association with the uniquely outstanding man whose name hangs on the school's football facility.

Fact is, that McFadden, who grew up in tiny Great Falls, S.C., leaned toward Duke University as his reputation grew in high school. He was wooed by Georgia Tech and South Carolina as well as Clemson. But Banks McFadden went to Clemson University because he was directed to school there — by his mother.

"My mother told me I was going to Clemson. It was a good school she said, and I would be treated well there. I liked Duke and may have gone there, but my mother knew best, and she made the decision. As it turned out, she made a wise decision for me," McFadden said.

In April of 1996, the Banks McFadden Building at Jervey Athletic Center on the Clemson campus was dedicated in McFadden's honor.

When McFadden came to Clemson he was a 6-foot-3 scarecrow who weighed 165 pounds sopping wet. Frank Howard, an assistant football coach at the time, took one look at McFadden and said that all McFadden needed do to become a thermometer was to drink a couple of cans of tomato juice. Howard wasn't impressed with the gangling rookie recruit.

"I remember the first time I saw Banks on the practice field," Howard recalled before his death. "He looked like one of those whooping cranes, and I thought sure as the devil that (head coach Jess) Neely had made a mistake giving this boy a scholarship. But he proved me wrong."

The two-sport All-American (football and basketball) remains the ultimate team member to this day. As any great athlete would say, McFadden credits the players who surrounded him for making the feats he accomplished possible.

"Everywhere I've been," he said, "I've been surrounded by people who want to do their best. It's not hard to be motivated when you're around folks with a common purpose, around people who want to succeed. I've been blessed by the Good Lord, and the teams I've played on were like diamonds in the rough when we started. But once we were all polished up and shining, it was a beautiful thing.

TIGERS QUIZ

17. What is the only Pac-10 team to play Clemson in a regular-season game?

"The thing that separated me, especially in football is that I wound up being the tailback and I got to run the ball a lot. Some folks think that the person running with the ball do what they do all on their own, but it was the people in front of me, doing the jobs they were taught to do — blocking and blocking, again and again — that makes anybody with the ball look better than they actually are. When my old teammates and me get together every year, and I still pat them on the back. I'll never forget them, and they never let me down."

McFadden, the only Clemson athlete in history to have both his football and basketball jerseys retired, is convinced that he matriculated to Clemson University

McFadden did it all in the 1940 Cotton Bowl victory against Boston College. He quarterbacked the Tigers, deflected four passes and averaged 45 yards a punt

"at the right time." The school was an all-male military school, and discipline was the order of the day. There were no scandals, and if some student broke the rules, they were unceremoniously dismissed and sent packing.

"I was blessed to have some athletic ability," McFadden said. "Back then we had great coaches, had great individuals on our teams, but we were always playing as a team. Sometimes in football today, that doesn't always happen."

There are certainly enough players nationally making headlines for the wrong reasons to support McFadden's claim. He said that being voted the most valuable player on the 1939 football team was the biggest compliment of his athletic life.

"To me, when your teammates vote you something, you feel pretty good," he said. "That award means more than anything to me."

McFadden was the first Clemson athlete to be invited to participate in the All-Star game in Chicago. By that time, McFadden had just graduated and was on the coaching staff. He was granted special leave by Howard to join other All-America selections at Soldier Field.

"I was a little uneasy at first, when we were practicing and getting things ironed out," McFadden said. "I was there playing with the best college athletes and against the greatest names I'd been reading about in the papers.

"I did all right, but I got a little cocky, I've got to tell you. The big thing is, I found out that I was as fast as some of the others. I felt good about my high school and college training. Before we all assembled for the game, I had no way to gauge my ability with them. When I realized I could compete, it gave me a good feeling inside, and I knew then that if I was called on to play, I would be comfortable about that. In fact, I caught a pass and scored a touchdown. They beat us 21-14, but we gave them a good game."

McFadden learned to develop his athletic skills from his half-brother, Tom Wallace. McFadden's mother lost her first husband to an incurable disease, and later remarried. McFadden wound up playing high school sports under the guidance of his older brother, his high school coach.

"We were good together," McFadden said. "We slept in the same bed together for years as we grew up. As it turned out, he ruled outside the home, and my momma ruled inside the house. I can't say I didn't work hard. He told me that I was an average player and that I would have to work harder than anybody on the team if I was going to amount to anything. I worked hard."

When McFadden was a sophomore, he got a telephone call saying that his brother was dying of cancer.

"I went to him," McFadden said. "He was in great pain. He was hurting. But, we laughed about some things anyway. He told me that he had always had pride in my ability. 'You can be an All-America in basketball if you play like I taught you. Football is harder to make All-America, but you can do it.' I told Tom that I'd always try my best.

"The next summer when I was in Alabama during ROTC training, I got a telegram sent to me informing me that I made All-America in basketball. I got a lot of credit for those things, but I didn't deserve a lot of it."

In 1941, after a year in the NFL and just blossoming as a college coach and recruiter, McFadden nearly lost his life. He was on his way home to Great Falls to visit

TIGERS QUIZ

18. Which offensive lineman recovered a fumble in mid-air and scored a touchdown in the Tigers' 35-10 win over South Carolina in 1966?

Banks McFadden stayed involved with Clemson athletics once his coaching days were over.

Danny Strong, who like McFadden is from Great Falls, S.C., poses with the legend. Strong led Great Falls to the Class A championship in basketball and was a senior at N.C. State in 1996. Strong, All-State in basketball and football, is the only Great Falls athlete since McFadden to be named All-State in several sports.

his mother from a recruiting trip. It was late and McFadden fell asleep at the wheel. The car crashed into a tree, lost a front wheel and pushed the dashboard into the seat. McFadden was thrown violently from the car, and found unconscious some time later.

Eventually, he healed completely, but it took time. McFadden lost the hearing in his right ear, but he was treated daily in the Clemson training room, and was given a clean bill of health.

"I was fortunate," he said. "It was a dumb thing to do, and it's a wonder that I wasn't killed from what the people who found me said. That was some lesson to learn. The car was demolished. It's a wonder I wasn't."

Clemson fans, and the rest of the football-loving

nation for that matter, will never know if McFadden would have been larger than, say, Red Grange, Vince Lombardi or Bart Starr. After one year of professional football with the Brooklyn Dodgers (both the football Dodgers and the baseball Dodgers played at Ebetts Field), McFadden retired.

"It might have been a crazy thing to do," McFadden confessed, "but I'd had enough. Basically, I was a country boy a long way from home. I called Coach Howard and Clemson gave me a chance to coach. That's who I was. And, I made the right decision. Jack Southerland was a great coach and I told him he did a great job with us. And I told him I was done, that I wasn't coming back. He asked why, and I said, 'This is just not for me.' Still, they sent me a contract to play for another year, but I sent it back."

The one year he spent with the Dodgers, he led the NFL in yards per carry. His talent attracted the Philadelphia Eagles coach, who came to Great Falls to make a deal with McFadden.

"I told them they were wasting their time," McFadden said. "He told me that they had bought my contract and was there to sign me that day. I told him he was wasting his time, but later they came back and wanted to get me to sign with them."

Looking back, McFadden knows he made the best decision for himself and his family when he left the bright lights and took up roots in rural South Carolina. "But, if I had it to do over again, I don't know. I couldn't have been that smart to turn down the kind of money I was being paid. There wasn't anywhere else I could make that kind of money, and certainly not at Clemson. When they were wanting to sign me, I turned down $8,000. They finally paid me $10,000.

"When they asked me to give them a figure, I said 'Nobody is worth $10,000.' They asked how long it would take for me to get to New York."

All he knew, after four seasons in New York, was that he was a country boy at heart, and likely would never fit into horns honking 24 hours a day, the rumble of subways rolling underground, people yelling epithets at one another, and restaurants that didn't serve grits or cornbread or a whole lot of good, ol' fried chicken.

When McFadden retired from playing, he went into coaching — not to make a killing financially or to live off his reputation. He went into coaching to give back some of what his brother, Tom, instilled in him, and to pass on some of the principals he learned as a player.

"I loved coaching and I believe to this day that the Clemson teams I performed on affected the future of Clemson University football," he said. "Our accomplishments were the first national impact teams,

TIGERS QUIZ

19. *Who was the first Clemson player ever drafted by an NFL team?*

TIGERS QUIZ

20. *Who was the first Clemson player to play professional football?*

TIGERS QUIZ

21. Who holds the Clemson record for most pass attempts in a game?

and we thought it was great. We didn't think we were the greatest, but we were good and were proud of what we accomplished."

McFadden coached Clemson's defensive backs during the 1941 football season, but when World War II broke out, he joined the Army Air Corps. He was sent to North Africa and spent four years there and in Italy.

When the war ended, McFadden resumed coaching. Along about that time, he married Aggie Rigsby. The couple had four daughters — Patsy, Lil, Mardia and Jan. Over the years, the couple has been blessed with nine grandchildren — five boys and four girls. In June of 1995, the McFaddens celebrated their 50th wedding anniversary, though Aggie McFadden has been stricken by Alzheimer's disease for more than four years. Since being moved to a resting home, McFadden has faithfully visited with his wife three hours every morning and three hours every evening.

"We have nice visits," McFadden said. "She knows I'm there, and we talk, but she cannot respond verbally."

Throughout his coaching profession, McFadden also

McFADDEN...

■ Led Clemson to its first conference basketball championship (1939).
■ Led Clemson to its first bowl game and victory (1940 Cotton Bowl).
■ Won three events in the South Carolina State Track meet in one afternoon, setting records in all three events. Earlier in the year McFadden placed first in five events in a dual meet, scoring 25 points while the opposing team's total score was 28 points.
■ Was Clemson's first No. 1 draft choice (1939 Brooklyn Dodgers).
■ Previously held the record for the longest punt in Clemson history (75 yards vs. Army, 1937).
■ Tied for the longest rushing play in Clemson history (90 yards vs. Presbyterian, 1939).
■ Holds the record for most punts of more than 50 yards in a

game (six vs. Tulane, 1939).
■ Held Clemson's punting record (43.5) for 40 years (1939-1979).
■ First Clemson player to be invited to play in the College All-Star game in Chicago.
■ Charter member in the Clemson Athletic Hall of Fame.
■ Charter member in the South Carolina Athletic Hall of Fame.
■ Only Clemson player ever chosen for the National Football Foundation Hall of Fame.
■ Highest NFL draft pick in Clemson history (No. 3 in entire 1940 draft).The list of credentials for Banks McFadden, who was named an All-American in both basketball and football in 1939, are the backbone of his incredible athletic legacy. The list is exhaustive. The list is epic. There might not be another on this globe like it.

served as varsity track coach, freshman basketball coach and spent 10 years as varsity basketball coach. After leaving football, McFadden stayed on as the university's director of intramurals for 15 years.

Although McFadden's legacy is anchored around football and basketball, his greatest love was track. He was especially drawn to the individual events, for he had only his dedicated athletic skills to lean on.

"The things I accomplished in track, I'm more proud of than the other things we did because in track it's an individual accomplishment," he said. "It's you against time. There's nobody else to rely on."

McFadden retired from coaching in 1969, the same year that Howard announced his resignation as head football coach. In 1996, McFadden was still serving the university as a goodwill ambassador. In April of 1996, the Banks McFadden Building at Jervey Athletic Center was dedicated in his honor.

RAY BROWN (1979-83) Ray Brown was a celebrity in his own right before he gave William Perry the nickname "The Fridge." When Brown was a rookie defensive end at Clemson, several of his hot postgame observations showed up in *Sports Illustrated's* They Said It. Throughout his career at Clemson, Brown's wry quotes continued to find their way to the magazine's "best quotes" section.

Ray Brown always had a good quote for the media, but it sometimes got him in trouble.

Fact is, his second-most clever line ever made for some hot news for SI as well as newspapers across the country. On a toasty fall Saturday afternoon at Chapel Hill, N.C. on November 7, 1981, ABC aired a halftime report that Clemson University was clearly headed toward NCAA probation for recruiting violations. Danny Ford was incensed by word that ABC was contemplating such an action. He drew his team together and commanded each member to ignore questions about the report.

Brown's sharp wit and quick tongue weren't able to contain themselves. He further fueled the network's fire. Shortly after the Tigers had beaten the Tar Heels, 10-8, at Kenan Stadium in a game that was decided by a UNC fumble deep in Clemson territory in the last few seconds, Brown took the plunge.

Jogging toward the dressing room, a sportswriter asked Brown what he thought of the dramatic finish. Brown turned toward the scribe, smiled a broad smile, and said, "What can I say? We work hard for the money." And he disappeared into the dressing room, somber-faced, as though he had not said one word.

That hit single by Donna Summer never had so much free pub, and Brown had never sunk so deep in Danny Ford's doghouse, either. But there it was, a virtually

Here Ray Brown taunts the South Carolina fans at Williams-Brice Stadium, who were throwing money onto the field in response to Brown's comments the week before that Clemson players "work hard for the money." The comment came while Clemson was being investigated for recruiting violations.

TIGERS QUIZ

22. Who holds the Clemson record for the longest touchdown run in a bowl game?

"innocent" comment hanging out on the line on a day that foreshadowed the inevitable — two years of probation following Clemson's dramatic upset of Nebraska in the Orange Bowl, a win that led to a national championship for the team, ranked No. 1 in the nation going into the game.

Brown's line about working hard for the money followed the Tigers the remainder of the season. There were hoots and howls from opposing fans. At Williams-Brice Stadium in Columbia, S.C., for the regular-season finale against archrival South Carolina, the diversion reached its pinnacle. USC fans began heckling the Clemson bench, as the Tigers were in the final minutes of rolling to a 29-13 victory. Brown, picking up on the catcalls and the money being tossed toward the string of Clemson players, turned to the crowd and encouraged it

Ray Brown signs autographs at the Tokyo Bowl.

to throw more cash his way.

Ford stemmed the sideshow before it got out of hand. Brown, again, became the center of attention, and the working hard for the money thing jumped back into newspaper, television and radio headlines.

WILLIAM "THE FRIDGE" PERRY (1981-84) Ray Brown was a sophomore in 1981 when William Perry brought all 300-and-some-odd pounds of himself to Clemson as a freshman, and also as a celebrity, for word of his considerable dimensions had preceded him.

The day that William Perry checked into the dormitory, Brown was waiting on the elevator to drop him off in the lobby. As the elevator door opened slowly, Brown's eyes popped wide open. Brown could barely believe what he saw — the wall-to-wall defensive lineman that Clemson players had heard so much about.

Weighing in at a lean 318 pounds, Perry was selected by the Chicago Bears in the first round of the NFL draft in 1985.

"William," spouted Brown, "you take up the whole elevator. You're as big as a refrigerator. I think I'm going to call you GE."

Perry smiled, and stepped off the elevator. Within days, Brown had modified Perry's nickname: "The Fridge." The legend had roots. Before he left Clemson for the pros, there were life-sized posters of the gentle giant. After all these years, there are still a few life-sized posters left of "The Fridge," yet, oddly enough, Perry has not set foot on campus since the day he left to add considerable dimension to the Chicago Bears roster. The posters suffice.

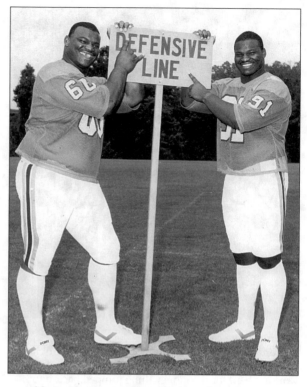

William Perry, left, and Michael Dean Perry show off their famous grins while posing for this shot.

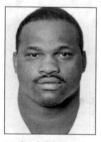

Michael Dean Perry was a 6-foot, 280-pound defensive end for Clemson.

Athletic administrators at Clemson claim Perry's refusal to accept invitations to come back to the university on special occasions is a personal thing that has to do with family. Perry's brother-in-law Crosby Broadwater was a two-year letterman as a reserve on the football team at Clemson and rarely played. It is said that Perry's wife, Sherry, has applied the brakes to any visits to that campus because her brother's talent was compromised.

At any rate, so much for campus Fridge sightings.

The most recent Fridge sighting was in 1996 in London, while Perry was a prominent member of the London Monarchs of the World Football League, competing for a spot in the World Bowl. Perry's almost royalty in England, and he filled up the airwaves and television signals with interviews here and interviews there, anything he could do to bolster the Monarchs' attendance and chances of making the title game.

The Brits built a love affair with "The Fridge" from the start, when he was a member of the Chicago Bears and played an NFL exhibition game in London against the Dallas Cowboys. So cuddly-looking and polite, any one of them would have hauled the gentle giant home.

Back then, some six or seven years ago, "The Fridge"

was larger than life, hawking McDonald burgers and
Swanson's Hungry Man TV dinners and soft drinks and
thermal long johns and, the most obvious, refrigerators.

Everywhere a fan turned, that gap-toothed smile was
labeled to something somebody was hawking, and Perry
ate it all up, even the controversial years with the Bears
when coach Mike Ditka rode him from sunrise to sunset
about his weight.

The awesome one, who literally can hold as much as
a refrigerator and still fill a gap in any line, escaped
Chicago because Ditka got tired of nagging Perry, whom
he called Bill (and that never stuck outside of Chicago),
and put him on waivers.

By that time, Perry had not only tired of Ditka's
nagging, the overwhelming, suffocating wave of publicity
wasn't nearly the fun it had once been, and Perry tired of
that too — partly because his popularity had waned and
he wasn't getting the commercial contracts he
commanded when he was the premier athletic national
novelty, and partly because he didn't want any more side
shows distracting from his personal life.

William "The
Fridge" Perry picked
up his nickname
from teammate Ray
Brown, who at first
proposed calling the
big guy by a brand
of refrigerators, GE
— for General
Electric.

Perry spikes the ball after scoring a touchdown in the 1986 Super Bowl.

William Perry was Chicago's biggest Bear.

Those things come and go, and Perry made his share off the commercials and other promotional contracts. According to NFL Properties, Perry merchandise outsold 18 of the 28 NFL teams during the span of 1985-86. In 1986, the year following the Bears' Super Bowl championship, Perry earned $4.5 million outside income. That figure tied him for fifth with golfer Greg Norman on the all-time list of additional revenue earned by sports personalities (at that time). He was joined in that group by such luminaries as Arnold Palmer, Michael Jordan, Jack Nicklaus, Boris Becker and John Madden, who earned a mere $3 million. The others earned only a few million more than "The Fridge" did.

"The Fridge" obviously didn't make the flight to Philadelphia wondering where his next meal was coming from. His bank account was solid. Perry was about to join a defensive line that was perhaps the softest in the NFL. The one thing Perry can do, and do with the best of them, is fill a gap in the line. At Philly, he was with some people he knew and liked, and people who wouldn't be getting on his case one day to the next.

Whatever happened to the new lease on Perry's life, he finished out the 1993 season, floundered around in '94 and announced his retirement in May of 1995. Of course, like any other celebrity, he didn't really and truly retire.

The London Monarchs bought his marketability, paid "The Fridge" handsomely and used his colorful personality and sense of humor to sway thongs of curiosity-seekers to the stadium to see the big guy, and his teammates, in action.

Plain and simple, Fridge still sells, but he has become recluse again, and may one day show up in a roped ring in a pair of tights staring up into Earthquake's fiery eyes wondering, perhaps wishing, that he had just opened up another McDonalds in his hometown Aiken instead.

As phony as most 9-to-5ers believe big time rasslin' is, it isn't all pitty-patty stuff. Although most of rasslin's basic themes seem to be predictable and recognizable, the Hulksters, and The Renegades, and Rick Flair's of the art have basic skills and instincts because not all of what you and I see on the television from time-to-time is fake.

At any rate, William "Fridge" Perry is hanging out at his Aiken castle on the edge of town and comes and goes without attracting a great deal of attention from the locals. Reports from Aiken claim that the big guy spends a lot of time at City B's, the hottest local greasy spoon and pool hall, where "The Fridge" has the reputation of, well, a pool shark.

At City B's and other hangouts, Perry comes and goes

Perry (72), who usually played defensive tackle for the Bears, crushes for short yardage over Dallas Cowboys linebacker Mike Hegman (57) in a 1985 game.

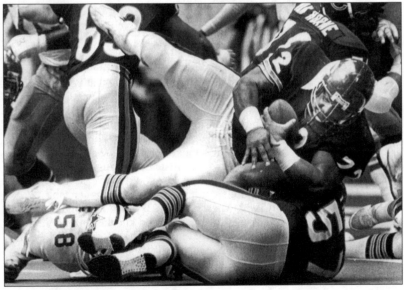

"The Fridge" has some fun in 1988, after returning to the Chicago Bears' camp after undergoing treatment for an eating disorder.

TIGERS QUIZ

23. Who was the first Clemson player to win a Super Bowl Championship?

as he pleases without all the hassle of signing autographs or having his picture snapped every other step he takes. Indeed, most of the townsfolk know that Perry has come back to his roots, but seldom run into him. The locals say that he likes his privacy and spends his time working to finish his mansion of a home, or fishing, or playing pool and wolfing down double cheeseburgers at B's.

Perry's eating habits are legend. When he played at Clemson, Perry's teammates, no strangers to smorgasbords themselves, would marvel at the big man's appetite. If he is at home anywhere, it is at a table.

In 1982, when Perry was a sophomore and a sportswriter's dream, Clemson knocked off the Virginia Cavaliers at Scott Stadium in Charlottesville, Va., 48-0, in a televised night game. Perry was besieged by scribes following the ho-hum romp.

Most of them had little interest in how many of

"The Fridge" was and is always a fan favorite.

Virginia's offensive personnel Perry had busted on the Cavaliers' artificial turf, but there were a number of bruises left behind in the wake of the Tigers' romp. The scribes wanted to know a little more about "The Fridge's appetite.

"William," one writer from Atlanta broke the silence, "some of us in the press box heard that you ate two whole chickens at the team meal last night after practice. Is that true?"

Perry looked up, and smiled a great big gap-toothed smile. "Nope," he said, "that ain't true. I ate five chickens last night, and I'm hungry enough right now to eat five more, but I doubt they got that many on the plane back home tonight. I'll have to find a place that stays open all night probably. Whatever they have for us on the plane will be an appetizer."

Perry's brother Michael Dean Perry also played for

Perry was always the main attraction during his NFL playing career. Maybe that's why he tries hard to stay out of the spotlight now that he is no longer playing in the NFL.

Clemson, lettering from 1984 through 1987. It has been said that Freddie, another Perry brother, has spoken on his famous brother's behalf on several occasions, telling inquirers that "The Fridge" is "just enjoying retirement. This is the first time in a long time he's been with his family so I guess he just wants to be by himself."

While Perry declines interviews, his wife tells inquirers that he is "just relaxing with the children, kind of following them around," referring to the Perry's 12- and 8-year-old daughters and their 3-year-old son.

Tending to their children "takes up a lot of our time. Our little boy doesn't even like to let his daddy out of his sight."

In a way, the spotlight may never have been intended for Perry, but it is doubtful, given his immense size and extraordinary talent, that he could have ducked outside its searing light. At Clemson, he was always considered larger than life, and Clemson fans felt most secure when he was busting offensive linemen and backs' noses and butts, more often than not in their own backfields.

At Chicago, when Perry confessed that he used to run the football for touchdowns in high school, and occasionally scored a coupe at Clemson in practice, Ditka decided to give the imposing former fullback a shot at glory when he ran the ball twice against the San Francisco 49ers, two weeks before his stunning shot at national glory, which came on a Monday Night Football telecast on October 21, 1985, against the Green Bay Packers.

Perry bulled one-yard into the end zone that night, and history became history. He was also used as a blocker for a couple Walter Payton touchdowns that night. In his career, Perry ran with the ball 10 times for four yards for four touchdowns. It was that celebrity that turned Perry into a marketing delight.

The momentum has followed Perry since, in ebb-and-flow fashion. Following Perry's metamorphosis as a an offensive "star," however short-lived, and given the Super Bowl championship that he helped bring to the Bears, Perry can never hope to escape his celebrity. He's stuck with it, and the best he can do is hide out in Aiken, where the people who have known him all their lives don't see him as that big a deal. William Perry is homefolk. He belongs.

He still smiles and waves in passing, and greetings are usually a relief, because there, "The Fridge" is still "William."

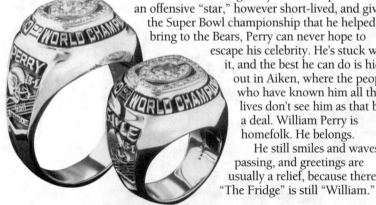

The ring on the right is size 10, the average ring size for a man. On the left, is Perry's size 23 Super Bowl ring. The ring, made by Jostens, is the largest Super Bowl ring ever made. It is the diameter of a half-dollar.

STEVE FULLER (1975-78) Steve Fuller has rewritten record books virtually every place he has landed. The lone exception would be the year he did time with the LA Rams, charting plays on a clipboard all season long, learning the Rams' system. At least that's what John Robinson told Fuller. Truth is, Fuller never dirtied his uniform in 1983; indeed, he never took a snap. Easy money, but Fuller was uneasy in Los Angeles and certainly had no idea he would be used as a bookend.

Happily, he jumped to the Chicago Bears, after, mind you, having several heart-to-hearts with Mike Ditka. Fuller not only respected Ditka, he liked the man and didn't see him as a dictator at all. But that's beside the point. The point is that with the Bears, a Super Bowl ring was included in the deal, as it turned out.

Chicago beat the Denver Broncos in the 1985 Super

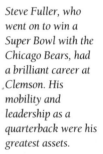

Steve Fuller, who went on to win a Super Bowl with the Chicago Bears, had a brilliant career at Clemson. His mobility and leadership as a quarterback were his greatest assets.

TIGERS QUIZ

24. Who holds the Clemson record for most passes caught in a game?

Bowl at the Super Dome in New Orleans, the crowning moment in Fuller's football career.

After a star-studded career at Clemson, Fuller the 23rd player chosen in the 1979 NFL Draft. He spent five years with the Chiefs, the one season with the Rams, and four years with the Chicago Bears. He also spent his last season in the pros (1988) with the San Diego Chargers.

Fuller became the Kansas City's starting quarterback his rookie season. After several seasons in the beef capital of the country, the Chiefs changed direction under head coach Marv Levy's command and that's how Fuller landed in Hollywood.

Fuller's story hardly ends with his days in the NFL, however. He had a solid career with significant mileposts, and today is a partner in an upscale real estate/Nicklaus-designed golf course development near Hilton Head Island, Colleton River Plantation.

Perhaps the crowning moment for Fuller after football was when he was one of three former outstanding Clemson figures whose names and jersey numbers were installed along the concrete buttress between Memorial Stadium's upper and lower decks in a touching ceremony in the fall of 1994, bringing life to the school's Ring of Honor circle.

The idea for Clemson's Ring of Honor came when a recruit was promised he could wear the No. 4 jersey when he signed with Clemson. That jersey, though, had once belonged to Steve Fuller and was retired in 1979. Only two players in school history have their jerseys retired — Fuller and Banks McFadden, the school's first ever All-American player.

The concept is to add names and numbers of only the most distinguished football players. Fuller certainly qualifies. His worth is also measured by being installed as a charter member along with legendary Frank Howard and Banks McFadden, the most decorated athlete in Clemson history. Fuller game along two generations behind those two Clemson giants.

Steve Fuller, second from left, is inducted into the Ring of Honor.

The Ring of Honor thing is a nice touch sparked by a recruiting flap over whether Anthony Downs had been promised he would be wearing No. 4 at Clemson, his high school number.

The problem was that Fuller's jersey, No. 4, was retired in 1979, Fuller being only the second athlete in Clemson history to have his jersey retired. McFadden, a two-sport All-American, was the first athlete to have jerseys retired in both football and basketball.

In the future, only highly distinguished Clemson greats with highly decorated careers on the field and in the classroom will be inducted into the Ring of Honor and have their names and numbers retired there, installed beside the elite few whose legends cast long shadows. There will not be a yearly induction program, flooding the wall with new names.

TIGERS QUIZ

25. Who was the MVP of the 1989 Gator Bowl?

Fuller, a shoo-in, was the man of the hour in his four seasons in the ACC. He helped give Clemson back its dignity in football, for the program suffered a swoon following Howard's retirement. Fuller quarterbacked the Tigers for four years and was captain his junior and senior years.

He became Clemson's top offensive performer as a junior with 3,932 yards running and passing, and padded that figure greatly as a senior.

While excelling on the football field, Fuller made mincemeat of his curriculum. He made the Dean's List six consecutive semesters, posting a GPA of 3.93 in pre-law. He made only two Bs while at Clemson, and made straight As otherwise.

He won an NCAA Top Five Award and made the acceptance speech for himself and on behalf of the other four recipients. He earned post-graduate scholarships, and awards for "achievement in bringing honor to Clemson University." Fuller was also a member of the Blue Key, Mortar Board, Tiger Brotherhood, Block C Club, Sigma Alpha Epsilon and Phi Eta Sigma.

DWIGHT CLARK (1975-78) Although Jerry Butler was Steve Fuller's favorite receiver, a fair share of Fuller's passes were directed to Dwight Clark, whose career

Dwight Clark, shown here during one of his "down" times at Clemson, was discovered when a pro football scout came to watch teammate Steve Fuller.

Dwight Clark (87) discusses "The Catch" with Joe Montana. The famous play vaulted San Francisco past the Dallas Cowboys in the 1981 NFC title game.

didn't really blossom until he was accidentally discovered by the San Francisco 49ers. Some 49ers scouts were at Clemson to check Fuller out and Clark was running routes for Fuller. The scouts were intrigued by Clark's hands, and signed him.

Clark played nine years for the 49ers and is best remember for "The Catch" that vaulted San Francisco past the Dallas Cowboys in the 1981 NFC title game, dragging the 49ers into the Super Bowl after eight years of missing the playoffs. Clark didn't live off just that one catch. He was a member of two 49ers Super Bowl teams, was an all-star on several occasions and retired in 1987 after three knee operations. He has also moved up to coordinator of football operations and player personnel.

Clark's career spanned from 1979 through 1987. He really blossomed as a pro, leading the NFC in receiving in 1981-82. He was a member of the Super Bowl championship team in 1981 and 1984 and was named to the NFL Pro Bowl in '81 and '82.

Fuller, Butler and Clark brought Clemson football back into prominence and paved the way for the Tigers to reclaim the glitter that had disappeared. (Butler went on to catch passes brilliantly for the Buffalo Bills from 1979 through 1987. He was the fifth player chosen in the first round of the NFL Draft and was the AFC Offensive Rookie of the Year.)

After his playing days were over, Dwight Clark became an executive with the San Francisco 49ers organization.

RODNEY WILLIAMS (1985-88) Finally, Rodney Williams is reaping respect. It should be pointed out to newcomers to the Clemson family of fans, that Williams, who just happens to be the Atlantic Coast Conference's quarterback of record when it comes to victories, is enjoying football more than ever.

Heading into the 1996 season, Williams was beginning his third year on the Clemson radio network as the roving sideline reporter.

So, what's all this business about No. 13 (that number might tell you something) getting a raw deal from some of the most ardent, loyal fans in the world of college football?

Well, good question; however, one without a good answer. Let's wing it. Williams, by his own admission, wasn't very talented. He may have been lying, but, to be honest, on the surface it didn't appear that he was lying. He wasn't fast. In fact, he was probably on the slow side. He couldn't pass. Heck, he couldn't even drop back and wing it, for goodness sake.

Clemson won 34 games during Rodney Williams' four-year career, with 32 of the wins coming with Williams as the starting quarterback.

What Williams could do was win football games. He even answered questions, some of them in the dumb category, after games about how inept he appeared to be. Game after game after game.

Some say Rodney Williams' No. 13 jersey was an omen.

Hang onto your seats with this one, lest you have forgotten the numbers. Basically, Williams was the starting quarterback for all four years of his eligibility. The Tigers won 32 games with that no-account rascal at the helm, and the question is still unanswered — until now. More on that later.

With Williams calling the signals, the Tigers went 6-6 in 1985 and finished third in the ACC. In 1986, Clemson went 8-2-2 and was ACC champion. (And can't you just recall the boos when the Tigers lost the home and season opener at Death Valley against Virginia Tech.)

The following two years, 1987 and '88, Clemson finished 10-2, and imagine this, won two more ACC championships. How could that be with Rodney Dangerfield still aboard?

Here's a sampling of how Williams' career went at Clemson:

A Sunday morning newspaper headline cries out:

"Williams crosses up critics with sparkling Wake effort."

Another reads:

"Can Tigers win with Williams?"

The theme, at least, is consistent:

"Clemson's Williams just might be in a QB class all his own;" "Clemson's Williams failing at passing;" "He wins, but critics persist 13's lucky for Williams."

Let's examine the last one.

Williams wore No. 11 in high school, but placekicker Mark Gettys had already claimed that jersey number at Clemson. Williams, obviously not superstitious, tempted fate by choosing No. 13.

"I just decided that I'd wear No. 13 and work my way up from there," Williams said. "I figured if I could beat the odds of wearing No. 13, I could beat anything. It worked out."

Not only did it "work out," Williams was the Gator Bowl's Most Valuable Player in 1986, the year the Tigers beat Stanford, 27-21.

The Tigers wound up with greater expectations going into Williams' senior season, ranked ninth in the Associated Press preseason poll.

"There was some pressure on us that year," Williams says, "but winning the ACC and going to the bowl game got us hungry. I felt like we would have to be lucky to win the ACC again, and in some cases we were."

By the end of the 1987 season, the Tigers had another conference title and were 10-2 overall. Williams capped the season with a 35-10 win over Penn State in the Citrus Bowl in Florida and another MVP trophy.

He capped his career with another 10-2 record and a 13-6 win over Oklahoma in the Citrus Bowl.

The dust had finally settled on Williams' career and he obviously had the last laugh.

He is still having the last laugh.

Williams teams up with Mike Eppley, also a former Tiger quarterback, on Clemson's radio broadcasts and brings insightful wisdom to the listeners along the network. Eppley, who has been behind on the radio several years longer that Williams, complements his younger compatriot very well.

"I really like doing the radio stuff," Williams said. "It keeps me in touch and I like getting real close to the action, anyway. I'm not a professional, but I think I can bring some things to the broadcast that shed light on what's going on. Mike and I work real good together. We've experienced a lot of the same things. He's a lot smoother than I am. I'm like a kid in the candy shop down there. It's fun. It's obvious that they guy who did the sideline reporter thing before me hadn't played football. I came along and added some dimension to the show, I believe."

TIGERS QUIZ

26. Who are the three Tigers to make first team All-ACC while wearing No. 99?

TIGERS QUIZ

27. When was the first televised broadcast of a Clemson home game?

Rodney Williams' tenure as Clemson quarterback immediately followed the career of Mike Eppley (shown here). Now the two former players cover Clemson on the radio.

Being a football family member, Williams has a carte blanche invitation to all football meetings, practices and functions. That certainly gives him a definite edge on what to expect and when to expect it.

"When I started, I vowed that I would never say anything negative about the Tigers, and I haven't," he said. "I know all about negativity surrounding any football program, and I'm not getting paid to hop on anybody's butt. For one thing, I told (athletic director) Bobby Robinson, Mike and Jim Phillips that I was going to be a Clemson fan on the radio. I do it because I love Clemson. I'm a 90 percent Clemson fan out there. I'm about 10 percent ojective.

"At the same time, I think things I say help some of the players when they listen to the broadcast later on. Even in the locker room, when I interview players, I interview them from a quarterback's standpoint, and I talk their language. I think they respect me, and some of them will talk to me about certain things. I'm not a reporter and I'm not going to ask what reporters ask."

Even he admits that his stature as a player has grown over the nine years that he has been out of football. He doesn't know why he was routinely booed over the various "down" segments of his career, but he wore his

TIGERS QUIZ

28. Who returned a missed field goal 108 yards for a touchdown at Georgia in 1968?

Mike Eppley was a two-sport athlete at Clemson. He quarterbacked the Tigers before Williams' career at the same position. Now the two can be heard making the calls together — on the radio.

dignity well, never showing much sign of frustration or anger by the mood swings that would take place in the stadium.

"I know I did some fool things on the field, but we were all out there busting our tails, and we made mistakes," he said. "Kids today make mistakes. It doesn't mean that they're not trying hard, it means that they are kids. These players today work as hard or harder than we did. Anytime I'm on the field as a reporter or whatever, I'm going to pat them on the back or the shoulder to let them know that I'm behind them. Clemson's my university and I'm going to stand behind it as long as I'm around."

By his junior year, Williams — while still the victim of some malcontents — was top dog. He wore a "Top Gun" hat, in not-so-subtle fashion, to preseason practice in the intense heat of August. Of course, there were those humorous moments in his first two years that were somewhat embarrassing, but also brought out Williams' human side.

During his sophomore season, one of Williams' passes conked an N.C. State guard in the back of the helmet. Despite the stunning 27-3 loss to the Wolfpack, Williams managed a slight smile when the misaligned pass was brought up in the dead silence of the visiting team's dressing room at Carter-Finley Stadium in Raleigh, N.C.

Rodney Williams was the Gator Bowl's Most Valuable Player in 1986, the year the Tigers beat Stanford, 27-21

Before he led the Tigers to the first of three straight ACC titles as a sophomore, Williams had to swallow hard over quotes like this one from then quarterback coach Jack Crowe: "Rodney Williams will never be a great

quarterback."

Even Danny Ford, who rarely stepped on his players' toes before the press, once said of Williams, "He ain't an Eppley yet," referring to the quiet, soft-spoken quarterback who preceded Williams at Clemson and had led the Tigers to a pair of 9-1-1 seasons, winning the ACC 1982 title with a 6-0 run and zipping through the 1983 season with a 7-0 league record (Clemson was ineligible for the '83 title because of ACC sanctions stemming from an NCAA probation for recruiting violations).

A season after Ford made the comparison to Eppley, Ford still wasn't extremely high on Williams when pressed for an answer. "I just don't know," said Ford. "Eppley was a very smooth quarterback at this stage (junior year) of his career. On the other hand, Rodney has to work every day on his footwork. On the other hand, I haven't ever seen Rodney throw the ball as well as he is throwing it now (in preseason practice.)"

Williams, who might not have looked picture perfect

Rodney Williams had to answer a lot of tough questions during his career.

Quarterback Rodney Williams watches the "henhouse" burn.

on the field (another of his passes beaned a referee), did compared favorably to quarterbacks of note. During his sophomore season, he completed 98 of 200 passes thrown. Steve Fuller completed roughly 50 percent of his passes as a sophomore; Homer Jordan completed 49.4 percent of his passes; and Eppley watched from the sidelines as Clemson cracked Nebraska for the national championship as a sophomore.

In a bottom-line sense, Williams was a clear winner. A quick check of the won-loss column takes care of that stat, and, in the end, that figure is the way all quarterbacks are measured.

Likely the most significant thing that was ever said of Williams during his career also came from Crowe, who said, "We can win with Rodney, and that's the most important thing."

One of Williams' principal assets was his work ethic. When he arrived on campus, he wasn't guaranteed one thing, and the early odds said that he had bitten off more than he could chew. During the off-seasons as a freshman and sophomore, he spent hours upon hours throwing footballs into a net strung between goalposts, the net having been spray-painted with targets. As a junior, he matured immeasurably.

"I thought that I didn't have a strong enough arm to

be a good passer, so I tried to put the muscle to every pass I threw, tried to throw passes with everything I had," he said his junior season. "Now, I throw easy and I throw better."

As a boy, Williams dreamed of playing football at Clemson. His family moved from Spartanburg to Columbia before he was a teenager, and he played high school ball in the shadow of the University of South Carolina.

He learned quickly that he wouldn't worry about what Clemson's fans thought of him, one way or the other.

"The one thing that pulled me through all of my experiences playing ball was something that my high school coach told me years and years ago, and I've applied it to my life today, as well as then. He said, 'If somebody becomes angry at you for whatever reason, and you let that anger eat away at you, the person who made you angry is the person controlling you. If you don't let anybody lead you to anger, you will be your own person. And that will lead you to be free to pursue success and become successful.' "

By anybody's standards, Williams, who has also earned his wings and is qualified to pilot twin engine airplanes, is the epitome of success.

And in 1996, Clemson fans have a respect for him that has aged nicely with time.

HAROLD VIGODSKY It's high time that Clemson fans get to know Dr. Harold Vigodsky, a Spartanburg optometrist, a little better. Poor, Doc. He's great at eye exams and prescriptions and all that, it's just that he has this hobby — stats, stats and more stats.

And that's all right, for the good Doc juggles his professional commitments like, well, a professional. You're likely thinking that he cuts out box scores and basketball boxes and football agate and you'd be partly right. But, it's not exactly that simple.

You see, Dr. V is a Clemson nut. It was a closet thing for a number of years, but it's out in the open and in high gear now. After spending some years in his den as an apprentice calling the *Spartanburg Herald-Journal* to point out math and other errors (minutes played errors in basketball box scores), Vigodsky hit the big time big.

In the fall of 1989, when Clemson opened its football season at home against Furman, Harold Vigodsky joined Jim Phillips and Mike Eppley in the broadcast booth. Vigodsky's been there since, tabulating stats and jotting down other tidbits for the broadcast team. Over the years, Vigodsky has mastered his sideline trade. He's meticulous and, what's more, he's quick, the key to keeping his seat in the booth.

TIGERS QUIZ

29. Who intercepted two passes against Miami in the 1951 Orange Bowl?

Dr. Harold Vigodsky is a walking Clemson record book.

The crowning glory of this time-consuming avocation of his has brought the eye doctor to the peak of the mountain. Last fall, when the Carolina Panthers played their home games at Death Valley, Vigodsky kept stats, and churned them out faster than the stat man the Panthers were paying.

Vigodsky's work happened to catch the attention of Charlie Dayton, the Panthers' media director. Dayton was impressed by the meticulous work, the accuracy and the dispatch of Vigodsky's work. Dayton asked Vigodsky if he would consider being the Panthers' stat man.

He didn't have to ask.

In 1996, the Panthers were to have a doctor in the press box — the Stat Doctor. He'd be paid for his work, of course, but what Dr. V does is a labor of love. He's smart enough to take the money and run, but putting all those little figures together that add up to the big picture cause Vigodsky's blood to bubble.

And what a year for the doc. On Saturdays, sandwiched between Eppley and Phillips, passing notes and figures to them right and left. On Sundays, surveying the Panthers from the new stadium in downtown Charlotte.

"It's quite a privilege for me to be able to do something I know something about and like very much to do," Vigodsky says. "I wasn't expecting the Carolina Panthers thing to happen. It took me by surprise, but I've been excited all year waiting for the season to start.

"I've always fiddled around with box scores and basketball boxes and all kinds of stats, but doing it when it's happening, and people are depending on you to deliver on the spot, well, it's a little more exciting than putting my patients in front of eye charts. Some of them know I keep Clemson stats. I've been doing it for a long time now.

"I also keep the book at Clemson basketball games, and the trips back and forth to Clemson from Spartanburg add up in mileage, and a fair amount of gasoline. But, the memories, the being there at courtside is something you can't buy, or beat."

Nor can he beat the support his partner, wife Gail, has given. "He's like a kid in a toy shop," Gail said. "Harold has done this kind of stuff all his life. I support him because he loves it. Besides, I have a hobby, too. I love to shop."

The unique thing about Vigodsky is that given the adoration he has for Clemson's athletic programs, coupled with the fact that he grew up a few miles west of Clemson in Westminster, Vigodsky never attended the university.

He became a Tiger fan some 30 years ago, while attending Emory University.

"When I was a freshman at Emory, I wanted to keep

TIGERS QUIZ

30. Who is the only former University of South Carolina player to be a Clemson assistant coach?

TIGERS QUIZ

31. Which opponent has the most wins in Death Valley?

up with what was going on at Clemson, so I asked my father to send me the IPTAY reports. He would have sent them, but he told me I should join IPTAY myself, and I did. It's hard to believe that was 35 years ago.

During his years in Atlanta, Vigodsky would relax at Braves and Falcons games. Of course, he would busy himself by keeping all the statistics the scribes in the press box were keeping. Vigodsky has spent eight years a couple booths down from the press box, and points out enough tidbits in one game's span to write a short story or two.

"I had always figured when you read it in the paper, it was gospel," he says. "But after I'd keep the stats, I'd pick up the paper the next day and my figures wouldn't match up with what was in the paper's figures. There would be glaring errors in the box scores, at least errors I considered glaring. And, more often than not, I'd be correct."

TOMMY WEST (1993-PRESENT)

Tommy West has apparently brought a troubled assemblage of Clemson fans back into Memorial Stadium and is slowly winning back their confidence in the program and its direction. Despite a spring that saw five football players run into trouble with the law, the promise of Clemson's future was looking up heading into the 1996 season.

The Tigers were ranked 10th by *Athlon* going into the season. The upward signs had Clemson fans on the brink of dreaming of championships recaptured and bowl games that don't end in 41-0 scores, as in the stunning Syracuse victory over the Tigers in the 1995 Gator Bowl.

Tommy West was a high school fullback who converted to tight end at the University of Tennessee.

Fans are certainly happier than they were in the 1993-94 season, when Ken Hatfield hoisted the white flag and resigned for primarily the same reason Frank Howard resigned 27 years ago — as Howard so plainly said "for health reasons. The alumni and fans were sick of me."

Longtime Clemson followers who loved Danny Ford weren't able to bring themselves to give Hatfield much of a chance. And so it was that the day Hatfield announced a hasty press conference at noon to announce his resignation, there were thousands of sighs of relief from Clemson fans.

The simple fact was that Hatfield had only one mediocre season, a 5-6 disappointment in which the Tigers lost by four points to Florida State, by another four to Georgia Tech, 20-6 to N.C. State, by three points to Wake Forest (you can still hear the boos if you bend your ear), by 30 to Maryland, and by 11 points to South Carolina at home, a definite no-no.

The big criticism was that Hatfield was winning with Danny Ford's troops and recruiting wasn't going well at all and that had he stayed the program would be in shambles. But, by the numbers, Hatfield's ledger in his

four years reflected this: 32-13-1.

There weren't many wet eyes when Hatfield left, and since West had been shaped under Ford's philosophy, he, at least, has a fighting chance, and likely will make it with the Tigers. Despite having five sophomores in starting positions in 1995, the Tigers were vastly improved on that side of the football.

"Now we want to take what we've done to another level," says West.

The Tigers were fourth in the nation in rushing in 1995, and hope to hold that position. The passing game should be stronger in 1996, another plus. The changes in coaches will also have an impact on the Tigers. Darrell Moody, offensive coordinator and quarterbacks coach at North Carolina, has changed his stripes after eight years with the powder blue Tar Heels. With Moody in charge of the UNC offense, the Tar Heels joined Florida State as the only two teams in the Atlantic Coast Conference to average at least 240 yards on the ground and 150 yards in the air per game.

"We want our offense to grow and Darrell can help us continue to move in that direction," West said. "He is experienced and has worked with many types of offenses. That will have to be an advantage for us."

Clemson's offense has picked up while the defense has held its course, including Top 10 rankings in scoring

Tommy West with his family at the news conference when he was introduced as Clemson's head coach in 1994.

Tommy West has brought talented assistants with him to the Clemson sideline.

TIGERS QUIZ

32. Who caught Harvey White's 68-yard touchdown pass to put Clemson ahead to stay in the 1959 Bluebonnet Bowl?

defense in 1994 and '95, the two years West has been head coach. Ellis Johnson, defensive coordinator, has 20 lettermen coming back and 10 players who have been starters at one time or another.

As for West, the growth is a healthy sign. He has been looking forward to the season, and putting the events of the summer involving players in trouble with the law behind the team. When he arrived as head coach two seasons ago, West moved three defensive players to the offensive line in order that the offensive line would have a starting unit.

"Now," he says, "we have at least two returning lettermen at every position in the offensive line. We can still say the same thing about the defense."

Overall, he sees the backfields as the strengths of the 1996 team. And with Nealon Greene and Emory Smith still around, there is reason for slight optimism.

He even shows that his humor is still intact. At an IPTAY meeting in the spring, West explained to his audience that his wife told him not to get too long-winded, that he had to cut something from his talk out.

"On the way down here," he said, "I decided to cut out the part about the Gator Bowl."

On a more serious note, West told the gathering that putting losses like that one in the rearview mirror was the only cure for the pain. "There were too many good things that happened last year, and I won't let our performance in the Gator Bowl take away from those good things.

"We were able to win five games in a row to end the (regular) season. We were unbeaten on Tobacco Road and we won the instate championship. We had a great year. In fact, last year we wanted to be able to compete with every team in the league and we were able to accomplish that as well."

West pushed the 1995 Tigers to an 8-4 finish, good for third place in the ACC. More importantly, that record put Clemson in the Gator Bowl, a New Year's Day game that, unfortunately for the Tigers, turned sour suddenly and stayed that way.

The fact that the Tigers were a middle of the pack pick in the preseason helped take some pressure off the Tigers, for there were no guarantees. And the 6-2 ACC record was the school's best finish since the ACC title in 1991. Eighteen freshmen from an impressive and productive class recruited by West when he took the job lettered in 1994, the most for a rookie class since the 1940s.

At times in '94, the Tigers started seven freshmen at skill positions, and over the winter, West and his staff recruited a second consecutive Top 20 recruiting class, according to many recruiting services.

Some say that Clemson fans still long for Danny Ford

Tommy West, shown here as a young assistant coach.

Tommy West talks on the air before the Tigers' game against Georgia Tech in 1995.

to be their coach, and Danny Ford likely is among that group, though he has been predictably successful at Arkansas. Ford, some say, left his heart at Clemson. But the point is that Ford is gone and West has some of the same charisma that Ford had. West is an easy interview, he is surrounding himself with good coaching stock, and most of the stuff he learned under Ford's wing.

Ford got off to a shaky start as a head football coach and it wasn't until he listened to some old heads tell him to hire an old hand to help him through the ropes that he started climbing the ladder to success. Ford hired

CLEMSON FANAMANIA

Clemson University football fans pride themselves on being the greatest. That reputation doesn't stop a fair share of them from doing a little booing from time to time, but for the most part, Clemson folks do have the spirit.

There are some who would walk through burning coals to keep up with their autumn heroes. Take Frazer "Jack" Grant of Chester, S.C., who followed the Tigers to Tampa, Fla., for the Hall of Fame Bowl in 1991, despite his doctor's warnings that he stood a high risk of losing a leg because of diabetic lesions.

Undaunted, Grant traveled by bus to Tampa for the New Year's Day game against Illinois. And, what a day it was for the Tigers during the Ken Hatfield reign. Clemson blanked Illinois 30-0, the largest ever margin for the Tigers in a bowl game. The win earned the Tigers an 18th place finish in the final Associated Press poll, capping a 10-2 record and a second place ACC finish.

At the time, Grant had five diabetic lesions on his left ankle. Convinced the lesions were healing, he made the trip. His wife, Lavinia, doctored him while they were in

Florida, and Grant did fine.

Grant made his way to and from bowl happenings and the game itself in an electric wheelchair. For the game, he wore a battery-operated cap with blinking orange lights in the shape of a Tiger Paw. His shirt, of course, was orange.

Jack Grant died April 25, 1996, of heart failure. "Jack had been doing so good," Lavinia Grant said. "We were looking forward to our 50th wedding anniversary. We were married 49 ½ years. We did get to go to the Gator Bowl last year, and he had such a good time. We didn't like the score, naturally, but we went on a tour bus and Jack used his little cart on the elevator and right up to the skybox where our seats were. He had to climb only four steps. He really enjoyed that game even though we lost."

The Grants spent a lifetime, more than 40 years, following the Tigers. Their first bowl game was the Gator Bowl in 1949, when Clemson beat Missouri, 24-23. Over the years, they skipped a few bowl outings, but they drove to Miami when Clemson beat Nebraska for the 1981 national championship.

Tom Harper, a salty, down-to-earth coach who led Danny Ford through some mazes and would have, at the same time, followed Ford to war.

West must have been born to be a football coach, for after a highly successful career as a player at the University of Tennessee, West spent a year as a graduate assistant at his alma mater. He followed that up with a year of high school football at White Country High in Sparta, Tenn. By 1979, West took a job as an assistant at Mississippi and for two years was an assistant at Appalachian State. He also coached South Carolina and

Spirit Blitz Day at Memorial Stadium.

took his first head coaching job at UT-Chattanooga. While there his team, which had won only two games in 1992, doubled the wins the following year and toward the end of the season upset the NCAA Division I-AA No. 1 ranked Marshall Thundering Herd.

West was born and raised in Gainesville, Ga. He earned his bachelor's degree from Tennessee in 1976 and

Coach Tommy West poses at Howard's Rock.

was drafted by the Tampa Bay Buccaneers.

West began his career as a player at Tennessee as a running back but became a tight end. As a junior, he caught an 81-yard pass from Condredge Holloway, still the longest non-scoring play in Tennessee history. West also played baseball for two years at Tennessee and had a career batting average of .305. He was an outfielder, and in basketball, he played guard. In the June 1972 baseball draft, Willie Randolph, who went on to an All-Star career with the New York Yankees, was drafted after West in the draft's regular phase.

Tommy West talks to the troops.

Glory — 1981

When Clemson opened the 1981 season at home against Wofford College, some of the Tiger faithful were understandably uneasy about what the 11-game schedule might bring, and understandably so.

Clemson limped into the final game of the 1980 season having lost four of its last five games and was a decided underdog against archrival South Carolina.

In that annual nail-biter, the only thing the Tigers had going for themselves was the home field advantage, a shaky insurance policy on that autumn day, for certain.

The salvation of the season had come down to beating USC, a critical juncture for second-year head coach Danny Ford. A win would give the faltering Tigers a 6-5 season, a loss would heap considerable pressure on Ford, whose fate would be determined on that very game.

The National Champs visit the White House. Ronald Reagan holds up a commemorative shirt while U.S. Senator Strom Thurmond watches.

In a stunning reversal on a bright, crisp November afternoon, the Tigers actually bullied the Gamecocks in a sterling performance that brought Clemson fans back to life. Their Tigers had administered a surprising 27-6 licking on the Gamecocks, taking the heat off Ford and setting the scene for the most memorable season in the school's history.

Clemson's varsity actually looked forward to spring practice that year. Ford outlined the prospects of the fall, which included the standard goals — winning one game at a time, winning the Atlantic Coast Conference title

and, naturally, making it to a bowl game, perhaps the bowl that would determine the national championship.

When wide receiver Perry Tuttle and other players began working out on their own before the spring workouts began, Tuttle was stunned to discover that his off-season workouts in the weight room meant advanced training with weights.

"I never thought that wide receivers had to lift weights like the other guys, but was I wrong," Tuttle, a crafty receiver and a senior leader, admitted. "Once I got used to doing more with weights, it wasn't that bad. I just worked to keep my muscles toned up. The important factor was to keep my speed up, and in the process, I actually increased my speed by several tenths in the 40-yard dash."

Given the reprieve that Ford forged for himself by whipping South Carolina in the season finale, he increased his efforts to bulletproof the Tigers against a similar collapse that nearly cost him his head coaching whistle.

"We opened up everything in the spring," Ford said in the fall of '81. "We looked at every possibility. Last year we were too limited by what we wanted the team to be. This year we're going to do what this team can do best."

Wide receiver Perry Tuttle was one of 11 returning offensive starters in 1981.

As it turned out, what the 1981 version of the Clemson Tigers did best was win, survive and out-maneuver the impossible. What turned the Tigers from jelly in 1980 to invincible in '81 were the numbers. By preseason practice, Ford counted 53 lettermen on the roster, and more importantly, all 11 starters on offense were back and brimming with confidence.

The key to the offense was quarterback Homer Jordan, who took some knocks in '80 but showed potential. Jordan had begun his climb to the top from the bottom of the quarterback ranks. But before he was able to take his place as the third-string quarterback, Jordan had to plead with Ford to give him his chance. Jordan had gotten word that he was being moved to a defensive back position. He reminded the head coach that he was told he would have a shot at quarterback. Following a pregnant pause, Ford gave Jordan a reluctant nod.

Some blamed the Tigers' 6-5 season in '80 on Homer Jordan, but in reality the athletic quarterback sparked Clemson's victory over South Carolina in the 1980 season finale. That victory was instrumental in turning around the football program.

Still, the journey to the starting position was an uphill trip. Jordan was naturally shy, reserved, and he dealt with being Clemson University's first starting black quarterback with poise, politely answering questions that cut straight to the point. He, of course, took much of the heat for Clemson finishing 6-5 in 1980, despite playing an instrumental role in the South Carolina win, which turned the program around.

"The fans here didn't know much about Homer, but we knew he was a football player," said Ford. "We didn't know he was a quarterback. Early on, he was very, very

Homer Jordan was the key to winning the national title. And just think, coaches nearly moved him from quarterback to defensive back before the 1980 season.

quiet and very, very shy. He didn't talk much at all. There was never a question of him having ability. He was always tight, nervous, and in the beginning, he deserved the criticism. He had to settle down."

By the time the Tigers lined up against Wofford College, a Division II team that was merely filling in as Clemson's season-opening opponent in '81, Jordan was firmly entrenched as quarterback. Only several months earlier, Villanova (Clemson's original season-opening opponent) had announced it was shutting down its football program and the Tigers searched desperately to find a suitable replacement.

The search was headed nowhere for the Tigers when Wofford, certainly no match for Clemson, volunteered for what most certainly would amount to wholesale slaughter. When the curtain rose on the season, Wofford not only showed up, they were juiced to play. At halftime, Wofford was trailing 7-3 and Danny Ford wasn't the only body in Memorial Stadium scratching his head. Clemson fans, still savoring the victory over South Carolina and expecting a routine blowout to begin the season, were shaking theirs.

As expected, the game rolled to a predictable conclusion. Clemson shifted gears and sailed to a 45-10 win, easing up on the Terriers in the second half. Jordan's stock grew.

Tuttle noticed the command that Jordan showed in the Wofford opener after Clemson's tentative performance in the first half.

"Homer started growing up in the last four games of the 1980 season," Tuttle noted. "Before that, Homer was never really sure of himself. He had to work hard to get the job in the first place. It took time. When he had to check off at the line, he wasn't sure of what to do all the time. He made mistakes. I would put my arm around him and say, 'Homer, don't worry. The coaches have confidence in you. Go with your instincts.' "

By the opening series of the fourth quarter, Clemson held a 31-3 lead. Ford had called off the dogs, and the Clemson community breathed a sigh of relief and already headed to their tailgates to celebrate the obvious.

"Wofford had an excellent game plan in the first half and ran us ragged with their misdirection plays," Ford said. "We just had a whole lot more depth than they did. If we hadn't thrown the big bomb, the score could have been 3-3 at halftime."

Tuttle went into the season-opener with a score of his own to settle. Despite an outstanding performance in 1980, Tuttle was overlooked on the '81 preseason All-ACC squad in a poll of ACC coaches. Tuttle picked up

Perry Tuttle poses at Howard's Rock on a trip back to Death Valley.

the paper with a headline that proclaimed 'Tuttle Left Out' and burned inside.

"It made me kind of mad and the first thought I had was that I still wasn't respected," he said.

"Some folks didn't know, but I knew how good Perry Tuttle is," Ford said then. "Pro scouts will give Perry a look very, very early in the draft." Indeed, Tuttle was a first round draft choice of the Buffalo Bills and played for nine years in the NFL and the CFL.

From the somewhat staggered start against Wofford College, the Tigers winged to the Big Easy to face Tulane and, alas, struggled to a 13-5 victory. Two wins are two wins, but things didn't look all that good for Clemsonites in the early going.

The Tigers were playing indoors for the first time ever — the SuperDome. Ford was understandably concerned, for depth perception was a possible problem for his players. The fear of misjudging, even losing the football against the Dome's ceiling prompted nightmares.

Clemson hadn't played Tulane since 1975, and the Green Wave beat the Tigers at Death Valley, 17-13. History began repeating itself. By the end of the first quarter, Tulane led on the strength of a 46-yard field goal and a safety.

The Tigers finally forged a 7-5 lead in the second quarter after Joe Glenn recovered a Tulane fumble and tailback Cliff Austin trotted the last four yards to draw blood. In the second half, Clemson had a 33-yard field goal attempt by Bob Paulling aborted on a poor snap. Paulling upped Clemson's tender lead to 10-5 on the first play of the fourth quarter on a 31-yard field goal.

Then, Clemson's defense took charge and Paulling drilled a 37-yard field goal to post the game's final points.

"I feel lucky to get out of here alive," Ford sighed afterward. "There were a lot of mistakes in the game. I don't know how many but they came from both sides. I thought that Tulane was a lot better team than they showed on film, and I was right. They were real physical. I'm glad we got out of this one alive."

Clemson fans, loyal as they are, still weren't able to determine which way the wind was blowing. The Tigers were 2-0, barely. What was worse, dread Georgia was next up for the Tigers. Orange disciples gnawed at their fingernails, geared for the worse.

GEORGIA ON HIS MIND The Bulldogs were defending national champions and ranked fourth nationally going into the Clemson game. Anxiety ran high all week on the Clemson campus. Georgia was a tough ticket for the Tigers, even at home — unranked, ranked, it didn't matter.

Despite the two wins, Clemson was still unranked.

Jeff Davis, nicknamed "The Judge," was selected an All-American at linebacker in 1981 after serving as captain of the national championship team. He still holds the school record for most tackles in a game (24) and in a season (175). Davis was a fifth-round draft pick for the Tampa Bay Buccaneers, where he played from 1982 through 1987. He was the leading tackler for the Bucs for four seasons.

Pollsters weren't looking the Tigers' way. Ford's seniors, sensing the urgency of beating the Bulldogs, pleaded with the head coach to don the orange pants they debuted in the stunning win over South Carolina the previous season.

Ford voted the request down. They would save the orange pants for the regular-season finale against South Carolina. His seniors persisted through the week and eventually wore Ford down.

"I didn't want them to wear the pants," Ford said, "and I still don't want them to wear 'em but once a year against South Carolina, but I got overruled. I knew it was coming. I knew they were going to ask. I told them I wanted to wear the orange pants again when I know we can win. They said, 'Well, we can wear them this week.' "

When the dust settled that afternoon in Death Valley, the Tigers had earned a respectable 13-3 win, and looked commanding getting there — in their all-orange outfits.

The Tigers forced nine turnovers, the most ever by a Clemson opponent. In the process, Clemson throttled

Ray Brown and the rest of the Tigers' defense roughed up Georgia and forced a record nine turnovers. Clemson's 13-3 victory over the Bulldogs in '81 started the ball rolling for the Tigers' best season ever.

James Farr was a starter at left guard as a sophomore in 1981. He went on to a stellar career, including third-team All-America honors from the Associated Press in 1983.

Herschel Walker, keeping the heralded tailback from scoring a touchdown on Clemson in his career at Georgia.

Clemson broke open a scoreless first half with 10 second quarter points. Tuttle scored on an 8-yard pass from Jordan and Donald Igwebuike booted a 39-yard field goal. Georgia got its only points in the third quarter on Kevin Butler's 40-yard field goal. Igwebuike capped the scoring on a 29-yard field goal early in the fourth quarter. Clemson's defense spent the remainder of time ensuring that Walker didn't penetrate the Tigers' goal line.

"This was probably the biggest game we were going to play all year," said linebacker Jeff Davis after the win over the Bulldogs. "When we lost to Georgia the year before, we kind of lost our morale; and it hurt us the rest of the season."

KENTUCKY Ford always feared the unknown, and though he knew a fair amount about Kentucky, he feared the Tigers would be prime for picking in Lexington, Ky.

There were reasons for Ford's fears.

Awakened by the stunning upset of Georgia the week before, the nation's pollsters ranked Clemson 18th. Frank Howard sweetened the suspense early in the week, which was normal routine for the retired Clemson coach.

"Danny, you dug yourself a hole Saturday, didn't you?" Howard drawled. "Now you got to win 'em all."

Kentucky was certainly no pushover, but the Tigers came back with a 21-3 win and Ford talked about how improved and tough the Wildcats were. It was certainly a victory in which the Tigers had to scrap for everything they got, he said.

The Wildcats held a psychological edge over the Tigers. Historically, Kentucky had won six of the seven games the two schools had played, the most recent a 13-10 win over the Tigers in 1971 at Death Valley.

Clemson was faced with the prospect of playing a team that had lost two of its first three games, but looked promising in the early going. Kentucky whipped North Texas State, 28-6, in the opener but lost heartbreakers to Alabama, 19-10, and Kansas, 21-16.

"Kentucky is a lot bigger game than we thought it would be at the time. Kentucky is so close, so close to

TIGERS QUIZ

33. Which team has Clemson defeated most often in football?

Homer Jordan as a sophomore in 1980, against WCU.

An important player on the '81 championship squad, Donald Igwebuike came to Clemson to play soccer but ended up setting all sorts of school records on the football field as a placekicker. He led the nation and the ACC in field goal percentage (.941) as a senior in 1984. He never missed a PAT in his career at Clemson and made 32 of 43 field goals.

A three-year starter on the offensive line for the Tigers, Lee Nanney was named a second-team UPI All-American in 1981.

winning. They are a team that's hungry to win," Ford said on the eve of the game.

Commonwealth Stadium was filled to the brim, and Kentucky fans were buoyed by the Wildcats early 3-0 lead in the first half. But Clemson's running game came to life in the second half and Kentucky was as good as sunk.

The Tigers took the second-half kickoff and drove 83 yards, sending Kevin Mack off-tackle for the final six yards that gave Clemson the lead for good. Minutes later, defensive end Andy Headen recovered a fumble at the Kentucky 21 and Jordan moved the Tigers to the 3-yard line before covering the final distance to provide Clemson with a 14-3 advantage.

Midway through the final quarter, the Tigers drove 87 yards in 12 plays that ran six minutes off the clock. Chuck McSwain covered 41 yards, scoring the final touchdown from two yards out.

VIRGINIA That put the Tigers at 4-0 and facing yet another psychological challenge — Virginia, the team that years before Howard had dubbed "white meat," a plump, easy prey.

The Tigers were back in Tigertown and the atmosphere was festive. Ardent fans began pouring into town early in the week camping out in recreational vehicles, checking into motels and getting primed for the Cavaliers.

As uncertain as Ford was going into the Kentucky game, he was doubly skittish as the Virginia game neared. The Tigers had vaulted into the ninth spot in the national polls. Virginia could make its season on the Clemson Tigers alone.

Ford played his cards close to the vest, as usual. "I'm very, very concerned about Virginia," he said. "The thing that worries me about Virginia more than anything else is that they know how to go out and beat people they're not supposed to beat. They beat Georgia in Athens a couple of years ago, and they beat Tennessee at Knoxville last year."

The Tigers had incentive. Virginia was Clemson's first conference foe, and the Cavaliers had been good at giving the Tigers some serious scares over the years. There was a bullet in the chamber. Ford pressed that point.

Despite getting off to a somewhat slow start, the Tigers posted a 10-0 halftime lead. Igwebuike kicked a 22-yard chip shot field goal in the first quarter and tailback Cliff Austin bolted for a 42-yard score down the right sideline to pad Clemson's lead late in the second quarter. The Tigers pressed onward in the second half, taking the second-half kickoff and driving 77 yards for a touchdown by Jeff McCall. Austin scored from a yard out, and Igwebuike capped the scoring with a 32-yard field goal, giving Clemson a solid 27-0 win before a soldout homecoming crowd.

DUKE Talk of a national championship still had not surfaced, and one prime reason was that Duke, Clemson's next opponent, more often than not gave the Tigers fits. The game was scheduled at Wallace Wade Stadium at Duke, a team that had a penchant for rubbing Clemson's nose in the grass at the Blue Devils' own stadium. Ford was as wary as he had been all season.

Typically, Ford said, "I'm very, very worried about playing them up there. They have one of the finest quarterbacks in the league and some youngsters who can run with it. Defensively, they match up well with our youngsters."

But by the middle of the week, Clemson was ranked sixth in the polls and bowl reps seemed to swarm all over the team. Talk of a shot at a national championship was surfacing, blunted by Ford, the eternal pessimist. Still, the thoughts of Clemson spending New Years Day in New Orleans was gaining credence, and there were other bowl scenarios that were brought to the table.

But Ford focused on the Blue Devils. His Tigers had dropped a dismal 34-17 decision to Duke at Death Valley the year before. The stakes were high.

Duke fell 38-10 that year, partly because Ford convinced his troops that they would be playing the college equivalent of the NFL All-Stars. It was part of Ford's motivational philosophy. He was convincing, a virtual football Will Rogers.

"They don't like Clemson," Ford said. "They're not impressed with Clemson and they don't have any reason to be impressed with Clemson. It ain't bragging when you come in and do what they did."

Clemson had a highly impressive defense going for it by then. The Tigers had allowed only one touchdown all season long, and had kept opponents out of their end zone for 16 consecutive quarters.

The Tigers sprang to a 7-0 lead in the first quarter, tacked on 17 additional points in the second quarter and patiently played out the second half, holding the Devils to 10 points. Clemson spread out its scoring assault. Paulling kicked a 20-yard field goal; Austin scored on a 15-yard run and a 2-yarder; Jordan hammered over from one yard out and he capped the point parade by hitting Tuttle on a 29-yard scoring strike.

Free safety Terry Kinard is the only Clemson player to be a unanimous All-American pick and was the first two-time Clemson All-American defensive back (1981 and '82). Kinard, who still holds numerous school records, was a first-round pick of the New York Giants in 1983, the 10th pick overall. He played with the Giants from 1983 through 1989, including the '86 Super Bowl championship season. He played with the Houston Oilers in 1990.

BACK-TO-BACK HOME VICTORIES By the time Clemson pasted N.C. State 17-7 and nuked Wake Forest 82-24 in back-to-back at home performances, the Tigers were humming, but no more so than their aroused fans.

Quarterback Homer Jordan rears back to throw a bomb against N.C. State. Clemson's 17-7 victory over the Wolfpack in '81 vaulted the Tigers to the No. 3 spot in the national rankings.

After stopping N.C. State in a game that was fairly evenly waged, the Tigers were ranked third nationally and poised to make history. Clemson was in the midst of its best football start in 33 years. Jordan had proven to be more than just a good quarterback, he was in command of a balanced attack that gave opposing defenses nightmares.

State took a 7-3 first quarter lead over the Tigers, but were shut out the rest of the way. Igwebuike put the Tigers on the board with a 39-yard field goal, and Austin sliced over from a yard out to give Clemson a 10-7 halftime lead. McCall capped the scoring in the fourth quarter on a 15-yard run that closed the door on the Wolfpack.

Against Wake, the Tigers defied some superstition by beating the Deacons on Halloween. In the process, Clemson broke 21 school, ACC or stadium records. Included in the new figures was 756 yards of total offense, 536 of those were rushing yards. This team, by consensus, was on destiny's track. Ford, of course, beat back any such talk, whether it came up at media functions, through the mail or just coincidentally. If thoughts of a national championship showdown danced around Danny Ford's head, nobody would have had a clue.

The Tigers scored 49 points in the first half, and scored on their first possession of the second half. Clemson's final points came on a 72-yard run by Craig Crawford on his first carry as a Tiger. It is the longest play in Clemson history for a player on his first play. In the 82-24 win, Clemson was 12-for-12 on third down conversions and racked up 12 touchdowns.

NORTH CAROLINA The North Carolina game, at Chapel Hill, snapped the Clemson crowd back to attention. The Tar Heels had the Tigers on their heels and a win in hand, until Clemson snatched the win away from UNC in the closing moments of the game. Clemson was leading 10-8 but the Tar Heels were literally at Clemson's end zone. A matter of yards. Time wasn't a factor until a muffed lateral was fumbled right into Jeff Bryant's hands. Clemson dodged a bullet.

The duel represented the only battle of Top 10 teams in ACC history. The game was basically a defensive struggle, with Clemson hanging onto a 7-5 lead at the half. Neither team scored a touchdown in the second half, but there were offsetting field goals in the third quarter.

Jeff Bryant was a second-team All-American defensive tackle on the '81 title team, which he led in sacks and tackles for loss. He was the sixth pick overall in the 1982 NFL Draft, going to the Seattle Seahawks. He played in Seattle from 1982 through 1993 and is second in Seahawks history in career sacks.

MARYLAND The following week Clemson was back at home and beat Maryland, 21-7, to win the ACC championship. Jordan completed 20 of 29 passes for 270 yards and that mark still stands as the most completions for a Tiger quarterback in a Clemson victory.

Ford, like many coaches, gave way to superstitions when it seemed reasonable. For instance, he grabbed a windbreaker with the number 21 on it early on as Clemson's head coach and the Tigers won on that particular day. Ford kept the jacket. Before the '81 season became the runaway it became, Ford had sucked on a lemon from a glass of iced tea, so he spent the rest of the season ritually sucking on a lemon.

Asked how sweet the lemon was, Ford smiled, "sweetest thing next to winning."

SOUTH CAROLINA Maryland turned out to be a piece of cake and Ford was able to spell some of his frontliners heading into the South Carolina game — a season unto itself — in Columbia at Williams-Brice Stadium. The die was cast. The Tigers were ranked No. 2 in the country; South Carolina was playing for pride.

Clemson rolled to a dramatic 29-13 win, and was ranked No. 1, no small potatoes. The Tigers had been shooting for the South Carolina game all season. In the backs of their minds, beating South Carolina would be a perfect finish to a picture perfect season. Nebraska was gravy — win or lose.

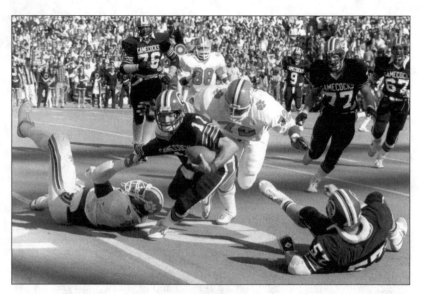

Defense was the key for Clemson's battle with South Carolina. Here, Ray Brown goes in for the kill and makes it.

Clemson jelled with Jordan at quarterback, while the Gamecocks were juggling quarterbacks and eventually settled on Gordon Beckham. As expected, the Tigers' defense proved the difference in the regular-season finale.

The stage was finally set when fans on both sides of the Clemson-Carolina fence read a quote by USC coach Jim Carlen: "There's more hatred here than in other rivalries. It's a stigma that has become hatred, and I'm not saying that's necessarily good for college athletics. I've been involved in rivalries before, but none of them compare to this one."

Naturally, Ford countered, "I heard the word 'hatred' mentioned," he said, "but we don't hate. Hatred might not be the word that we would use because you're not supposed to hate people. We just dislike them this week. I think that's the way they feel about Clemson. It's a good rivalry, an enjoyable one and one I like to be associated with. I just hope it doesn't get ugly."

South Carolina was primed to knock Clemson from the mountaintop. The Tigers received the opening kickoff, but punted after three downs. The Gamecocks rocked the stadium and the USC family by driving the football straight down the Tigers' vaunted defense, gracefully moving 51 yards in seven plays and sending Johnnie Wright over from a yard out to zip to a 7-0 lead.

Clemson sputtered on offense a second time, and USC took over. But the Gamecocks weren't able to move the ball and were forced to punt. The Tigers blocked the kick, however, and Clemson's Johnny Rembert covered the ball in the end zone for a touchdown. Unfortunately for the Tigers, Paulling missed his first extra point conversion of the season and USC held the lead at 7-6.

In the second quarter, Paulling atoned himself. He converted a 23-yard field goal to put Clemson ahead, 9-7, for good. Jordan was intercepted on the following series, but Clemson scored again after a Hollis Hall interception at the South Carolina 28-yard line. Jordan closed that deal on an 11-yard scamper around left end, giving the Tigers a 15-7 lead at the half.

South Carolina spiced up the second half by taking the opening kickoff and driving 67 yards for a touchdown when Beckham hit Horace Smith in the end zone with a 10-yard pass. The Tigers clung to a 15-13 lead when the Gamecocks' two-point conversion failed.

Clemson countered. On the kickoff, Jordan set the Tigers on an 86-yard drive that ended on McSwain's surge from one yard out.

Clemson sealed South Carolina's fate early in the fourth quarter, cruising for another 80 yards, punctuated by McSwain's 21-yard run up the middle for the touchdown. Clemson's band wore out "Tiger Rag" through the night.

The Tigers weren't just going bowling, they were going for a national title.

"I've told our youngsters all along they could be a great team if they continued to work and improve every week," Ford said. "Now, I'm ready to say it. This is a great football team."

On that day, after beating South Carolina, Clemson officials accepted the invitation from the Orange Bowl to play Nebraska for the national title.

Johnny Rembert made a big play in Clemson's victory over South Carolina in 1981 when he recovered a blocked punt in the end zone for a touchdown. Rembert, a junior college transfer who played just two years at Clemson, was a third-team All-America selection by the Associated Press in 1982. He played with the New England Patriots for a decade after being taken in the fourth round of the NFL Draft.

After a season of humble-speak, Danny Ford finally admitted his true feelings after Clemson wrapped up the Orange Bowl bid. "Now, I'm ready to say it. This is a great football team."

TIGERS QUIZ

34. Who is the only Tiger to be both a first team All-American and a first team Academic All-American?

THE ORANGE BOWL There was some down time between the South Carolina game and Clemson's preparations for the Orange Bowl. Ford gave his players a week off following the USC win. They, like Ford and his staff, needed to recuperate. Basically, Ford wanted his players to bask in the limelight of Clemson's first unbeaten season and the school's highest ranking in 33 years.

Clemson was the only unbeaten team in the country, and the Tigers were poised to challenge powerhouse Nebraska in the Orange Bowl at Miami for all the marbles. The Tigers, ranked No. 1 but pegged by oddskeepers as a decided underdog, upset the Cornhuskers 22-15 on a balmy night by the Atlantic Ocean.

For the Tigers, the Florida experience began after working out on campus for several weeks before heading to New Smyrna Beach, Fla., where the Tigers began seriously focusing on the Cornhuskers. The trip to Florida was no vacation. Ford drilled his troops hard. He was stern, unforgiving. The players understood. Everything was on the line.

"Everybody on the team and everybody associated with Clemson University understands what is ahead — the national championship," said Jeff Davis. "You can't make a better present for yourself than winning the national championship. There's always time for fun after you've finished your hard work."

As the game drew nearer, Clemson players read more and more newspaper stories that knocked the soft schedule the Tigers had played. The ACC was a basketball league. Wofford was a minor league program. Nebraska was the college equivalent of the NFL. Conclusion: Clemson had no business at the Orange Bowl, and time would prove that point.

Legendary Frank Howard countered: "I thought we had done outgrew that stuff, but I guess not. A lot of people think Clemson has never been anywhere, but Clemson has been to the Cotton Bowl, two Orange Bowls and a bunch of Gator Bowls. We'll show up."

In fact, the first face-to-face meeting between players of both teams on the Orange Bowl field was eye-opening. The Huskers were imposing, practically larger-than-life compared to Clemson players, who didn't appear to be intimidated despite the obvious physical disparity.

The game was late starting, bending to the completion of the Sugar Bowl in New Orleans. The Miami air was humid and the crowd of 72,748 began buzzing over Clemson's use of the orange pants for only the third time that season.

Nebraska, which hadn't had the jitters in the days before the game, bobbled the football into Clemson hands on its opening possession. Suddenly, Clemson was in control at the Nebraska 28-yard line. Clemson sputtered somewhat in that series, but Igwebuike gave the Tigers an early 3-0 lead on a 41-yard field goal.

Nebraska took the following kickoff at the goal line and Mike Rozier ran and ran until he was dragged down at the Clemson 31-yard line. Nebraska slipped and slid, but eventually scored on a 25-yard pass from Rozier to Anthony Steels. Nebraska had a 7-3 lead.

Igwebuike added another field goal to bring Clemson to within 7-6 after one quarter. The game see-sawed through the second quarter, but tailback Austin's 2-yard touchdown run gave the Tigers a 12-7 lead at the half, a lead that had orange diehards in the stands buzzing, and waving those signature two-dollar bills.

Clemson sputtered early in the second quarter. But, Nebraska wasn't clicking on all cylinders, either. Clemson still led by five points, but it obviously wasn't enough. Jordan took over, throwing 12 yards to Tuttle at the 37-yard line. Jordan converted a third down play and passed 16 yards to Tuttle to the Nebraska 42-yard line. The Tigers ran for several more yards, and Jordan threw for seven more. The Tigers sputtered, but only momentarily. Facing turning the ball back over to the Huskers, Jordan found Tuttle in the end zone from 13 yards out for the points that gave Clemson an 19-7 lead.

The scoring slowed down, with Igwebuike adding

Punter Dale Hatcher was just a freshman when Clemson won the national championship, but he made an impact and his numbers that year ranked him 19th in the nation. Hatcher is the only player to lead Clemson in punting four straight years. He was a second-team All-America selection in 1984, and he was the 77th player chosen in the 1985 NFL Draft. He played with the Los Angeles Rams for six years and spent one year with Miami.

another field goal in the final minutes of the third quarter to pad Clemson's lead, 22-7.

But the Cornhuskers weren't dead. Nebraska scored on a 26-yard run by Roger Craig (who also completed a successful run for the two-point conversion) to pull within seven points with more than nine minutes remaining in the game. The Tigers relied on defense to get the job done, but Clemson's offense ran valuable time off the clock. By the time the clock showed only 1:53 left, Clemson could smell a win — and a national championship.

Jordan kept Clemson's offense alive. Finally, with 17 seconds left on the clock, Jordan took the ball himself, and scrambled from one side to the other until he was dropped for a 2-yard loss. Six seconds remained.

Nebraska couldn't stop Homer Jordan's run to a national championship. Here, he breaks away from Nebraska's Henry Waechter in the fourth quarter.

The Huskers had time for one play. Clemson covered up the end zone and Headen put an end to the drama, knocking down the desperation pass at the Clemson 15-yard line.

"We finally proved that there is more to the ACC than basketball," said Ford. "They didn't believe this team in Las Vegas. They didn't believe this team in Nebraska. Newspapers were asking if we belonged in the big time.

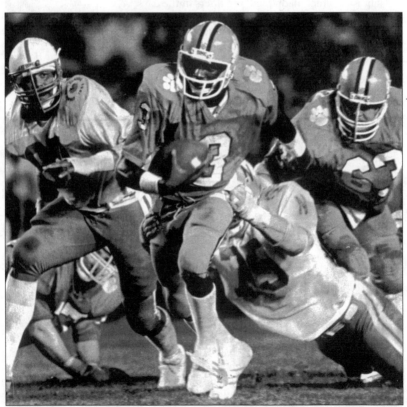

Well, you can brag until you've proved your facts. We've proved ours. Now we can brag.

"No matter what they all say, nobody else in America has done what we have done this year. We played 11 and whipped 11 to get to be No. 1. Now, we've played 12 and whipped 12 and it's over."

Ford secured a place in college football history, and Tiger fans had a lifelong memory of an enchanted season despite the two-year NCAA probation that followed. Ford howled long and loud that the program had been framed and turned even more bitter when the ACC added its own sanctions to Clemson's program. Ford defended Clemson's position, and the following two years the Tigers, ineligible for postseason play, cruised through the league like a thrashing machine.

Yet, on that January night in 1982, Clemson had gone the distance. Not only were the Tigers the only team in the country with a 12-0 record, the Tigers were the only team to defeat three other AP Top 10 teams.

Linebacker Jeff Davis was named the ACC Most Valuable Player, and led the league with 175 tackles. He was a first-team Kodak All-America, UPI, Football Writers Association and *Football News* selection.

Perry Tuttle was a first-team All-America selection by NEA and *Sporting News*. In that championship season, Tuttle became Clemson's career leader in receptions and reception yardage.

Jeff Bryant was tabbed second-team All-America by *Football News* and was drafted by the Seattle Seahawks as the No. 6 pick. He played 12 years for the Seahawks

Quarterback Homer Jordan was the Orange Bowl's MVP and first-team All-ACC.

Danny Ford was named National Coach of the Year by the Football Writers Association, UPI, Kodak and the Washington Touchdown Club. Ford also became the youngest coach to win the national championship. He was 33 at the time the Tigers won the Orange Bowl match.

TIGERS QUIZ

35. The 1950 season saw Clemson go 9-0-1, defeat Miami in the Orange Bowl, and finish the year ranked 10th in the nation. Can you name the team that tied the Tigers?

The Bowl Years

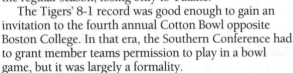

1940 COTTON BOWL

CLEMSON 6, BOSTON COLLEGE 3

January 1, 1940, at Dallas, Texas

Jess Neely coached Clemson to its first bowl game.

Charlie Timmons racked up 115 rushing yards and the game's only touchdown in the 1940 Cotton Bowl.

Jess Neely's last Clemson squad won eight games in the regular season, losing only to Tulane.

The Tigers' 8-1 record was good enough to gain an invitation to the fourth annual Cotton Bowl opposite Boston College. In that era, the Southern Conference had to grant member teams permission to play in a bowl game, but it was largely a formality.

The bowl game was the first for Clemson, a team that sported the school's first All-American, Banks McFadden.

On the last play of the first quarter, the Tigers punted to Boston College. The Eagles' Charlie O'Rourke fielded the punt at the Clemson 40-yard line and was finally brought down at the Tigers' 13. Two running plays pushed BC back 10 yards, but the Eagles gained back six of those yards before Alex Lukachik kicked a 34-yard field goal to give BC an early 3-0 lead.

Banks McFadden was the star of the 6-3 Clemson victory over Boston College in 1940.

McFadden, who had four pass deflections on defense, put the Tigers in gear a couple of series later, hauling an Eagle punt back to the BC 33-yard line. Charlie Timmons picked up 15 yards in two plays, and two plays later McFadden hit Wister Jackson with a 16-yard pass to the Eagle 20-yard line. Timmons covered the final 20 yards in three thrusts, putting Clemson ahead 6-3 following Shad Bryant's missed extra point attempt.

Later in the second quarter, a 51-yard punt by McFadden saddled the Eagles at their own 20-yard line. On first down, BC fumbled and Clemson's George Fritts recovered at the 24. The Tigers gained several yards before fumbling the ball back to BC.

The second half was a defensive struggle. Boston was able to knife deep into Clemson territory twice. The Eagles took the second half kickoff to Clemson's 19 but a holding penalty and an incomplete pass ended the threat.

Late in the game, the Eagles drove to the Clemson 11-yard line, but Bryant and McFadden each batted down two passes and the Tigers took over on downs, averting a disaster. McFadden's punting was one of the keys to Clemson's winning its first ever bowl appearance. His 45-yard average on nine kicks included one for 51 yards and another for 55 yards in the second half. Those boomers prevented BC from establishing field position,

TIGERS QUIZ

36. Who tackled Miami's Frank Smith for a safety to give the Tigers a 15-14 win over the Hurricanes in the 1951 Orange Bowl?

and Clemson's defense was solid enough to make the 6-3 score stand up.

TIGERS QUIZ

37. Four Tigers have scored touchdowns in two different bowl games. Who are they?

Clemson	0	6	0	0	—	6
Boston	0	3	0	0	—	3

BC — Lukachik 34 FG
CU — Timmons 2 run (Bryant kick failed)
Attendance — 20,000

Team Statistics	CU	BC
First Downs	11	9
Rushes/Yards	47-204	37-102
Passing Yardage	35	75
Total Offense	239	177
Yards/per Play	4.69	2.95
Punts	11-44.0	10-42.0
Passes	2-4-1	4-23-1
Fumbles/Lost	5-3	3-2
Penalties/Yards	8-80	9-85
Turnovers	4	3

Individual Rushing (Att-Yds)
CU — Timmons 27-115, Bryant 14-56, McFadden 6-33
BC — Ananis 11-43, O'Rourke 8-41
Individual Passing (Comp-Att-Int-Yds-TD)
CU — McFadden 2-3-0-35-0, Blalock 0-1-1-0-0
BC — Toczlowski 4-23-1-73-0
Individual Receiving (Catches-Yds-TD)
CU — Blalock 1-19-0, Jackson 1-6-0

1949 GATOR BOWL

CLEMSON 24, MISSOURI 23

January 1, 1949, at Jacksonville, Fla.

Jack Miller kicked Clemson's only field goal of the season and it resulted in a 24-23 victory over Missouri in the 1949 Gator Bowl.

Clemson University opened the 1948 season with a 53-0 shutout of Presbyterian College in the first-ever night home game. The Tigers closed the regular season with a 20-0 win over The Citadel in the first game played at the Bulldogs' Johnson Hagood Stadium.

In between those bookend games, the Tigers shut out

three more opponents and beat five other foes on the way to a 10-0 record, a ninth-place ranking in the polls and an invitation to play Missouri in the fourth annual Gator Bowl.

Clemson took the early advantage but the lead see-sawed through all four quarters. Clemson kicked off to Missouri but three plays into its first possession, Missouri fumbled at its 19-yard line. A defensive pass interference call put Clemson on the Missouri 1-yard line, and Fred Cone scored the game's first touchdown.

Later in the quarter, Ray Mathews recovered a Missouri fumble, and Clemson took command at its 35-yard line. The Clemson Tigers gobbled up 26 yards on their first play from scrimmage and added 19 more yards on a pass from Bobby Gage to Bob Martin. Cone duplicated his 1-yard plunge into the end zone. The Tigers, Southern Conference champs, had parlayed Missouri miscues into a 14-0 lead.

Missouri countered, though, launching an 80-yard drive to pull within seven points of the Clemson Tigers. Harold Entsminger capped the 13-play drive with a quarterback sneak from the 2-yard line. Robertson Dawson kicked the extra point.

Gage was intercepted on Clemson's ensuing drive and Wilbur Volz set the Missouri offense up on the Missouri 46-yard line. MU kept the ball on the ground, and Entsminger popped into the end zone from the 1-yard line to tie the game at 14-14.

Clemson's Tigers wasted little time in scoring again. They ran six minutes off the clock on the opening drive of the second half and scored on a flea-flicker from Cone to Gage to John Poulos in the end zone.

Clemson's lead was 21-14, and while Missouri's drive died, its punt wobbled to a stop at Clemson's 1-yard line. But Clemson wasn't able to take advantage. Gage threw an incomplete pass, and another that hit the ground in the end zone that was ruled a safety. Clemson's lead shrunk to 21-16.

The next time Clemson got its hands on the football, the Tigers launched an 11-play assault that bogged down at the 12-yard line. Miller came on to kick the 32-yard field goal that proved to be the difference in the end.

The game might have been decided at that point, but the drama was far from over. Missouri returned the football to its 40-yard line. Seven plays later, halfback Richard Braznell's pass found Kenneth Bounds for a 20-yard touchdown. Dawson added the point after to pull Missouri within a point of Clemson.

Clemson took the kickoff, and was able to milk the clock to the buzzer.

The Tigers, nine years between their first and second

Bobby Gage, who lettered from 1945 through 1948, didn't have a perfect game in his career finale, the Gator Bowl played on January 1, 1949, but he did throw for 112 yards and one touchdown in the victory.

TIGERS QUIZ

38. Chester McGlockton recovered a fumble by West Virginia's Major Harris for a touchdown in the Tigers' 27-7 win in the 1989 Gator Bowl. Who caused the fumble?

bowl games, had run up a 2-0 record in postseason play.

Clemson	14	0	7	3	—	**24**
Missouri	0	14	2	7	—	**23**

CU — Cone 1 run (Miller kick)
CU — Cone 1 run (Miller kick)
MU — Entsminger 2 run (Dawson kick)
MU — Entsminger 1 run (Dawson kick)
CU — Poulos 9 pass from Gage (Miller kick)
MU — Safety, Gage pass grounded in end zone
CU — Miller 32 FG
MU — Bounds 20 pass from Braznell (Dawson kick)
Attendance — 35,273

Team Statistics	CU	MU
First Downs	19	16
Rushes/Yards	42-186	52-225
Passing Yardage	112	73
Total Offense	298	298
Passes	10-23-1	4-8-0
Punts	1-35.0	3-31.0
Fumbles/lost	1-0	3-2
Penalties/Yards	2-10	4-42

Individual Rushing (Att-Yds)
CU — Matthews 11-73, Cone 14-72, Gage 15-25
MU — Entsminger 17-77, Carras 12-73, Braznell 15-37
Individual Passing (Com-Att-Int-Yds-TD)
CU — Gage 10-23-1-112-1
MU — Braznell 2-2-0-57-1, Entsminger 2-6-0-16-0
Individual Receiving (Catches-Yds-TD)
CU — Thompson 4-48-0, Poulos 3-28-1, Martin 1-19-0
MU — Bounds 2-57-1, Wren 1-8-0, Sheehan 1-8-0

1951 ORANGE BOWL

CLEMSON 15, MIAMI 14
January 1, 1951, at Miami, Fla.

Clemson's attempt at another perfect season (like 1948) was shattered when the Tigers scrambled to tie South Carolina in October. They opened the season with three straight shutouts before relying on Charlie Radcliff's extra points for the 14-14 tie with the Gamecocks.

Clemson was able to recover from the setback by inching past Wake Forest. Then, the Tigers won their remaining four games in convincing fashion. An 8-0-1 mark gave the Tigers a second-place finish in the Southern Conference and a trip to play Miami — also unbeaten — in the 17th annual Orange Bowl.

Following a scoreless first quarter, Clemson quarterback Billy Hair threw a 45-yard pass to Bob Hudson, putting the Tigers at the Miami 1-yard line. Fred Cone, as he had done so often, capped the 76-yard drive on a sweep. Radcliff added the extra point.

Clemson scored its second touchdown in the third quarter. Hair threw 31 yards to Ray Matthews, who, as the Miami newspaper reported the following day, made "a circus catch with two men on his back," to move the Tigers to the Miami 28-yard line. Hair tossed another pass to Glenn Smith at the Miami 7-yard line and Smith

TIGERS QUIZ

39. What is the only team that the Tigers have played more than once in a bowl game?

TIGERS QUIZ

40. From 1957 through 1962, Clemson was led by three quarterbacks who were all from Greenwood, S.C. Can you name them?

Sterling Smith, wearing No. 33, made this key tackle of Miami's Frank Smith in the 1951 Orange Bowl that helped preserve a 15-14 Clemson victory.

managed to scramble into the end zone. Radcliff's extra point, however, was blocked, giving Clemson a 13-0 lead.

Miami woke up minutes later when Jack Delbello intercepted a pass in the Clemson end zone and returned it to the 40-yard line. Clemson was further penalized 10 yards for unnecessary roughness. On the following play, Frank Smith ran a reverse for 45 yards, moving the Hurricanes to the Clemson 5-yard line.

Harry Mallios took a pitch from quarterback Bob Schneidenbach for the score. The Hurricanes cut the Clemson lead to 13-7.

Coach Frank Howard celebrates with the hero, Smith.

Miami covered 95 yards for its next touchdown. Ed Lutes caught a midfield pass and dashed to the 17-yard line before being hauled down there. On fourth down, Jack Hackett threw to Frank Smith for the score. The extra point have the Hurricanes a 14-13 lead.

Mallios' 80-yard punt return was called back, a flag that definitely changed the complexion of the game. On top of the flag, Miami was charged with two clipping infractions and an unnecessary-roughness penalty. There were six minutes left on the clock when a second-team defensive guard for Clemson, Sterling Smith, saved the day for the Tigers. Smith tripped Miami's Frank Smith in the end zone for a safety, and Clemson suddenly had the lead back, 15-14.

Don Wade ended the final Miami threat with an interception, his second of the game, and Clemson ran out the clock.

Clemson	0	7	6	2	—	**15**
Miami	0	0	14	0	—	**14**

CU — Cone 1 run (Radcliff kick)
CU — G. Smith 21 pass from Hair (kick blocked)
UM — Mallios 5 run (Watson kick)
UM — F. Smith 17 pass from Hackett (Watson kick)
CU — Safety, F. Smith tackled in end zone by Sterling Smith
Attendance — 65,181

Team Statistics	**CU**	**UM**
First Downs	19	7
Rushes/Yards	57-152	31-122
Passing Yardage	178	100
Total Offense	330	222
Yards Per Play	4.4	4.83
Passes	9-18-3	5-15-4
Punts	4-30.0	5-40.2
Fumbles/Lost	3-1	0-0
Penalties	2-20	5-55
Turnovers	4	4

Individual Rushing (Att-Yds)
CU—Cone 31-81, Hair 10-48, Calvert 7-29
UM—F. Smith 15-87, Mallios 9-25, Czaplinski 2-6
Individual Passing (Comp-Att-Int-Yds-TD)
CU—Hair 9-16-3-178-1, Calvert 0-1-0-0-0, Mathews 0-1-0-0-0
UM—Schneidenbach 3-9-3-78-0, Hackett 1-5-1-17-1
Individual Receiving (Catches-Yds-TD)
CU—G. Smith 6-93-1, Hudson 1-46-0, Mathews 2-39-0
UM—Lutes 1-78-0, F. Smith 2-19-1, Mallios 1-(-2)-0

1952 GATOR BOWL

MIAMI 14, CLEMSON 0
January 1, 1952, in Jacksonville, Fla.

If statistics won football games, Clemson would have snared its fourth straight bowl game in the '52 Gator Bowl. The Tigers had the statistics, but Miami had the points to avenge Clemson's win in the Orange Bowl a year earlier.

The Tigers outgained Miami on the ground by 26 yards and had 33 more passing yards. But four interceptions paralyzed Clemson's chances.

TIGERS QUIZ

41. Who are the two Tigers who have scored at least 100 points in a season?

TIGERS QUIZ

42. Jimmy Addison threw a 75-yard touchdown pass with 3:49 remaining to give Clemson a 40-35 come-from-behind win over Virginia in the 1966 opener. Who caught the pass?

Clemson's chances looked good when Billy Hair took the opening kickoff of the 1952 Gator Bowl 72 yards, but Miami's defense held the Tigers scoreless.

Frank Howard's troops opened the 1951 season with three straight wins and clinched the last four, including South Carolina in Columbia on Big Thursday.

When invitations from the Gator Bowl Committee were dispatched to Clemson and Miami, the school had a hard and fast decision before it. Earlier, the Southern Conference had voted to ban its teams from bowl games. However, both Clemson and Maryland ignored the edict. By league sanction, the two schools were ordered to play only each other in the league in the 1952 season, thus costing either school a chance at the conference title. (The Tigers posted a 2-6-1 record the next season, beating only Presbyterian and Boston College.)

Against Miami, the Tigers looked like they were going to make short work of the day. Billy Hair took Elmer Tremont's kickoff and returned it 72 yards to the Miami 26-yard line. The next four downs turned out to be a clearer picture of what would unfold. Clemson's drive died on downs after the Tigers gained only six yards.

The first quarter turned into a punting exchange, but Miami mounted an 82-yard drive, putting the Hurricanes on top. In that drive, Miami quarterback Jack Hackett threw his only passes of the game — a 15-yarder to Frank McDonald and a 40-yarder to Ed Lutes. Several plays later, fullback Harry Mallios took a pitch and jogged 11 yards into the end zone and Miami took a 7-0 lead.

Clemson mounted a serious attack before the halftime break, but Miami's Jim Dooley intercepted the first of four Clemson passes to kill the Tigers' drive at the Miami 15-yard line. Then Clemson reclaimed the ball, but turned the ball over on a blocked punt at its 32-yard line. The miscue was fatal. Mallios converted fourth-down plays on two occasions to keep the Hurricanes' drive alive. He eventually crashed over from the 2-yard line

TIGERS QUIZ

43. Whose diving touchdown catch gave Clemson a 6-0 win and its first victory ever over Duke in 1959?

Attendance at the Gator Bowl in 1952 was 37,208.

and Miami took a 14-0 cushion into the third quarter.

Clemson's defense was tough in the second half. The Tigers kept Miami from penetrating deeper than their 35-yard line, and the Hurricanes spent the last two quarters without a first down. But the handwriting was on the scoreboard. Clemson's offense moved well enough, but mistakes, like a fumble at the Miami 18, cut deep. Three more Dooley interceptions inside the Miami 18 cut deeper.

The Tigers suffered their first bowl loss in four appearances.

TIGERS QUIZ

44. Which Clemson player was named 1982 NFL Player of the Year by Sports Illustrated?

Clemson	0	0	0	0	—	**0**
Miami	7	7	0	0	—	**14**

UM — Mallios 11 run (Tremont kick)
UM — Mallios 2 run (Tremont kick)
Attendance—37,208

Team Statistics	**CU**	**UM**
First Downs	14	5
Rushes/Yards	44-145	50-119
Passing Yardage	88	55
Total Offense	64-233	52-174
Yds/Play	3.64	3.35
Passes	6-20-4	2-2-0
Punts	4-30.5	9-44.4
Fumbles/Lost	4.1	0-0
Penalties	0.0	4-30
Turnovers	5	0

Individual Rushing (Att-Yds)
CU — Gressette 16-64, Hair 12-35, Shirley 7-33
UM — Mallios 20-50, Bow 13-33, Dolley 8-18
Individual Passing (Comp-Att-Int-TD)
CU — Hair 6-20-4-88-0
UM — Hackett 2-2-0-55-0
Individual Receiving (Catches-Yds-TD)
CU — Smith 4-55-0, Kempson 1-31-0, Gressette 1-2-0
UM — Lutes 1-40-0, McDonald 1-15—0

1957 ORANGE BOWL

COLORADO 27, CLEMSON 21

January 1, 1957, at Miami, Fla.

By the time Clemson went bowling again, the Tigers had been charter members of the Atlantic Coast Conference for four years. The Tigers, indeed, were in a swoon. The first year they competed under the new conference banner, the Tigers finished a depressing sixth. The following year the Tigers moved up a notch, finishing fifth. By 1955, Clemson was bouncing back, climbing to a third-place finish. By 1956, the Tigers were 7-1-2 and ACC champs for the first time.

A surprise choice, Clemson was offered a postseason pass to play Colorado in Miami, another New Year's Day appearance. The Tigers dropped a close decision in a game in which Frank Howard locked the dressing room door at halftime and told his players that he would resign, then and there, if they did not perform better in the game's second half.

"I told them I didn't want to be associated with any team that played like they did in the first half," Howard said.

When Howard and Colorado coach Dal Ward met at midfield following the game, Ward asked the Baron what went wrong with Clemson. Howard, for once at a loss for words, simply said, "Dal, I just don't know."

At least one Clemson player, Joel Wells, was clicking on most cylinders. Wells rushed for 125 yards and scored two touchdowns to spur Clemson's comeback in

Bob Spooner (with ball, bottom right) carried the ball 18 times for 65 yards and one touchdown against Colorado in the 1957 Orange Bowl.

TIGERS QUIZ

45. Which Clemson All-American was the first Tiger to play in the Japan Bowl and the last Tiger to play in the College All-Star game?

TIGERS QUIZ

46. Who was the first Clemson player to play in the East-West Shrine game (he won the award as the Most Outstanding Defensive Player in the game)?

the final two quarters. At the half, the Tigers were looking down the barrel of the Buffaloes' 20-0 lead. In the second half, Clemson's defense held Colorado to seven points, while the offense generated 21 points.

Well's rushing total still ranks as the second-best in Clemson history in a bowl game and his 58-yard touchdown run with 27 seconds left in the third quarter is the longest by a Clemson tailback in a bowl game.

The two teams got off to a dead-even start. Neither team was able to crack the scoreboard in the first period. However, Colorado put together an impressive 75-yard drive that began with a 26-yard run by Bob Stransky, moving the Bisons to Clemson's 23-yard line. It took Colorado only four plays to cover the remainder of the distance, when John "The Beast" Bayuk plunged over from the 2-yard line.

Charley Bussey very likely became a target of Howard's halftime tirade for throwing a pass to Colorado's Stransky near midfield only minutes after the Buffaloes took their 7-0 lead. Stransky moved the ball 36 yards to the Clemson 10-yard line, and Boyd Dowler, who went on to star with the Green Bay Packers, lumbered from six yards out to up Colorado's lead to 14-0.

Clemson's troubles mounted. Horace Turbeville's punt on the ensuing Clemson drive was blocked and Colorado took over on Clemson's 26-yard line. Howard Cook took a right angle into the end zone, but missed the extra point, giving the Buffaloes a 20-0 cushion at intermission.

After Howard's tirade at halftime, the Tigers marched 69 yards in 15 plays to light up their side of the scoreboard on Wells' 3-yard run.

After stopping the Buffaloes on the next series, Wells did his 58-yard touchdown thing and, suddenly, Clemson was down only 20-14, with a full quarter of football to go. And the rallying procedure got much brighter moments later when Clemson recovered its onsides kick. Colorado threw water on that opportunity by stopping the Tigers on four downs.

The Tigers were not done, however. Colorado fumbled at its 11-yard line and Clemson's Tommy Sease covered the ball at the 10. Clemson moved to the one and Spooner dove over for the score. Bussey's third extra point put Clemson ahead 21-20 with 11:22 left on the clock.

The Tigers went back to the onsides kick strategy, but Colorado sniffed that one out, and turned the field position into an eight-play touchdown from 53 yards out. The remainder of the clock was spent with the two teams trading turnovers.

Clemson	0	0	14	7	—	**21**
Colorado	0	20	0	7	—	**27**

UC — Bayak 2 run (Indorf kick)

UC — Dowler 6 run (Cook kick)
UC — Cook 26 run (kick failed)
CU — Wells 3 run (Bussey kick)
CU — Wells 58 run (Bussey kick)
CU — Spooner 1 run (Bussey kick)
UC — Bayuk 1 run (Indorf kick)
Attendance — 72,552

Team Statistics	CU	UC
First downs	14	16
Rushes/Yards	60-217	52-279
Passing Yardage	25	27
Total offense	69-242	56-306
Yards/play	3.51	5.46
Passes	4-9-2	2-4-0
Punts	7-37.8	5-36.6
Fumbles/lost	0-0	8-3
Penalties/yards	4-40	5-55
Turnovers	2	3

Individual Rushing (Att-Yds)
CU — Wells 18-125, Spooner 18-65, Hayes 9-28
UC — Bayuk 23-121, Stransky 7-59, Dove 6-36
Individual Passing (Comp-Att-Int-Yds-TD)
CU — Bussey 3-8-2-9-0, Turberville 1—1-0-16-0
UC — Morley 1-1-0-18-0, Stransky 1—1-0-0-0
Individual Receiving (Catches-Yds-TD)
CU — Lawrence 1-16-0, W. Smith 1-16-0, Horne 2-(-7)-0
UC — Clark 1-18-0, Dowler 1-9-0

1959 SUGAR BOWL
LOUISIANA STATE UNIVERSITY 7, CLEMSON 0
January 1, 1959, at New Orleans, La.

Clemson went 8-2, with losses to South Carolina and Georgia Tech, on its way to the ACC title. The reward was a matchup with the No. 1 team in the nation, Louisiana State University, in the Sugar Bowl. It was the 25th anniversary of the Sugar. Clemson's Frank Howard was

In the '59 Sugar Bowl, Clemson wore dark blue jerseys for the first time.

TIGERS QUIZ

47. *Who played quarterback as a sophomore, became an All-ACC wide receiver as a senior, and later became an NFL All-Pro safety?*

pitted against LSU's Paul Dietzel, who left Louisiana to coach at Army. He was lured to the University of South Carolina in the 1970s to reverse USC's football fortunes.

The precursor to the Dietzel era in Columbia was quite a battle royal. The No. 1 Bayou Bengals slid by Clemson, and Dietzel praised the Tigers' performance.

Clemson got off to a slow start. In the first half, LSU drove deep into Clemson territory three times, but two fumbles and a thwarted fake field goal killed LSU's chances. On the other hand, Clemson's six drives never made it past midfield.

Clemson drove to the LSU 27-yard line on the first drive of the second half. A fumble stemmed any momentum the Tigers were searching for, though, and the swing went to LSU, which recovered a fumble at the Clemson 11-yard line.

From there, LSU halfback Billy Cannon, the Tigers' All-American back, hit tight end Mickey Mangham in the corner of the end zone for the only score of the game. It was Cannon who kicked the extra point that gave LSU the lead.

The Tigers were down, but not KO'd. Late in the fourth quarter, the Tigers launched a drive from their 17-yard line and 17 plays later were in business at the LSU 28-yard line. Facing fourth down, quarterback Harvey White's fourth-down pass to George Usry was incomplete. LSU regained possession

Dietzel was elated. "It was a wonderful victory. They're just as fine when you win 7-0 as 30-0. I'm very happy that we won," said Dietzel, who at 34 years old won the national championship. "Clemson proved tougher than most people figured. But we knew we would have to play at our top peak to beat them. They were a good team."

Howard was pleased that his squad played the top-ranked team in the nation, but couldn't pass up saying what was churning in his mind not long after the game ended.

TIGERS QUIZ

48. *Can you name the player who lettered five times, was team captain twice, and served as an assistant coach for two years?*

"Hell!" Howard spouted. "I think we'd have beat them if that boy had held onto that little screen pass. I was going for those two points and beat them. I didn't think we would hold them to one touchdown, but I didn't think they would shut us out, either."

Clemson	0	0	0	0	—	0
LSU	0	0	7	0	—	7

LSU — Mangham 9 pass from Cannon (Cannon kick)
Attendance — 82,000

Team Statistics	CU	LSU
First Downs	12	9
Rushes/Yards	64-168	37-114
Passing Yardage	23	68
Total Offense	68-191	48-182
Passes	2-4-0	4-11-0

Punts	6-32.8	6-41.7
Punt Returns	3-11	2-19
Kickoff Returns	2-53	1-31
Fumbles/Lost	3-2	4-2
Penalties/Yards	2-20	5-35

Individual Rushing (Att-Yds)
CU — Hayes 17-55, Usry 10-29, Morgan 10-28
LSU — Cannon 13-51, Davis 2-17, Purvis 3-13, Broadnax 3-17
Individual Passing (Comp-Att-Int-Yds-TD)
CU — White 1-3-0-11-0, Shingler 1-1-0-12-0
LSU — Rabb 2-7-0-33-0, Cannon 1-1-0-9-1, Matherne 1-3-0-26-0
Individual Receiving (Rec-Yds)
CU — Cox 1-12, Anderson 1-11
LSU — Mangham 2-33-1, McClain 1-26, Cannon 1-9

1959 BLUEBONNET BOWL

CLEMSON 23, TCU 7

December 19, 1959, at Houston, Texas

The year 1959 was a milestone year for Clemson. The Tigers won the last Big Thursday game, 27-0, putting an end to Clemson having to bus to Columbia each year to play South Carolina on its home turf.

The 9-2 record posted by the Tigers was the school's third ACC championship squad and Frank Howard's last bowl team. After the season-ending win over Furman that year, Clemson was invited to play Texas Christian in the inaugural Bluebonnet Bowl, the Tigers' second postseason appearance in the calendar year of 1959. The 23-7 win over the Horned Frogs was Clemson's 300th football triumph.

Alternate quarterback Lowndes Shingler guided

Clemson scored 20 points in the fourth quarter to win the 1959 Bluebonnet Bowl, a feat that is still a school bowl record. Ron Scrudato put the game out of reach with this 1-yard run.

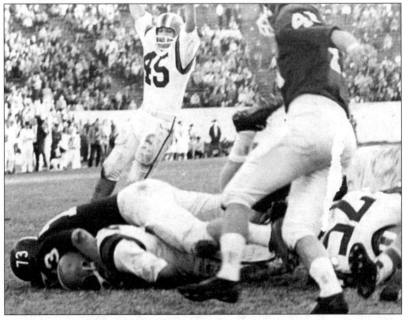

Clemson on a 12-play, 63-yard drive straight to the TCU 5-yard line, but the Tigers stalled. Lon Armstrong's 22-yard field goal to open the second quarter gave Clemson a 3-0 lead, but there was still some life in TCU.

The Horned Frogs, led by second-string quarterback Donald George, moved the home team on an identical drive, only TCU's drive didn't die at the Clemson 5-yard line. The Frogs drove the ball deep into the red zone and scored on a 19-yard pass from Jack Reding to Harry Moreland to take a 7-3 lead.

The third quarter was scoreless but Clemson penetrated to the TCU 29-yard line midway through the quarter. The drive died on a fourth-down pass that was caught a yard short of a first down.

TCU wasn't able to muster any offense and Clemson took to the air in the final quarter. The pass-happy Tigers scored two touchdowns and built a comfortable lead. The game turned into business for the Tigers. Facing third-and-18 at its 32-yard line, Clemson's White threw to Tommy King slashing across the middle and sprinted the distance for a touchdown.

Following a TCU interception, Shingler threw to King for a 23-yard touchdown. Shingler's point after try was wide and Clemson's lead was 16-7.

Clemson went back to its running game for its final score. Shingler, Doug Daigneault and Ron Scrudato moved the Tigers to the TCU 1-yard line and Scrudato slanted off right tackle for the score. Armstrong's kick put the game out of reach and capped a 20-point quarter for the Tigers.

49. In 1996, Clemson plays at Missouri for the second time in school history. When was the first time and what was the score?

Clemson	0	3	0	20	—	**23**
TCU	0	7	0	0	—	**7**

CU — Armstrong 22 FG
TCU — Moreland 19 pass from Reding (Dodson kick)
CU — Barnes 68 pass from White (Armstrong kick)
CU — King 23 pass from Shingler (kick failed)
CU — Scrudato 1 run (Armstrong kick)
Attendance — 55,000

Team Statistics	CU	TCU
First Downs	16	12
Rushes/Yards	55-203	39-89
Passing Yardage	103	70
Total Offense	67-306	56-159
Yds/Play	4.57	2.84
Passses	6-13-1	7-17-4
Punts	3-37.0	5-32.0
Fumbles/Lost	3-1	1-0
Penalties/Yards	3-23	5-35
Turnovers	2	4

Individual Rushing (Att-Yards)
CU — Shingler 3-65, Daigneault 12-50, Cline 9-33
TCU — Spikes 11-33, Harris 8-29, Moreland 7-18
Individual Passing (Comp-Att-Int-Yds-TD-Lng)
CU — White 4-9-1-69-1-68, Shingler 2-4-0-34-1-23
TCU — George 3-7-2-37-0-18, Dawson 2-4-1-4-0-7
Individual Receiving (Catches-Yds-TD-Long)
CU — Barnes 1-68-1-68, King 1-23-1-23, Usry 2-5-0-6
TCU — Moreland 2-37-1-19, Harris 2-17-0-10, Meyer 1-14-0-14

50. Can you name the only Clemson non-lineman to win the ACC Jacobs Blocking Trophy and who later played linebacker for seven seasons with the Houston Oilers and San Diego Chargers?

1977 GATOR BOWL
PITTSBURGH 34, CLEMSON 3
December 30, 1977, at Jacksonville, Fla.

Eighteen years passed between Clemson's bowl appearances. It was not a fruitful meeting with Pittsburgh, and Clemson was no match for the Panthers, quarterbacked by Matt Cavanaugh. Cavanaugh spent the night in Jacksonville filling the Gator Bowl air with passes. He completed 23 of 36 passes for 387 yards and four touchdowns. It was a long night for the Tigers.

The Tigers finished the season with an 8-3 record under first-year coach Charley Pell. The Tigers had been

Jerry Butler's twisting, off-balance catch allowed the Tigers to beat South Carolina and receive the invitation to play in the 33rd annual Gator Bowl.

Quarterback Steve Fuller couldn't get the offense going in the '77 Gator Bowl.

forged on several key performances through the season, edging Georgia 7-6 early and giving Notre Dame a healthy scare. The Tigers came within an extra point of winning the ACC championship, tying North Carolina, 13-13.

Jerry Butler made a twisting, diving catch to beat South Carolina and earn a berth in the Gator. Clemson won the opening coin toss that chilly December night, but that was about it for the Tigers. The Panthers, spurred by Cavanaugh, scored on six of their 12 possessions, set seven Gator Bowl records, and handed Clemson one of its worst defeats in school history.

Cavanaugh threw for a Clemson opponent record of 387 yards and accounted for 402 yards in total offense.

Pitt's defense kept Clemson's offense bottled up all night. Steve Fuller rushed for 34 yards and threw for 158, but the Tigers weren't able to find a successful seam. The Panthers were up 17-0 before Clemson finally posted a 49-yard field goal by Obed Ariri in the second quarter. Pittsburgh added another 17 points in the second half, but Clemson learned from the Pittsburgh loss. It was the dawn of a new era.

In his first season at the helm, coach Charley Pell made the Tigers the "Cinderella" story of college football.

| Clemson | 0 | 3 | 0 | 0 | — | **3** |
| Pittsburgh | 10 | 7 | 7 | 10 | — | **34** |

UP — E. Walker 39 pass from Cavanaugh (Schubert kick)
UP — Schubert 24 FG
UP — E. Walker 10 pass from Cavanaugh (Schubert kick)
CU — Ariri 49 FG
UP — Jones 10 pass from Cavanaugh (Trout kick)
UP — Schubert 21 FG
UP — E. Walker 25 pass from Cavanaugh (Trout)
Attendance — 72,289

Team Statistics	CU	UP
First Downs	14	30
Rushes/Yards	36-110	51-179
Passing Yardage	158	387
Total Offense	59-268	88-566
Yards/Play	4.54	6.43
Passes	10-23-4	23-37-1
Punts	4-33.3	3.43.5
Fumbles/Lost	1-0	5.1
Penalties/Yards	3-24	10-91
Turnovers	4	2

Individual Rushing (Att-Yds)
CU — Fuller 13-34, Callicutt 7-32, Perry 4-22
UP — E. Walker 15-53, Hawkins 2-43, Heath 3-23
Individual Passing (Comp-Att-Int-Yds-TD-Long)
CU — Fuller 10-23-4-158-0-46
UP — Cavanaugh 23-36-0-387-4-41
Individual Receiving (Catches-Yds-TDs-Long)
CU — Butler 4-64-0-22, Weddington 2-57-0-46, King 3-30-0-15)
UP — Jones 10-163-1-41, E. Walker 6-121-3-39

1978 GATOR BOWL
CLEMSON 17, OHIO STATE 15
December 29, 1978, at Jacksonville, Fla.

Danny Ford, who had been presented a brand spanking new Jaguar originally intended for Charley Pell, launched his head coaching career against Ohio

State in the Gator Bowl against one of the fiery legends of the college football game.

Ford had little enough time to prepare his squad to face the Buckeyes, having inherited the reins to Clemson's football program when Pell suddenly announced he was leaving Clemson for the University of Florida shortly after the regular season ended.

The Tigers had just completed an 11-1 season and a

Danny Ford's first game as Clemson's head coach was the 1978 Gator Bowl.

Bubba Brown (47) recorded 22 tackles against Ohio State, which is still the second highest single game total in school history.

6-0 sweep of the ACC. Clemson quickly tabbed Ford as Pell's successor, and some Clemson fans wondered if the decision was too hasty. Their fears were allayed on that New Year's Eve in Jacksonville, when Clemson, ranked No. 6 in both the AP and UPI polls, stunned both Woody Hayes and the Buckeyes.

The Gator Bowl that year was infamous for Hayes' behavior. The fact that Clemson beat a Big Ten team for the first time was very secondary to the night on the banks of the St. John's River. It could be that Ohio State didn't take the Tigers, a football team from a "basketball league," seriously enough. The better bet is that the Tigers were the better team.

Toward the game's end, Clemson held a 17-15 advantage. But faced with third-and-5 at the Clemson 24-yard line, the bowl game turned into the game that ended Woody Hayes' coaching career. Second-team middle guard Charlie Bauman intercepted a pass that killed the threatening drive. Bauman was run out of bounds on the Ohio State sideline, and Hayes moved in the direction of Bauman, swinging and hitting the Clemson player. The moment was frozen in time for fans at the stadium, and those watching on national television.

Bauman, understandably stunned, wasn't hurt, and shook the incident off. For Hayes' action, Ohio State was stung with a pair of unsportsmanlike conduct penalties

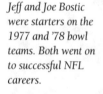

Jeff and Joe Bostic were starters on the 1977 and '78 bowl teams. Both went on to successful NFL careers.

that gave Clemson enough field position for quarterback Steve Fuller to run the clock out.

The game began with Ohio State looking like it would make duck soup of the Tigers. The Buckeyes marched to the Clemson 1-yard line in the first quarter, but the Tigers' defense stopped the drive on fourth down.

The second quarter saw each team score twice. Ohio State drove to the Clemson 9-yard line but had to settle for a 27-yard field goal. Fuller put Clemson in gear, engineering an 80-yard, 15-play drive that gave Clemson the lead. Fuller capped the drive with a 4-yard end run, and the Tigers were up 7-3 following Obed Ariri's point after.

Schlichter moved the Buckeyes in for a touchdown, but Clemson end Steve Gibbs blocked the extra point attempt. Still, OSU moved into a 9-7 lead.

With 75 seconds left in the half, Clemson scored again. Fuller directed the Tigers to the Buckeye 30-yard line and Ariri hit a 47-yard field goal to put the Tigers up 10-9 at the half.

The Tigers hit the scoreboard again in the third quarter, grinding out 83 yards on 18 plays and Cliff Austin knifed over from the 1-yard line. With Ariri's kick, the Tigers held a 17-9 cushion. Schlichter's touchdown with eight minutes left pulled Ohio State within two points, but Jim Stuckey brought the Buckeyes' quarterback down on a sweep to prevent the tying two-point play.

TIGERS QUIZ

51. Who was the Tiger linebacker known as "The Judge"?

| Clemson | 0 | 10 | 7 | 0 | — | **17** |
| Ohio State | 0 | 9 | 0 | 6 | — | **15** |

OSU — Atha 27 FG
CU — Fuller 4 run (Ariri kick)
OSU — Schlichter 4 run (kick blocked)
CU — Ariri 47 FG
CU — Austin 1 run (Ariri kick)
OSU — Schlichter 1 run (Run failed)
Attendance — 72,011

TIGERS QUIZ

52. Who holds the Clemson career record for most passes caught in a season by a tight end?

Team Statistics	**CU**	**OSU**
First Downs	20	16
Rushes/Yards	60-207	44-150
Passing Yardage	123	205
Total Offense	80-330	64-355
Yds/Play	4.1	5.6
Passes	9-20-0	16-20-1
Punts	6-38.3	4-41.5
Fumbles/Lost	5-1	1-0
Turnovers	1	1
Punt Returns	1-(-8)	3-7
Kickoff Returns	2-38	4-94
Penalties/Yards	7-65	7-83

Individual Rushing (Att-Yds)
CU — Perry 14-54, Ratchford 10-54, Fuller 17-38
OSU — Schlichter 18-70, Springs 10-42, Campbell 11-26
Individual Passing (Comp-Att-Int-Yds-TD-Long)
CU — Fuller 9-20-0-123-0-28
OSU — Schlichter 16-20-1-205-0-37
Individual Receiving (Catches-Yds-TD-Long)
CU — Butler 4-44-0-27, Tuttle 3-41-0-20, Clark 1-28-0-28
OSU — Barwig 2-51-0-34, Hunter 2-49-0-37, Donley 3-44-0-34

1979 PEACH BOWL

BAYLOR 24, CLEMSON 18

December 31, 1979, in Atlanta, Ga.

TIGERS QUIZ

53. Who is the current Clemson assistant coach whose brother played for the Tigers?

The Tigers finished in a tie for second place in the ACC race, closing out the regular season with an 8-3 record, including losses to Maryland, N.C. State and South Carolina. The Tigers also whipped eventual ACC champion North Carolina, which won the league and played in the Gator Bowl. Clemson also came from behind to beat Notre Dame, 16-0.

The regular-season work gave Clemson its third consecutive bowl appearance, against Baylor, where the Bears' Mike Singletary spent a large part of the afternoon in Clemson's backfield.

The Tigers were in the battle until the final buzzer. They scored first with an eight-play, 66-yard drive in which quarterback Billy Lott hit Lester Brown with a 27-yard toss to put the Tigers inside Baylor's 5-yard line. Brown scored two plays later on a 1-yard dive over the middle. Obed Ariri's kick put the Tigers up 7-0 with six minutes left in the first quarter.

The Bears clawed back, taking the lead on two second-quarter touchdown passes from Mike Brannon to Bo Taylor and from Brannon to Robert Holt. By intermission, Baylor held a 14-7 advantage.

Clemson drove to the Baylor 22-yard line with the opening kickoff of the second half, but the drive died there and Ariri's foot accounted for the 40-yard field goal that kept Clemson within striking distance.

However, the third quarter belonged to the Bears, who ticked off 10 points. Baylor squeezed out a field goal and quarterback Mickey Elam threw a 7-yard touchdown to

Future pro players Terry Kinard (43), Jeff Davis (45), and Jeff Bryant (99) join Rex Varn (13) in swarming Baylor's Walter Abercrombie, but it was Clemson's Willie Underwood who made the stop. The star-studded defense wasn't enough, though, as the Bears won the Peach Bowl 24-18.

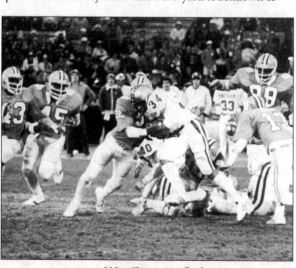

Raymond Cockrell with four minutes left in the quarter.

Singletary led the Bears defense with 20 tackles, primarily for holding Clemson's rushing yardage to 67 yards in 51 attempts.

Despite the lack of a more potent ground assault, Andy Headen spurred Clemson's comeback with a blocked punt that was recovered by James Robinson at the Baylor 1-yard line. Chuck McSwain scored with 20 seconds left in the game and Lott passed to Jeff McCall for the two-point conversion.

Headen pounced on the ensuing onsides kick, and Lott completed a 30-yard pass to Perry Tuttle, moving the Tigers to the Baylor 33. Clemson's hopes for a comeback win were dashed when Lott threw and interception and the Bears ran out the remaining ticks on the clock.

Baylor's Mike Singletary had a big day against the Tigers in the '79 Peach Bowl. He recorded 20 tackles.

Clemson	7	0	3	8	—	**18**
Baylor	0	14	10	0	—	**24**

CU — L. Brown 1 run (Ariri kick)
BU — Taylor 3 pass from Brannon (Bledsoe kick)
BU — Holt 24 pass from Brannon (Bledsoe kick)
CU — Ariri 40 FG
BU — Bledsoe 29 FG
BU — Cockrell 7 pass from Elam (Bledsoe kick)
CU — McSwain 1 run (McCall pass from Lott)
Attendance — 57,731

Team Statistics	CU	BU
First Downs	20	11
Rushes/Yards	51-67	45-62
Passing Yardage	213	172
Total Offense	85-280	62-234
Yds/Play	3.29	3.77
Passes	17-34-3	8-17-0
Punts	9-31.5	9-40.7
Fumbles/Lost	1-0	4-2
Penalties/Yards	7-47	4-30
Turnovers	3	2

Individual Rushing (Att-Yds)
CU — L. Brown 25-76, Perry 5-28, M. Sims 3-15
BU — Abercrombie 12-32, Elam 7-13, Brannon 6-12
Individual Passing (Comp-Att-I-Yds-TD-Long)
CU — Lott 17-34-3-213-0-27
BU — Elam 4-11-0-86-1-63, Brannon 4-6-0-86-2-31
Individual Receiving (Catches-Yds-TD-Long)
CU — Tuttle 8-108-0-30, Gaillard 4-48-0-17, Brown 3-43-0-27
BU — Abercrombie 1-63-0-63, Holt 2-52-1-28, Taylor 2-34-1-31

1982 ORANGE BOWL

CLEMSON 22, NEBRASKA 15
January 1, 1982, at Miami, Fla.

The crowning glory of Clemson's bowl heritage manifested itself on a hot, sticky night at the Orange Bowl when the unbeaten Tigers, ranked No. 1 by both the AP and UPI, upset — yes, upset — the Nebraska Cornhuskers, who were the odds-on favorite by oddsmakers to easily breeze by Clemson.

Clemson's schedule, which included a season-opening game against Division II Wofford College

TIGERS QUIZ

54. Who holds the Clemson career record for the most games started?

Homer Jordan, who quarterbacked the Tigers to the national championship, was big on football sandwiches. In the Orange Bowl game, Jordan racked up 180 yard of total offense and garnered offensive MVP honors.

Perry Tuttle, shown here as a Buffalo Bill, was the only Clemson athlete ever featured on the cover of Sports Illustrated while still a Clemson athlete. A photo of Tuttle, an All-American wide receiver, celebrating a touchdown in the 1982 Orange Bowl was the cover shot. Tuttle's 13-yard touchdown reception in that game was the last of his college career.

because Villanova canceled its football program, was one of the factors the bookies fed on. The prevailing wisdom was that Clemson's schedule was overall a weak one and Nebraska by far had the superior program.

Early in the week of the game, Frank Howard was inducted into the bowl's Hall of Fame. All week long, Howard, who kept up with the comings and goings of college football, felt the Tigers could match up with the beefier Huskers. The folks clad in orange had their fingers crossed, and perhaps the rest of the caring spectators were snickering under their breath.

Clemson began its national championship quest by knocking off defending national champion Georgia, 13-3, early in the season. The Tigers ran through the ACC unscathed and sunk archrival South Carolina, 29-13, to close the regular season.

The Cornhuskers sputtered at the start of the game when Clemson middle guard William Devane recovered a fumble at the Nebraska 33-yard line. The Tigers didn't score a touchdown with the gift, but after stalling at the Nebraska 24-yard line, Donald Igwebuike drilled home a 41-yard field goal that gave the Tigers a lift as well as a 3-0 lead.

Not to be outdone, Nebraska roared back, driving 69 yards in eight plays to score on a 25-yard halfback pass from Mike Rozier to Anthony Steels. With just more than six minutes remaining in the first quarter, the Huskers had a 7-3 lead. The script was unfolding on schedule.

Clemson managed another field goal, a 37-yarder, to pull within a point. And then fate, or something similar, kicked in. The Cornhuskers bobbled the ball for a second time, at the Nebraska 27-yard line, and Clemson took advantage. Three bullrushes landed the football at the Nebraska 2-yard line. Cliff Austin, who had been stuck in the team's hotel elevator for two hours earlier in the day, slithered through the stacked line for the score that gave Clemson a 12-7 lead that it would not relinquish.

The Tigers turned on the heat in the second half, driving 75 yards in 12 plays to score its final touchdown, a 13-yard pass from Homer Jordan to All-American receiver Perry Tuttle, whose backward, diving catch was captured on the cover of *Sports Illustrated*. It was Tuttle's eighth touchdown catch of the season, setting a school record. With that score, Clemson led Nebraska 19-7 with close to seven minutes left in the third quarter. The game wasn't a lock, but Clemson was in high gear and didn't appear to be running out of gas.

Nebraska's Mike Rozier gave it everything he had — he rushed for 75 yards on 15 carries, threw a 25-yard scoring pass, caught one pass for 11 yards and returned three kickoffs for 78 yards — but it wasn't enough to hold off the Tigers' march to the national title.

Before the end of the third quarter, Igwebuike kicked a 36-yard field goal that inflated Clemson's lead to 22-7. By the final quarter, Nebraska came to life, but it was too little, too late. Following a near-interception by John Rembert, the Cornhuskers capped a 69-yard touchdown drive that cranked up the Nebraska fans. The Huskers ran for the two-point conversion to close the gap to 22-15 with nine minutes left.

Clemson's defense, however, shut down the Cornhuskers on their final drive, and Jordan milked the clock for more than five minutes, running it down to six seconds before giving Nebraska one final fling. Andy Headen deflected the desperation pass and preserved the win for the Tigers, voted No. 1 by the major polls the following day.

Clemson	6	6	10	0	—	**22**
Nebraska	7	0	0	8	—	**15**

CU — Igwebuike 41 FG
UN — Steels 25 pass from Rozier (Seibel kick)
CU — Igwebuike 37 FG
CU — Austin 2 run (pass failed)
CU — Tuttle 13 pass from Jordan (Pauling kick)
CU — Igwebuike 36 FG
UN — Craig 26 run (Craig run)
Attendance — 72,748

Team Statistics	CU	UN
First Downs	17	13
Rushes/Yards	52-155	40-193
Passing Yardage	134	63
Total Offense	74-289	57-256
Yds/Play	3.90	4.49
Passes	11-22-1	6-17-0
Punts	4-45.8	6-43.0
Fumbles/Lost	3-0	3-2
Turnovers	1	2

Individual Rushing (Att-Yds)
CU — McCall 12-49, Jordan 16-46, C. McSwain 12-24

UN — Craig 10-87, Rozier 15-75, Bates 6-24
Individual Passing (Comp-Att-I-Yds-TD-Long)
CU — Jordan 11-22-1-134-1-42
UN — Mauer 5-15-0-38-0-13, Rozier 1-1-0-25-1-25
Individual Receiving (Catches-Yds-TD-Long)
CU — Tuttle 5-56-1-16, Magwood 1-42-0-42, Gaillard 3-26-0-16
UN — Steels 1-25-1-25, Brown 1-13-0-13, Rozier 1-11-0-11

1985 INDEPENDENCE BOWL

MINNESOTA 20, CLEMSON 13

December 21, 1985, at Shreveport, La.

This was a bowl game the Tigers likely should have passed up. Clemson carved out a 6-6 season, and Clemson's tradition of bringing fans to the four corners nabbed the Tigers a chance to close the season out on a winning note and a winning record.

The Independence Bowl was only the second time the Tigers faced a Big Ten school. Both clubs gained more than 200 rushing yards. The game was a see-saw match, and Clemson held a 13-10 lead heading into the fourth quarter. But the Gophers scored on a 1-yard run with five minutes left and held Clemson's offense at bay the rest of the way.

The cameras caught Clemson defensive end Michael Dean Perry, the younger brother of William "The Refrigerator" Perry, sunning during a practice session for the Independence Bowl. Minnesota won the contest.

Four Tigers threw passes in the '85 Independence Bowl, but it was the main job of quarterback Rodney Williams. Williams wasn't able to connect with a touchdown pass, but he finished with 171 yards of total offense.

Clemson	0	6	7	0	—	**13**
Minnesota	3	7	0	10	—	**20**

MN — Lohmiller 22 FG
MN — Anderson 9 pass from Foggie (Lohmiller kick)
CU — Treadwell 39 FG
CU — Treadwell 21 FG
CU — Jennings 3 pass from Driver (Treadwell kick)
MN — Lohmiller 19 FG
MN — Baylor 1 run (Lohmiller kick)
Attendance — 42,800

Team Statistics	CU	MN
First Downs	18	20
Rushes/Yards	48-211	55-257
Passing Yardage	162	123
Total Offense	77-373	77-380
Yds/Play	4.84	4.95
Passes	10-29-1	9-22-0
Punts	4-41.5	6-37.5

Individual Rushing (Att-Yds)
CU — Flowers 27-148, Driver 13-37, Rod Williams 5-12
MN — Baylor 13-98, Puk 15-69, Foggie 18-60
Individual Passing (Comp-Att-I-Yds-TD-Long)
CU — Rod Williams 9-23-1-159-0-48, Driver 1-3-0-3-1-3, Anderson 0-2-0-0-0-0
MN — Foggie 9-22-0-123-1-27
Individual Receiving (Rec-Yds-TD-Long)
CU — Ray Williams 5-58-0-21, Jennings 3-41-1-21, Roulhac 2-63-0-21
MN — Anderson 4-34-1-10, Otto 2-31-0-22, Couch 2-41-0-27

TIGERS QUIZ

55. Who was the first Clemson lineman to win the Jacobs Blocking Trophy for the State of South Carolina?

1986 GATOR BOWL

CLEMSON 27, STANFORD 21

December 27, 1986, at Jacksonville, Fla.

All-American David Treadwell nailed a 22-yarder and a 46-yarder in Clemson's win against Stanford in the 1986 Gator Bowl. He came up big during the season, too, kicking a 46-yard field goal on the last play of the game to beat Georgia.

Christmas came several days late for the Tigers as they snapped a bad-luck string and won their first bowl game since the 1982 Orange Bowl. After a brilliant first-half display of offense and defense, Clemson held off a Stanford rally in the second half.

Rodney Williams was voted MVP of the game, and his mastery of the option helped Clemson to a healthy 27-0 lead by the half. Clemson was conservative in the second half, going scoreless in the final two quarters, while the Cardinal posted 21 points to close to within a touchdown.

Tailbacks Terrence Flagler and Kenny Flowers combined for 149 yards. The game also marked the offensive debut of Michael Dean Perry, who was used as a blocking back on a goal-line situation in the first half.

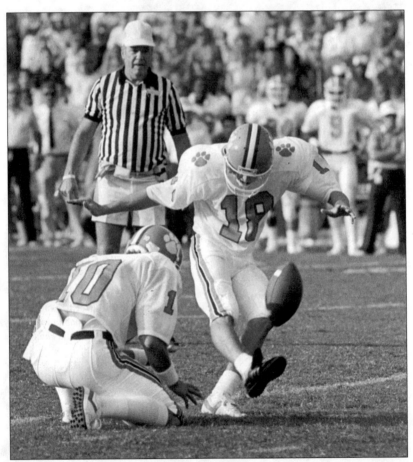

David Treadwell had Georgia's number. In 1986, he beat the Bulldogs with a 46-yard field goal on the last play. A year later, his 21-yarder with two seconds left gave the Tigers a 21-20 win over Georgia.

Clemson	7	20	0	0	—	**27**
Stanford	0	0	7	14	—	**21**

CU — Lancaster 5 run (Treadwell kick)
CU — Rodney Williams 1 run (Treadwell kick)
CU — Treadwell 22 FG
CU — Ray Williams 14 run (Treadwell kick)
CU — Treadwell 46 FG
SU — Muster 1 run (Sweeney kick)
SU — Muster 13 pass from Ennis (Sweeney kick)
SU — Muster 37 pass from Ennis (Sweeney kick)
Attendance — 80,104

Team Statistics	CU	SU
First Downs	19	18
Rushing	57-238	29-114
Passing	12-19-1	20-40-1
Passing Yards	135	168
Total Offense	76-373	69-282
Yards per Play	4.91	4.09
Fumbles	4-0	1-1
Penalties	5-49	3-28

Individual Rushing (Att-Yds-TD)
CU — Flagler 12-82-0, Flowers 14-67-0, Lancaster 7-31-1, Johnson 7-26-0, Rod Williams 16-18-1, Ray Williams 1-14-1
SU — Muster 17-70-1, Dillard 3-13-0, Morris 3-12-0
Individual Passing (Comp-Att-I-Yds-TD)
CU — Rod Williams 12-19-1-135-0
SU — Ennis 20-40-1-168-2
Individual Receiving (Red-Yds-TD)
CU — Hooper 2-44-0, Flagler 3-25-0, J. Riggs 2-23—0, Roulhac 3-22-0, Ray Williams 1-11-0
SU — Muster 4-53-2, Snelsen 4-42-0, James 4-41-0

TIGERS QUIZ

56. Who won the Swede Nelson Sportsmanship Award in 1953?

TIGERS QUIZ

57. Raymond Priester set a new Clemson single-season rushing record in 1995 with 1,322 yards. Whose record did he break?

1988 CITRUS BOWL

CLEMSON 35, PENN STATE 10

January 1, 1988, at Orlando, Fla.

Clemson's day in the Florida sun went well as the Tigers routed Penn State. Quarterback Rodney Williams was named the game's most valuable player, leading a brilliant attack that took the Nittany Lions by surprise.

The win was Danny Ford's fourth bowl victory in only nine years as Clemson's head coach. It also marked Williams' second bowl victory in his career, and it was also the second consecutive time that he was named the MVP of a postseason bowl. Williams, also named the offensive player of the game, completed 15 of 24 passes for 214 yards. Keith Jennings caught seven passes for 110 yards, a career best.

Defensively, Clemson was led by cornerback James Lott's eight tackles. Linebacker Dorian Mariable was selected as the defensive player of the game. He had five tackles and intercepted a pass in the end zone.

Clemson	7	7	7	14	—	**35**
Penn State	0	7	3	0	—	**10**

CU — Johnson 7 run (Treadwell kick)
PS — Alexander 39 pass from Knizner (Etze kick)

The Tigers held Penn State to just 10 points in the '88 Citrus Bowl, and Dorian Mariable, shown here closing in on a Nittany Lion runner, was named defensive MVP.

Rodney Williams picked up his second bowl MVP honor in the 1988 Citrus Bowl. His first MVP award was in the 1986 Gator Bowl.

CU — Johnson 6 run (Treadwell kick)
PS — Etze 27 FG
CU — Johnson 1 run (Treadwell kick)
CU — Allen 25 run (Treadwell kick)
CU — Henderson 4 run (Treadwell kick)

Team Statistics	CU	PSU
First Downs	25	12
Net Rushing	54-285	28-111
Passing	15-24-0	14-23-2
Passing Yards	214	194
Total Offense	74-499	51-305
Yard per Play	6.4	5.9
Fumbles	0-0	2-1
Penalties	8-44	4-26

Individual Rushing (Att-Yds-TD)
CU — Allen 11-105-1 T. Johnson 18-88-3, Henderson 6-54 -1, McFadden 12-38-0.
PSU — Thompson 6-55-0, Brown 13-51-0 Green 4-6-0
Individual Passing (Comp-Att-I-Yds-TD)
CU — R. Williams 15-24-0-214-0
PSU — Knizner 13-22-2-14
Individual Receiving (Rec-Yds-TD)
CU — Jennings 7-110-0, Cooper 4-56-0, Coley 1-19-0, Hooper 1-17-0
PSU — Thompson 4-81-0, Alexander 2-43-1

TIGERS QUIZ

58. Raymond Priester set a new Clemson single-game rushing record in 1995 with 263 yards against Duke. Whose record did he break?

1989 CITRUS BOWL

CLEMSON 13, OKLAHOMA 6
January 2, 1989, at Orlando, Fla.

The Tigers rang in the New Year in fine form, moving into the Top 10 after sailing by the Oklahoma Sooners. The victory gave Danny Ford a win over the winningest active coach in Division I, Barry Switzer.

Levon Kirkland (44) was a defensive standout throughout his career at Clemson. He still ranks high on several defensive record lists and was a second-round draft pick of the Pittsburgh Steelers in 1992.

Although the Tigers faced the Wishbone offense for the first time since Ford became coach, the Clemson defense played very well, holding the Sooners to 116 yards and no touchdowns.

Oklahoma took a 3-0 lead in the first quarter after driving to the Clemson 1-yard line and stalling there.

Doug Brewster intercepted an Oklahoma pass early in the second quarter to set up Clemson's first score, a 20-yard field goal by Chris Gardocki. With time running out in the first half, Gardocki booted a 46-yard field goal to give the Tigers a 6-3 lead at the half.

Clemson fumbled early in the second half, but the

defense held the Sooners to another field goal, a 30-yarder. The Tigers bowed up and scored the game's only touchdown on the next series, moving 80 yards in 15 plays, sending Terry Allen over from four yards out.

Clemson's Jesse Hatcher was named the game's MVP. He caused and recovered a fumble on the Sooners' next drive and had another chance on a final drive, but the Tigers held. Dexter Davis secured the win by knocking down an Oklahoma pass in the end zone to seal the win.

TIGERS QUIZ

59. Who is Clemson's career leader in touchdown responsibility with 44?

Clemson	0	6	0	7	—	**13**
Oklahoma	3	0	3	0	—	**6**

OU — Lasher 35 FG
CU — Gardocki 20 FG
CU — Gardocki 46 FG
OU — Lashar 30 FG
CU — Allen 4 run (Seyle kick)

Team Statistics	**CU**	**OU**
First Downs	12	17
Net Rushing	48-187	43-116
Passing	5-11-0	10-24-1
Passing Yards	57	138
Total Offense	59-244	67-254
Yards per Play	4.14	3.79
Fumbles	1-0	4-1
Penalties	7-76	5-50

Individual Rushing (Att-Yds-TD)
CU — McFadden 9-55-0, Allen 17-53-1, T. Johnson 10-31-0, R. Williams 8-29-0, Henderson 3-10-0
OU — Perry 12-52-0, Gaddis 12-37-0, Holieway 15-17-0
Individual Passing (Comp-Att-I-Yds-TD)
CU — R. Williams 5-11-0-57-0
OU —Holieway 10-24-1-38-1
Individual Receiving (Red-Yds-TD)
CU — Allen 4-47-0, Hooper 1-10-0
OU — Carl Cabbiness 3-78-0, Guess 2-25-0, Chris Cabbiness 1-12-0

Clemson's defense was stellar against the Sooners in the 1989 Citrus Bowl. Here, linebacker Levon Kirkland answers questions from reporters.

1989 GATOR BOWL

CLEMSON 27, WEST VIRGINIA 7

December 30, 1989, at Jacksonville, Fla.

The Tigers squashed Heisman Trophy finalist Major Harris with a dominant defense that held the high-powered Mountaineers' offense virtually helpless. West Virginia had only 237 yards in total offense and the win gave Clemson's senior class the ACC record for victories as they became the first class in conference history to record 38 wins and the first Clemson team ever to win four straight bowl games.

Harris came into the game ranked eighth nationally in total offense and ninth in passing efficiency. His figures dropped drastically against the Tigers, led by outside linebacker Levon Kirkland. Harris gained only 17 yards on the ground and 119 in the air. Kirkland was named MVP.

At the half, Clemson held a 10-7 lead. Following a scoreless third quarter, the Tigers tacked on 17 points in the fourth quarter to take the guesswork out of the final score.

Placekicker Chris Gardocki was named an All-American in 1989-90. He was the second player in the NCAA to finish in the Top 10 in both punting and placekicking in the same season and the first to do it twice.

Sophomore Levon Kirkland holds the MVP trophy from the 1989 Gator Bowl. He took the honor after recording nine tackles, a sack and three quarterback pressures in Clemson's 27-7 victory over West Virginia.

Chris Gardocki never missed a PAT in his career at Clemson. He made three PATs and two field goals in the '89 Gator Bowl.

Chris Gardocki kept the Tigers in excellent field position with a 46-yard punting average, including a long kick of 63 yards.

Clemson	0	10	0	17	—	**27**
W. Virginia	7	0	0	0	—	**7**

WV — Jett 12 pass from Harris (Carroll kick)
CU — Gardocki 27 FG
CU — McFadden 1 run (Gardocki kick)
CU — Henderson 4 run (Gardocki kick)
CU — McGlockton fumble recovery in end zone (Gardocki kick)
CU — Gardocki 24 FG

Team Statistics	CU	WV
First Downs	21	13
Net Rushing	61-257	31-118
Passing	6-11-1	11-25-1
Passing Yards	91	119
Total Offense	72-348	56-237
Yards per Pay	4.83	4.23
Fumbles	0-0	3-3
Penalties	4-30	4-37

Rushing (Att-Yds-TD)
CU — Henderson 22-92-1, Morocco 11-65-0, Kennedy 9-57-0, Lawrence 5-16-0, McFadden 8-12-1
WV — Ford 8-45-0, Napolean 6-24-0, Tyler 4-18-0

Passing (Comp-Att-I-Yds-TD)
CU — Morocco 5-9-0-57-0, Cameron 1-1-0-34-0
WV — Harris 11-21-1-119-1

Receiving (Rec-Yds-TD)
CU — Fletcher 3-66-0, Cooper 2-15-0, Fields 1-10-0
WU — Rembert 4-57-0, Dykes 2-27-0

TIGERS QUIZ

60. Nelson Welch finished his career with a Clemson-record 72 field goals. Who previously held the Clemson career record?

1991 HALL OF FAME BOWL

CLEMSON 30, ILLINOIS 0

January 1, 1991, at Tampa, Fla.

Ken Hatfield's brightest hour came at Tampa Bay when the Tigers lashed the Illini to bits and pieces. John Mackovic, who coached with Hatfield when they were both graduate assistants at Army, had one of the longest days of his coaching career as Clemson racked up 30 points in a flawless performance.

DeChane Cameron was the game's MVP. Cameron's passing yardage totaled 141 yards and he completed touchdown passes to Doug Thomas and Howard Hall.

Clemson caught fire right away, moving 71 yards to the Illinois 2-yard line where Chris Gardocki kicked a chip shot. The Tigers had built a 24-0 lead at the half, and put the game out of reach when Arlington Nunn picked off a pass and raced 34 yards for the score, deflating Illinois.

The Clemson defense earned its third shutout of the season, and posted the first Hall of Fame Bowl shutout. The win was a Tiger record for margin of victory in a bowl game.

Quarterback DeChane Cameron, shown here running the option, set a Hall of Fame Bowl completion percentage record while Clemson's defense dominated the Fighting Illini 30-0 on January 1, 1991.

Clemson	10	14	3	3	—	**30**
Illinois	0	0	0	0	—	**0**

CU — Gardocki 18 FG
CU — Thomas 14 pass from Cameron (Gardocki kick)
CU — Hall 17 pass from Cameron (Gardocki kick)
CU — Nunn 34 interception return (Gardocki kick)
CU — Gardocki 26 FG
CU — Gardocki 43 FG
Attendance — 63,154

Team Statistics	**CU**	**UI**
First Downs	18	14
Rushing	44-148	33-59
Passing	16-23-0	18-36-2
Passing Yards	157	185
Total Offense	305	247
Yards per Play	4.5	3.6
Fumbles	1-0	2-2
Penalties	10-75	2-28

Rushing (Att-Yds-TD)
CU — Cameron 17-76, Williams 14-27, Harris 3-10, Blunt 4-10, Moncrief 3-9
UI — Griffin 15-59, Feagin 5-28, Bell 3-14

Passing (Comp-Att-Yds-I-TD)
CU — Cameron 14-19-141-0-2, Moncrief 2-4-16-0-0
UI — Verduzco 13-25-121-2-0

Receiving (Rec-Yds-TD)
CU — Thomas 5-57-1, Smith 3-43, Hall 1-17-1, Blunt 1-16
UI — Wax 6-77, Muller 3-76, Finke 3-23

Chris Gardocki gets a little help from the sidelines on this one (notice the coach kicking, too).

1992 CITRUS BOWL

CALIFORNIA 37, CLEMSON 13
January 1, 1992, at Orlando, Fla.

61. Who holds the Clemson career record for the most extra points kicked without ever missing one?

Clemson's string of bowl wins was halted at five as the favored Tigers spent a snakebit afternoon in Orlando, virtually helpless as the Golden Bears rung up one score after another. Clemson, ranked No. 13, had entered the game favored over California, ranked 14th entering the game.

Defense, a hallmark for Clemson under Danny Ford, let the Tigers down in this one. Clemson had 50 yards more offense on the ground, but California stacked up 230 yards in the air. On the ground, Tiger defenders were crisscrossed. The Bears scored every which way — on a 1-yard bolt to light up the scoreboard to cap a 76-yard drive, a 31-yard field goal, a 72-yard punt return, a 23-yard pass.

The Tigers were dazed by the end of the first quarter. Nelson Welch hit a 32-yard field goal as the clock expired in the first quarter, but the Bears commanded a 17-3 lead that stretched to 24-3 early in the second

In his last game as a Tiger, quarterback DeChane Cameron had 189 yard of total offense and scored Clemson's only touchdown in a 37-13 Citrus Bowl loss to California.

quarter. By the half, Clemson trailed 27-10, and the numbers wouldn't have been that close had it not been for a 62-yard touchdown sprint late in the second quarter by Clemson quarterback DeChane Cameron.

However, California continued its domination in the second half.

Two Clemson players, participating in their last Clemson game, were named team MVPs in the loss. Defensive tackle Chester McGlockton, who had six tackles, was chosen on defense. Cameron was the offensive pick. Cameron had the Tigers' only touchdown and totaled 189 yards in total offense.

DeChane Cameron, who lettered from 1989 through 1991, still ranks among the Top 10 of nearly every passing category in the Clemson record books.

Clemson	3	7	3	0	—	13
California	17	10	10	0	—	37

UC — Zomalt 1 run (Brien kick)
UC — Brien 31 FG
UC — Treggs 72 punt return (Brien kick)
CU — Welch 32 FG
UC — White 2 run (Brien kick)
CU — Cameron 62 run (Welch kick)
UC — Brien 33 FG
CU — Welch 36 FG
UC — Brien 34 FG
UC — Dawkins 23 pass from Pawlawski (Brien kick)
Attendance — 64,192

Team Statistics	CU	UC
First Downs	19	22
Rushing	44-206	42-146
Passing	15-36-3	21-33-0
Passing Yards	123	230
Total Offense	80-329	75-376
Yards per Play	4.2	5.0
Fumbles	1-0	3-0
Penalties	6-62	8-60

Rushing (Att-Yds-TD)
CU — Harris 14-83-0, Cameron 12-66-1, Blunt 15-41-0
UC — White 22-103-1, Chapman 5-25-0, Mahlum 1-16-0, Edwards 2-14-0
Passing (Com-Att-Yds-I-TD)
CU — Cameron 15-33-123-1-0, Moncrief 0-1-0-1-0
UC — Pawlawski 21-32-30-0-1
Receiving (Rec-Yds-TD)
CU — Smith 7-71, Blunt 3-28, Gibson 2-15
UC — Dawkins 5-55-1, Zomalt 6-41-0, White 3-39-0, Chapman 1-36-0

1993 PEACH BOWL

CLEMSON 14, KENTUCKY 13

December 31, 1993, at Atlanta, Ga.

The Tommy West era brought some color back to the cheeks of Clemson's fans, most of whom had withstood the "agony" of Ken Hatfield's time at Clemson's football helm with little or no patience. To see West make a successful debut — reminding the orange contingent of Danny Ford's similar beginning — was the dose of medicine the faithful needed.

Going into the Peach Bowl, Clemson had established itself by having the seventh-best bowl winning percentage in college football. That mark moved up a tad with the win over the Wildcats, and West became the

TIGERS QUIZ

62. Who holds the Clemson career record for most touchdown passes caught?

Nelson Welch's PAT gave the Tigers a 14-13 victory over Kentucky in the '93 Peach Bowl.

63. Who is second on Clemson's career list for passes intercepted with 15 and also was an outstanding base stealer for the baseball team?

first coach in NCAA history to win his first game for a school in a bowl game without serving as an assistant coach in that program during the regular season.

West's first game as Clemson's head coach was replete with drama. With time running out, the Tigers sealed the victory with a 21-yard touchdown pass from quarterback Patrick Sapp to wideout Terry Smith.

Clemson carried a 7-3 lead into the halftime break, and the third quarter was a back-and-forth struggle that produced no points by either team, setting the stage for a nail-biting finish. Kentucky gained the lead early in the final quarter, scoring on a 46-yard drive on a 5-yard pass. The next two possessions put Clemson on the ropes. Dexter McCleon was intercepted and the Cats bumped their lead another three points on a 26-yard field goal. Clemson trailed 13-7 with seven minutes remaining.

Time had become a crucial factor, and West pulled McCleon in favor of Sapp, who had played only a few minutes in the first half. With 3:50 left, and 82 yards between the Tigers and the Kentucky end zone, Sapp seized the moment. A screen pass to fullback Emory Smith clicked for 57 yards.

The Tigers were poised at Kentucky's 25. With less than a minute to go, Sapp was zapped by Kentucky linebacker Marty Moore, who intercepted the ball while thousands of Clemson hearts fell. Fate intervened, however. As Moore began his flight in the opposite direction, Clemson tackle Stacy Seegars separated Moore from the football. Clemson's Brent LeJeune recovered.

Clemson had a final shot. The game clock was 20 ticks from expiring. Sapp stepped back and drilled a bullet to Smith. Welch drilled the clinching extra point.

The West era was off to a rousing start.

With the Peach Bowl victory, Tommy West became the first coach in NCAA history to win his first game for a school in a bowl game without serving as an assistant coach in that program during the regular season.

Clemson	7	0	0	7	—	**14**
Kentucky	0	3	0	10	—	**13**

CU — E. Smith 2 run (Welch kick)
UK — Nickles 34 FG
UK — Chatman 5 pass from Jones (Nickles kick)
UK — Nickles 26 FG
CU — T. Smith 21 pass from Sapp (Welch kick)

Team Statistics	CU	UK
First Downs	14	20
Rushing	46-119	34-139
Passing	8-16-3	16-32-0
Passing Yards	129	154
Total Offense	62-248	66-293
Yards per Play	4.0	4.4
Fumbles	1-0	2-2
Penalties	10-75	3-25

Rushing (Att-Yds-TD)
CU — Blunt 15-58, E. Smith 8-45-1, Witherspoon 5-17, Sapp 4-10, Franklin 5-8, McCleon 8-2
UK — Williams 13-58, Hood 8-36, Jones 8-19

Passing (Comp-Att-I-Yds-TD)
CU — McCleon 3-7-2-20-0, Sapp 5-9-1-109-1
KU — Jones 16-32-0-154-1

Receiving (Rec-Yds-TD)
CU — T. Smith 4-56-1, Blunt 3-16, E. Smith 1-57
UK — Wyatt 2-28, Chatmon 3-27-1, Calvert 2-32

1996 GATOR BOWL

SYRACUSE 41, CLEMSON 0

January 1, 1996, at Jacksonville, Fla.

History suggests that Clemson was due for a letdown, despite the fact that the Tigers were considered something of a favorite over the Orangemen. Clemson made the trip to one of its favorite bowling spots with a string of five straight wins in the regular season. The Tigers were percolating, to say the least.

The euphoria didn't last long. Syracuse, as former coach Red Parker was wont to say, put something on the Tigers that "soap and water wouldn't wash off." Before the clock died in the first quarter, Syracuse had a 20-0 lead, and it wouldn't get any better for Clemson, which posted goose eggs across the board on that miserable afternoon for the southern "orange" contingent.

TIGERS QUIZ

64. Who is the only player to lead Clemson in punting for four consecutive years?

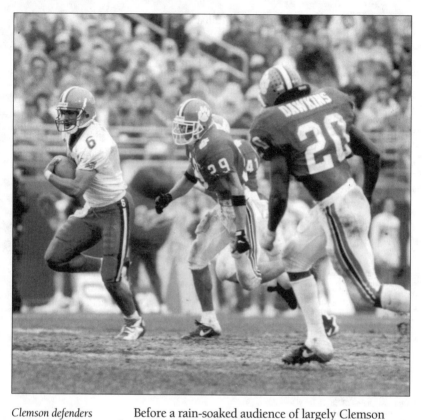

Clemson defenders were chasing the Orangemen all day, and rarely did they catch them.

TIGERS QUIZ

65. Who was the last Tiger to lead the ACC in passing?

Before a rain-soaked audience of largely Clemson fans, Syracuse handed the Tigers their worst bowl defeat in the school's 20-year history.

Syracuse quarterback Donovan McNabb ran and passed his way over, under and around Clemson's defense. The unquestionable MVP of the Gator, McNabb was unstoppable. He threw three touchdown passes and ran for another. He completed 13 of 23 passes for 309 yards, and Marvin Harrison was on the receiving end of most of McNabb's tosses. Harrison nabbed seven passes for 173 yards.

Clemson appeared to have gotten a grip on the situation early in the second quarter, moving 53 yards on 11 plays to the Syracuse 6-yard line, facing a critical fourth-and-2. Down by 20 points, the Tigers gambled on a down-and-out pattern that was just out of reach of Lamont Hall's outstretched hands.

The beat went on through the second quarter and on into the second half. The humiliating loss spoiled the homecoming of Jacksonville natives Brian Dawkins and Patrick Sapp. Clemson, which entered the game with the nation's fourth best rushing attack, managed just 90 yards on 34 attempts, and Syracuse held Raymond

Priester, the ACC's leading rusher, to a mere 36 yards on 15 catches.

The Orangemen added insult to injury in the fourth quarter when McNabb threw a 15-yard strike to Kaseem Sinceno for the game's final points.

TIGERS QUIZ

66. Who are the only Tigers to lead the ACC in pass receiving?

Syracuse	20	0	14	7	—	**41**
Clemson	0	0	0	0	—	**0**

SU — Thomas 1 run (Mare kick)
SU — McNabb 5 run (kick blocked)
SU — Harrison 38 pass from McNabb (Mare kick)
SU — Thomas 2 run (Mare kick)
SU — Harrison 56 pass from McNabb (Mare kick)
SU — Sinceno 15 pass from McNabb (Mare kick)
Attendance — 45,202

Team Statistics	CU	SU
First Downs	12	21
Rushing	34-90	50-158
Passing	11-24-2	13-23-1
Passing Yards	69	309
Total Offense	58-159	73-467
Yards per Play	2.7	6.4
Fumbles	1-0	1-0
Penalties	1-16	7-65

Individual Rushing (Att-Yds-TD)
CU — Priester 15-36, Smith 6-30, Greene 8-16, Solomon 4-8
SU — Thomas 14-71-2, Downing 6-37, Jones 10-25, Konrad 6-24
Individual Passing (Cmp-Att-I-TD)
CU — Greene 9-19—2-63-0, Solomon 2-4-0-6-0
SU — McNabb 13-23-1-309-3
Individual Receiving (Rec-Yds-TD)
CU — Wyatt 3-21, Priester 2-16, Crooks 2-10
SU — Harrison 7-173-2, Wilson 2-70-Sinceno 2-47-1

By the Numbers

The statistics, lists and records that appear in this chapter are taken from Clemson University football media guide, which is produced by the Clemson University Sports Information Office. This list has been updated through the 1995 season.

SEASON-BY-SEASON

Year	Conf. W-L-T	Conf. Finish	Overall W-L-T	Overall Pct	Scoring CU-Opp	Coach	Captain
1896	—	—	2-1-0	.667	36-18	W.M. Riggs	R.G. Hamilton
1897	—	—	2-2-0	.500	30-58	W.M. Williams	W.T. Brock
1898	—	—	3-1-0	.750	110-20	John Penton	A.B. Shealy
1899	—	—	4-2-0	.667	109-50	Walter Riggs	J.N. Walker
1900	—	—	6-0-0	1.000	222-10	John W. Heisman	J.N. Walker
1901	—	—	3-1-1	.700	190-38	John W. Heisman	Claude Douthit
1902	—	—	6-1-0	.857	152-22	John W. Heisman	Hope Sadler
1903	—	—	4-1-1	.750	167-22	John W. Heisman	Hope Sadler
1904	—	—	3-3-1	.500	50-45	A.B. Shealy	John B. Holland
1905	—	—	3-2-1	.583	101-63	Eddie Cochems	O.L. Derrick
1906	—	—	4-0-3	.786	38-4	Bob Williams	Fritz Furtick
1907	—	—	4-4-0	.400	67-45	Frank Shaughnessy	J.M. McLaurin
1908	—	—	1-6-0	.143	26-104	John Stone	Sticker Coles
1909	—	—	6-3-0	.667	93-43	Bob Williams	C.M. Robbs
1910	—	—	4-3-1	.563	106-54	Frank Dobson	W.H.Hankel
1911	—	—	3-5-0	.375	71-108	Frank Dobson	Paul Bissell
1912	—	—	4-4-0	.500	177-123	Frank Dobson	W.B. Britt
1913	—	—	4-4-0	.500	112-98	Bob Williams	A.P. Gandy
1914	—	—	5-3-1	.611	168-123	Bob Williams	W.A. Schilletter
1915	—	—	2-4-2	.375	113-48	Bob Williams	W.K. McGill
1916	—	—	3-6-0	.333	81-147	Wayne Hart	S.S. Major
1917	—	—	6-2-0	.750	183-64	Edward Donahue	F.L. Witsell
1918	—	—	5-2-0	.714	198-101	Edward Donahue	Stumpy Banks
1919	—	—	6-2-2	.800	152-55	Edward Donahue	Stumpy Banks
1920	—	—	4-6-1	.409	98-146	Edward Donahue	Boo Armstrong
1921	0-3-0†	14th	1-6-2	.222	48-187	E.J. "Doc" Stewart	J.H. Spearman
1922	1-2-0	11th	5-4-0	.556	170-109	E.J. "Doc" Stewart	E.H. Emanuel
1923	1-1-1	12th	5-2-1	.688	91-65	Bud Saunders	Butch Holohan
1924	0-3-0	T18th	2-6-0	.250	80-96	Bud Saunders	Charlie Robinson
1925	0-4-0	T20th	1-7-0	.125	27-160	Bud Saunders	G.I. Finklea
1926	0-3-0	18th	2-7-0	.222	20-169	"Bud Saunders, Cul Richards, Bob Williams	B. C. Harvey
1927	2-2-0	8th	5-3-1	.611	73-84	Josh Cody	Bud Eskew
1928	4-2-0	T7th	8-3-0	.727	192-77	Josh Cody	O.K. Pressley
1929	3-3-0	12th	8-3-0	.727	236-110	Josh Cody	O.D. Padgett
1930	3-3-0	12th	8-2-0	.800	239-82	Josh Cody	Johnnie Justus
1931	1-4-0	20th	1-6-2	.250	19-164	Jess Neely	A.D. Fordham
1932	0-4-0	20th	3-5-1	.389	89-111	Jess Neely	Bob Miller
1933	1-1-0	6th	3-6-2	.400	50-98	Jess Neely	John Heinemann
1934	2-1-0	5th	5-4-0	.556	89-85	Jess Neely	Henry Woodward
1935	2-1-0	4th	6-3-0	.667	147-99	Jess Neely	Henry Shore
1936	3-2-0	5th	5-5-0	.500	98-95	Jess Neely	Net Berry
1937	2-0-1	3rd	4-4-1	.500	128-64	Jess Neely	H.D. Lewis
1938	3-0-1	2nd	7-1-1	.833	145-56	Jess Neely	Charlie Woods
1939	4-0-0	2nd	9-1-0	.900	165-45	Jess Neely	Joe Payne
1940	4-0-0	1st	6-2-1	.722	182-73	Frank Howard	Red Sharpe
1941	5-1-0	3rd	7-2-0	.778	233-90	Frank Howard	Wade Padgett
1942	2-3-1	9th	3-6-1	.350	100-138	Frank Howard	Charlie Wright
1943	2-3-0	T7th	2-6-0	.250	94-185	Frank Howard	Ralph Jenkins
1944	3-1-0	3rd	4-5-0	.444	165-179	Frank Howard	Ralph Jenkins
1945	2-1-1	4th	6-3-1	.650	211-73	Frank Howard	Ralph Jenkins
1946	2-3-0	11th	4-5-0	.444	147-174	Frank Howard	Chip Clark
1947	1-3-0	12th	4-5-0	.444	206-146	Frank Howard	Cary Cox
1948	5-0-0	1st	11-0-0	1.000	274-76	Frank Howard	Bob Martin, Phil Prince
1949	2-2-0	8th	4-4-2	.500	232-216	Frank Howard	Gene Moore
1950	3-0-1	2nd	9-0-1	.950	344-76	Frank Howard	Fred Cone
1951	3-1-0	4th	7-3-0	.700	196-97	Frank Howard	Bob Patton
1952	—	—*	2-6-1	.278	112-157	Frank Howard	George Rodgers

Year	Conf. W-L-T	Conf. Finish	Overall W-L-T	Overall Pct	Scoring CU-Opp	Coach	Captain
1953	1-2-0‡	6th	3-5-1	.389	139-172	Frank Howard	Dreher Gaskin, Nathan Gressette
1954	1-2-0	5th	5-5-0	.500	193-121	Frank Howard	Clyde White, Buck George, Scott Jackson, Mark Kane
1955	3-1-0	3rd	7-3-0	.700	206-144	Frank Howard	Don King
1956	4-0-1	1st	7-2-2	.727	167-101	Frank Howard	Charlie Bussey
1957	4-3-0	T3rd	7-3-0	.700	216-78	Frank Howard	John Grdijan, Leon Kaltenback
1958	5-1-0	1st	8-3-0	.727	169-138	Frank Howard	Bill Thomas
1959	6-1-0	1st	9-2-0	.818	285-103	Frank Howard	Paul Snyder, Harvey White
1960	4-2-0	4th	6-4-0	.600	197-124	Frank Howard	Lowndes Shingler, Dave Lynn
1961	3-3-0	T3rd	5-5-0	.500	199-126	Frank Howard	Ron Andreo, Calvin West
1962	5-1-0	2nd	6-4-0	.600	168-130	Frank Howard	Dave Hynes
1963	5-2-0	T3rd	5-4-1	.550	181-140	Frank Howard	Tracy Childers
1964	2-4-0	7th	3-7-0	.300	105-135	Frank Howard	Ted Bunton, John Boyette
1965	4-3-0	T3rd	5-5-0	.500	117-137	Frank Howard	Bill Hecht, Floyd Rogers
1966	6-1-0	1st	6-4-0	.600	174-177	Frank Howard	Mike Facciolo
1967	6-0-0	1st	6-4-0	.600	166-128	Frank Howard	Jimmy Addison, Frank Liberatore
1968	4-1-1	2nd	4-5-1	.450	184-179	Frank Howard	Billy Ammons, Ronnie Ducworth
1969	3-3-0	T3rd	4-6-0	.400	178-250	Frank Howard	Charlie Tolley, Ivan Southerland
1970	2-4-0	T6th	3-8-0	.273	164-313	Hootie Ingram	B.B. Elvington, Jim Sursavage, Ray Yauger
1971	4-2-0	2nd	5-6-0	.455	155-202	Hootie Ingram	Larry Hefner, John McMakin
1972	2-4-0	5th	4-7-0	.364	143-245	Hootie Ingram	Wade Hughes, Buddy King, Frank Wirth
1973	4-2-0	3rd	5-6-0	.455	231-263	Red Parker	Mike Buckner, Ken Pengitore
1974	4-2-0	T2nd	7-4-0	.637	246-250	Red Parker	Willie Anderson, Mark Fellers, Jim Ness, Ken Peeples
1975	2-3-0	5th	2-9-0	.182	177-381	Red Parker	Bennie Cunningham, Neal Jetton, Dennis Smith, Jimmy Williamson
1976	0-4-1	7th	3-6-2	.367	172-237	Red Parker	Malcolm Marler, Mike O'Cain, Randy Scott, Joey Walters
1977	4-1-1	2nd	8-3-1	.708	228-163	Charley Pell	Steve Fuller, Randy Scott, Steve Godfrey
1978	6-0-0	1st	11-1-0	.917	368-131	Charley Pell (11) Danny Ford (1)	Steve Fuller, Randy Scott
1979	4-2-0	T2nd	8-4-0	.667	205-116	Danny Ford	Billy Lott, Bubba Brown
1980	2-4-0	T4th	6-5-0	.545	217-222	Danny Ford	Lee Nanney, Willie Underwood
1981	6-0-0	1st	12-0-0	1.000	338-105	Danny Ford	Jeff Davis, Perry Tuttle, Lee Nanney
1982	6-0-0	1st	9-1-1	.864	289-147	Danny Ford	Terry Kinard, Homer Jordan
1983	7-0-0	—*	9-1-1	.864	338-200	Danny Ford	James Robinson, James Farr
1984	5-2-0	—*	7-4-0	.636	346-215	Danny Ford	William Perry, Mike Eppley
1985	4-3-0	T3rd	6-6-0	.500	244-222	Danny Ford	Steve Reese, Steve Berlin
1986	5-1-1	1st	8-2-2	.750	296-187	Danny Ford	Terence Mack, Terrence Flager
1987	6-1-0	1st	10-2-0	.833	333-176	Danny Ford	Michael Dean Perry, John Phillips
1988	6-1-0	1st	10-2-0	.833	342-157	Danny Ford	Donnell Woolford, Rodney Williams
1989	5-2-0	3rd	10-2-0	.833	368-138	Danny Ford	Wesley McFadden, Otis Moore
1990	5-2-0	T2nd	10-2-0	.833	333-109	Ken Hatfield	Stacy Fields, Vance Hammond
1991	6-0-1	1st	9-2-1	.792	317-185	Ken Hatfield	Levon Kirkland, Rob Bodine, DeChane Cameron
1992	3-5-0	7th	5-6-0	.455	261-213	Ken Hatfield	Robert O'Neal, Ashley Sheppard, Wayne Simmons
1993	5-3-0	3rd	9-3-0	.750	198-192	Ken Hatfield (11) Tommy West (1)	Richard Moncrief
1994	4-4-0	6th	5-6-0	.455	164-188	Tommy West	Tim Jones, Louis Solomon
1995	6-2-0	3rd	8-4-0	.667	303-219	Tommy West	Louis Solomon

Tot. 240-135-12   539-366-45 .591 17,272-12,804

* Indicates Clemson Ineligible for Conference Title

† 1st year of Southern Conference. Clemson's Southern Conference Record: 61-52-6 (.538), 2 Conf. Champions

‡ 1st year of Atlantic Coast Conference; Clemson's Record vs. ACC Opponents (Including 18 games vs. South Carolina) 170-78-6 (.683); 12 ACC Championships, 1 Co-Championship

COACHING RECORDS

No.	Coach	Alma Mater	Years	Overall Rcd.	Pct.
1	Walter Riggs	Auburn 1893	1896, 1899	6-3	.667
2	William Williams	Auburn 1896	1897	2-2	.500
3	John Penton	Auburn 1898	1898	3-1	.750
4	John Heisman	Pennsylvania 1892	1900-03	19-3-2	.833
5	Shack Shealy	Clemson '00	1904	3-3-1	.500
6	Eddie Cochems	Wisconsin '01	1905	3-2-1	.583
7	Bob Williams	Virginia '02	1906, 19, 13-15	21-14-6	.585
8	Frank Shaughnessy	Notre Dame '05	1907	4-4	.500
9	John Stone	Vanderbilt, '08	1908	1-6	.143
10	Frank Dobson	Peddie Inst.	1910-12	11-12-1	.479
11	Wayne Hart	Georgetown, KY '12	1916	3-6	.333

No.	Coach	Alma Mater	Years	Overall Rcd.	Pct.
12	Edward Donahue	Washington & Lee '16	1917-20	21-12-3	.625
13	E.J. Stewart	Case Westrn Reserve	1921-22	6-10-2	.389
14	Bud Saunders	Missouri '11	1923-26	10-22-1	.318
15	Josh Cody	Vanderbilt '17	1927-30	29-11-1	.720
16	Jess Neely	Vanderbilt '23	1931-39	43-35-7	.547
17	Frank Howard	Alabama '31	1940-69	165-118-12	.580
18	Hootie Ingram	Alabama '55	1970-72	12-21	.364
19	Red Parker	Arkansas A&M '53	1973-76	17-25-2	.409
20	Charley Pell	Alabama '61	1977-78	18-4-1	.804
21	Danny Ford*	Alabama '70	1979-89	96-29-4	.760
22	Ken Hatfield	Arkansas '65	1990-93	32-13-1	.706
23	Tommy West†	Tennessee '76	1993-95	14-10-0	.583
	Totals			**539-366-45**	**.591**

* Coached one game in 1978   † Coached one game in 1993

BOWL HISTORY

Year	Bowl	Site	Opponent	W/L	Score
1939	Cotton	Dallas, TX	Boston College	W	6-3
1948	Gator	Jacksonville, FL	Missouri	W	24-23
1950	Orange	Miami, FL	Miami (FL)	W	15-14
1951	Gator	Jacksonville, FL	Miami (FL)	L	0-14
1956	Orange	Miami, FL	Colorado	L	21-27
1958	Sugar	New Orleans, LA	LSU	L	0-7
1959	Bluebonnet	Houston, TX	TCU	W	23-7
1977	Gator	Jacksonville, FL	Pittsburgh	L	3-34
1978	Gator	Jacksonville, FL	Ohio State	W	17-15
1979	Peach	Atlanta, GA	Baylor	L	18-24
1982	Orange	Miami, FL	Nebraska	W	22-15
1985	Independence	Shreveport, LA	Minnesota	L	13-20
1986	Gator	Jacksonville, FL	Stanford	W	27-21
1987	Citrus	Orlando, FL	Penn State	W	35-10
1988	Citrus	Orlando, FL	Oklahoma	W	13-6
1989	Gator	Jacksonville, FL	West Virginia	W	27-7
1990	Hall of Fame	Tampa, FL	Illinois	W	30-0
1991	Citrus	Orlando, FL	California	L	13-37
1993	Peach	Atlanta, GA	Kentucky	W	14-13
1995	Gator	Jacksonville, FL	Syracuse	L	0-41

YEARLY LEADERS

SCORING

Year	Name	TDS	FG	PAT	TOT
1927	Bob McCarley, FB	5	0	1	31
1928	O.D. Padgett, BB	7	0	0	42
1929	Goat McMillan, TB	9	0	0	54
1930	Maxcey Welch, TB	10	0	4	64
1931	J.M. Lambert, WB	1	0	0	6
	E.R. Patterson, RB	1	0	0	6
	Fred Hook, TB	1	0	0	6
1932	Henry Woodward, RB	5	0	0	30
1933	Gene Willimon, TB	2	0	0	12
	Bill Dillard, RB	2	0	0	12
1934	Randy Hinson, RB	3	0	0	18
1935	Mac Folger, BB	6	0	0	36
1936	Mac Fogler, BB	8	0	0	48
1937	Red Pearson, BB	3	1	8	29
1938	Banks McFadden, TB	5	0	0	30
	Shad Bryant, WB	5	0	0	30
1939	Shad Bryant, WB	4	0	8	32
1940	Aubrey Rion, RB	4	0	4	28
1941	Charlie Timmons, FB	9	0	23	77
1942	Marion Butler, TB	6	0	0	36
1943	James Whitmire, WB	4	0	0	24

Year	Name	TDS	FG	PAT	TOT
1944	Bill Rogers, FB	6	0	1	37
1945	Jim Reynolds, BB	5	0	0	30
	Marion Butler, TB	5	0	0	30
1946	Dutch Leverman, RB	4	0	0	24
	Chip Clark, WR	4	0	0	24
1947	Jim Reynolds, EB	8	0	0	48
1948	Ray Mathews, WB	13	0	0	78
1949	Fred Cone, FB	9	0	1	55
1950	Fred Cone, FB	15	0	2	92
1951	Glenn Smith, WR	7	0	0	42
1952	Billy Hair, TB	3	0	0	18
	Don King, RB	3	0	0	18
	Red Whitten, FB	3	0	0	18
	Buck George, WB	3	0	0	18
1953	Dreher Gaskins, WR	5	0	0	30
1954	Jim Coleman, RB	5	0	1	31
1955	Joe Pagliei, RB	7	0	1	43
1956	Joel Wells, RB	8	0	0	48
1957	Bob Spooner, RB	5	0	0	30
	Bill Mathis, RB	5	0	0	30
1958	Harvey White, QB	5	0	0	30
1959	Bill Mathis, RB	11	0	4	70

Year	Name	TDS	FG	PAT	TOT
1960	Bill McGuirt, RB	9	0	0	54
1961	Ron Scrudato, RB	8	0	0	48
1962	Rodney Rogers, PK	0	7	13	34
1963	Frank Pearce, PK	0	4	21	33
1964	Hal Davis, RB	5	0	0	30
1965	Hugh Mauldin, RB	4	0	0	24
	Thomas Ray, QB	4	0	0	24
1966	Jacky Jackson, TB	8	0	0	48
1967	Buddy Gore, TB	9	0	0	54
1968	Ray Yauger,TB	7	0	2	42
1969	Ray Yauger, TB	11	0	2	68
1970	Eddie Seigler, PK	0	8	16	40
1971	Eddie Seigler, PK	0	11	14	47
1972	Eddie Seigler, PK	0	11	14	47
1973	Smiley Sanders, RB	10	0	0	60
1974	Mark Fellers, QB	9	0	0	54
1975	Steve Fuller, QB	6	0	0	36
1977	Lester Brown, TB	9	0	0	54
1978	Lester Brown, TB	17	0	0	102
1979	Obed Ariri, PK	0	16	14	62
1980	Obed Ariri, PK	0	23	18	87
1981	Cliff Austin, TB	9	0	0	54
1982	Cliff Austin, TB	14	0	0	84
1983	Bob Paulling, PK	0	18	36	90
1984	Donald Igwebuike, PK	0	16	41	89
1985	Kenny Flowers, TB	13	0	0	78
1986	Terrence Flagler, TB	13	0	0	78
1987	David Treadwell, PK	0	18	33	87
1988	Terry Allen, TB	10	0	0	60
1989	Chris Gardocki, PK	0	22	41	107
1990	Chris Gardocki, PK	0	22	30	96
1991	Nelson Welch, PK	0	19	31	88
1992	Nelson Welch, PK	0	22	23	89
1993	Nelson Welch, PK	0	15	17	62
1994	Nelson Welch, PK	0	16	14	62
1995	Emory Smith, FB	15	0	0	90

RUSHING

Year	Name	Att.	Gain	Avg.
1935	Joe (Net) Berry, TB	99	457	4.5
1936	Mac Fogler, FB	144	522	3.6
1937	Don Willis, WB	99	329	3.3
1938	Don Willis, FB	103	483	4.7
1939	Charlie Timmons, FB	146	556	3.8
1940	Chippy Maness, FB	86	472	5.4
1941	Charlie Timmons, FB	149	635	4.3
1942	Marion Butler, TB	145	616	4.2
1943	James Whitmire, WB	72	376	5.2
1944	Sid Tinsley, TB	126	479	3.8
1945	Dewey Quinn, FB	89	392	4.4
1946	Bobby Gage, TB	58	264	4.5
1947	Bobby Gage, TB	114	502	4.4
1948	Ray Mathews, WB	113	646	5.7
1949	Ray Mathews, TB	118	728	6.0
1950	Fred Cone, FB	184	845	4.6
1951	Billy Hair, TB	160	698	4.4
1952	Red Whitten, FB	115	445	4.0
1953	Don King, QB	79	243	3.1
1954	Joel Wells, RB	74	352	4.8
1955	Joel Wells, RB	135	782	5.8
1956	Joel Wells, RB	174	803	4.6
1957	Bob Spooner, RB	88	358	4.1
1958	Doug Cline, FB	103	450	4.3
1959	Doug Cline, FB	119	482	4.1
1960	Bill McGuirt, FB	99	320	3.2
1961	Ron Scrudato, FB	99	341	3.4
1962	Pat Crain, FB	94	348	3.7
1963	Pat Crain, FB	137	513	3.7
1964	Hal Davis, RB	87	533	6.1
1965	Hugh Mauldin, RB	194	664	3.4
1966	Buddy Gore, TB	186	750	4.0
1967	Buddy Gore, TB	230	1045	4.5
1968	Buddy Gore, TB	184	776	4.2
1969	Ray Yauger, TB	223	968	4.3
1970	Ray Yauger, TB	183	711	3.9
1971	Rick Gilstrap, TB	144	514	3.6
1972	Wade Hughes, RB	177	761	4.3
1973	Smiley Sanders, RB	113	627	5.5
1974	Ken Callicutt, RB	161	809	5.0
1975	Ken Callicutt, RB	145	572	3.9
1976	Warren Ratchford, TB	119	676	5.7
1977	Warren Ratchford, TB	118	616	5.2
1978	Lester Brown, TB	202	1022	5.1
1979	Marvin Sims, FB	158	743	4.7
1980	Chuck McSwain, TB	114	544	4.8
1981	Cliff Austin, TB	163	824	5.1
1982	Cliff Austin, TB	197	1064	5.4
1983	Kevin Mack, FB	151	862	5.7
1984	Stacey Driver, TB	139	627	4.5
1985	Kenny Flower, TB	227	1200	5.3
1986	Terrence Flagler, TB	192	1258	6.6
1987	Terry Allen, TB	183	973	5.3
1988	Terry Allen, TB	216	1192	5.5
1989	Joe Henderson, TB	178	848	4.8
1990	Ronald Williams, TB	178	941	5.3
1991	Rodney Blunt, TB	175	747	4.3
1992	Rodney Blunt, TB	149	812	5.4
1993	Derrick Witherspoon, TB	111	519	4.7
1994	Lamont Pegues, TB	92	390	4.2
1995	Raymond Priester, TB	231	1322	5.6

Leaders based on total net yards

RECEIVING

Year	Name	No	Yds	Avg
1938	Gus Goins, RE	8	123	15.4
1939	Joe Blalock, LE	15	322	21.5
1940	Joe Blalock, LE	10	211	21.1
1941	Joe Blalock, LE	13	240	18.5
1942	Marion Craig, BB	14	173	12.4
1943	Eddis Freeman, RE	8	175	21.9
1944	Eddis Freeman, LE	9	162	18.0
1945	Eddis Freeman, RE	7	156	22.3
1946	Eddis Freeman, RE	15	181	12.1
1947	John Poulos, LE	6	169	28.2
1948	Oscar Thompson, RE	19	333	17.5
1949	Glenn Smith, RE	25	446	17.8
1950	Glenn Smith, RE	22	498	22.6
1951	Glenn Smith, LE	39	632	16.2
1952	Otis Kempson, LE	15	220	14.7
1953	Dreher Gaskin, E	21	426	20.3
1954	Scott Jackson, E	11	151	13.7
1955	Joe Pagliei, RB	10	233	23.3
1956	Dalton Rivers, E	5	76	15.2
1957	Whitey Jordan, E	12	369	30.7
1958	George Usry, RB	18	171	9.5
1959	Bill Mathis, RB	18	319	17.7
1960	Harry Pavilack, RB	17	272	14.2
1961	Elmo Lam, RB	17	237	13.9
1962	Johnny Case, E	13	213	16.4
1963	Lou Fogle, E	17	218	12.8
1964	Hoss Hostetler, E	8	103	12.9
1965	Phil Rogers, FLK	36	466	12.9
1966	Phil Rogers, FLK	42	574	13.7
1967	Phil Rogers, FLK	28	429	15.3
1968	Charlie Waters, WR	22	411	18.6
	Jack Anderson, WR	22	344	15.6
1969	Charlie Waters, FLK	44	738	16.9
1970	John McMakin, TE	40	532	13.3
1971	John McMakin, TE	29	421	14.5
1972	Dennis Goss, FLK	21	385	18.3
1973	Bennie Cunningham, TE	22	341	15.5
1974	Bennie Cunningham, TE	24	391	16.3

Year	Name	No	Yds	Avg
1975	Joey Walters, WR	26	394	15.2
1976	Jerry Butler, WR	33	484	14.7
1977	Jerry Butler, WR	47	824	17.5
1978	Jerry Butler, WR	58	908	15.7
1979	Perry Tuttle, WR	36	544	15.1
1980	Perry Tuttle, WR	53	915	17.3
1981	Perry Tuttle, WR	52	883	17.0
1982	Jeff Stockstill, WR	25	247	9.9
1983	Ray Williams, WR	19	342	18.0
1984	Terrance Roulhac, WR	26	512	19.7
1985	Terrance Roulhac, WR	31	533	17.2
1986	Ray Williams, WR	20	280	14.0
	Terrance Roulhac, WR	20	228	11.4
1987	Gary Cooper, WR	34	618	18.2
1988	Keith Jennings, WR	30	397	13.2
1989	Rodney Fletcher, WR	35	556	15.9
1990	Terry Smith, WR	34	480	14.1
1991	Terry Smith, WR	52	829	15.9
1992	Terry Smith, WR	38	596	15.7
1993	Terry Smith, WR	38	776	20.4
1994	Antwuan Wyatt, WR	30	282	9.4
1995	Antwuan Wyatt, WR	45	683	15.2

Leaders based on number of receptions

PASSING

Year	Name	Att.	Cmp.	Pct.	Yds
1935	Joe (Net) Berry	72	42	.583	422
1936	Joe (Net) Berry	99	32	.323	434
1937	Bob Bailey	88	35	.398	579
1938	Bob Bailey	35	18	.514	272
1939	Banks McFadden	70	31	.443	581
1940	Chippy Maness	51	19	.373	388
1941	Booty Payne	90	36	.400	582
1942	Butch Butler	90	38	.422	504
1943	Butch Butler	34	12	.353	166
1944	Sid Tinsley	51	11	.216	248
1945	Butch Butler	45	11	.244	239
1946	Dutch Leverman	62	26	.419	501
1947	Bobby Gage	109	47	.413	1002
1948	Bobby Gage	105	42	.400	799
1949	Ray Mathews	72	24	.333	487
1950	Billy Hair	71	29	.408	644
1951	Billy Hair	164	67	.409	1004
1952	Don King	69	23	.333	317
1953	Don King	98	46	.469	706
1954	Don King	72	32	.444	468
1955	Don King	79	33	.418	586
1956	Charlie Bussey	68	26	.382	330
1957	Harvey White	95	46	.484	841
1958	Harvey White	87	43	.494	492
1959	Harvey White	107	56	.523	770
1960	Lowndes Shingler	145	61	.441	790
1961	Jim Parker	98	46	.469	735
1962	Jim Parker	67	30	.448	431
1963	Jim Parker	117	52	.444	728
1964	Thomas Ray	59	21	.356	253
1965	Thomas Ray	175	74	.423	1019
1966	Jimmy Addison	186	103	.554	1491
1967	Jimmy Addison	174	82	.471	924
1968	Billy Ammons	162	74	.457	1006
1969	Tommy Kendrick	227	107	.471	1457
1970	Tommy Kendrick	267	133	.498	1407
1971	Tommy Kendrick	152	64	.421	1040
1972	Ken Pengitore	131	55	.420	831
1973	Ken Pengitore	188	82	.436	1370
1974	Mark Fellers	92	42	.457	783
1975	Willie Jordan	73	40	.548	728
1976	Steve Fuller	116	58	.500	835
1977	Steve Fuller	205	106	.517	1655
1978	Steve Fuller	187	101	.540	1515
1979	Billy Lott	174	90	.517	1184
1980	Homer Jordan	172	85	.494	1311
1981	Homer Jordan	196	107	.546	1630
1982	Homer Jordan	100	55	.555	674
1983	Mike Eppley	166	99	.596	1410
1984	Mike Eppley	213	116	.545	1494
1985	Randy Anderson	123	63	.512	703
1986	Rodney Williams	200	98	.490	1245
1987	Rodney Williams	209	101	.483	1486
1988	Rodney Williams	186	78	.419	1144
1989	Chris Morocco	134	79	.590	1131
1990	D. Cameron	194	98	.505	1185
1991	D. Cameron	226	126	.557	1601
1992	Patrick Sapp	144	60	.417	750
1993	Patrick Sapp	133	66	.496	1084
1994	Nealon Greene	94	51	.543	524
1995	Nealon Greene	202	116	.574	1537

Leaders based on efficiency rating.

PUNTING

Year	Name	No.	Yds	Avg
1938	Bob Bailey	44	1631	37.1
1939	Banks McFadden	65	2828	43.5
1940	Chippy Maness	51	1989	39.0
1941	Bootyy Payne	47	1931	41.1
1942	Butch Butler	73	2679	36.7
1943	Butch Butler	32	1316	41.1
1944	Sid Tinsley	52	2070	39.8
1945	Butch Butler	50	1864	37.3
1946	Gerald Leverman	30	1067	35.5
1947	Bobby Gage	52	2054	39.5
1948	Bobby Gage	37	1317	35.6
1949	Jackie Calvert	26	1087	41.8
1950	Billy Hair	18	610	33.9
1951	Billy Hair	39	632	29.7
1952	Jack Shown	55	2073	37.7
1953	Don King	18	668	37.1
1954	Joe Pagliei	26	955	36.7
1955	Joe Pagliei	20	782	39.1
1956	Charlie Bussey	39	1410	36.1
1957	Charlie Horne	22	695	31.6
1958	Bill Mathis	22	787	35.8
1959	Lowndes Shingler	24	858	35.8
1960	Eddie Werntz	38	1376	36.2
1961	Eddie Werntz	56	2249	40.2
1962	Eddie Werntz	41	1667	40.7
1963	Hugh Mauldin	37	1157	31.3
1964	Don Barfield	60	2191	36.5
1965	Don Barfield	62	2503·	40.4
1966	Don Barfield	55	2132	38.7
1967	Sammy Cain	64	2423	37.9
1968	Sammy Cain	60	2235	37.3
1969	Sammy Cain	48	1785	37.3
1970	Jack Anderson	35	1434	41.0
1971	Tony Anderson	73	2714	37.2
1972	Tony Anderson	71	2724	38.4
1973	Mitch Tyner	61	2552	41.8
1974	Mitch Tyner	66	2649	40.1
1975	Richard Holliday	31	1083	35.0
1976	Mike O'Cain	55	2110	38.4
1977	David Sims	64	2462	38.7
1978	David Sims	50	2010	40.2
1979	David Sims	79	3468	43.9
1980	Richard Hendley	52	2001	38.5
1981	Dale Hatcher	44	1908	43.4
1982	Dale Hatcher	46	1871	40.7
1983	Dale Hatcher	47	2051	43.6
1984	Dale Hatcher	54	2361	43.7
1985	Andy Newell	57	2276	39.9
1986	Bill Spiers	59	2310	39.2
1987	Rusty Seyle	53	2011	37.9
1988	Chris Gardocki	45	1924	42.8

Year	Name	No.	Yds	Avg
1989	Chris Gardocki	48	2062	43.0
1990	Chris Gardocki	58	2580	44.5
1991	Chuck Lynch	58	2146	37.0
1992	Nelson Welch	63	2525	40.1
1993	Nelson Welch	41	1579	38.5

Year	Name	No.	Yds	Avg
1994	Nelson Welch	76	2980	39.2
1995	Chris McInally	50	2136	42.7

Leaders based on 3.6 punts per game or largest number of punts that season if no one attempted 3.6 per game.

TEAM OFFENSIVE RECORDS

MOST RUSHES
Game: 78 vs. Duke, 1979
Season: 741 in 1978
Per Game: 61.8 (741 in 12 games), 1978

MOST RUSHING YARDS
Game: 615 vs. Georgia Tech, 1903; 536 vs. Wake Forest, 1981
Season: 3469 in 1978
Per Game: 289.1 (3469 in 12 games), 1978
200-Yard Games: 11 in 1978 and 1986
300-Yard Games: 5 in 1978

RUSHING YARDS/ATTEMPT
Game: 7.898 (68-536) vs. Wake Forest, 1981
Season: 5.25 (504-2648) in 1950

MOST PASSING ATTEMPTS
Game: 55 at Maryland, 1992
Season: 302 in 1970
Per Game: 27.5 (302 in 11 games), 1970

MOST PASS COMPLETIONS
Game: 25 vs. Florida State, 1970, at Maryland, 1992
Season: 145 in 1970
Per Game: 13.2 (145 in 11 games), 1970

PASSING YARDS PER ATTEMPT
Game (min 15): 17.5 (16-280) vs. Furman, 1947
Season: 9.8 (126-1233) in 1950

PASSING YARDS PER COMPLETION
Game (min 10): 25.5 (11-280) vs. Furman, 1947
Season: 23.3 (53-1233) in 1950

MOST YARDS PASSING
Game: 364 vs. Duke, 1963
Season: 1858 in 1984
Per Game: 175. 5 (1755 in 10 games), 1969
200-Yard Games: 4 in 1969, 1970
300-Yard Games: 1 in 1963, 1965, 1966, 1975

COMPLETION PERCENTAGE
Game (min 15 att): 88.2 (15-17) vs. The Citadel, 1978
Season: 60.0 (117-195) in 1989

PASSING EFFICIENCY
Game (min 15 att): 269.4 (15-17-245-1-0) vs. The Citadel, 1978
Season: 148.23 (53-126-1233-14-8), 1950

MOST INTERCEPTIONS THROWN
Game: 7 vs. South Carolina, 1945
Season: 24 in 1969
Per Game: 2.4 (24 in 10 games)1969

TOTAL PLAYS
Game: 98 at Maryland (55 pass, 43 rush), 1992
Season: 946 in 1978
Per Game: 78.8 (946 in 12 games), 1978

TOTAL OFFENSE
Game: 756 vs. Wake Forest, 1981
Season: 5134 in 1978
Per Game: 427.8 (5134 in 12 games), 1978
400-yard Games: 7 (1950, 1978, 1982)
500-yard Games: 3 (1950, 1978, 1988)

OFFENSIVE YARDS PER PLAY
Game: 8.7 (87-756) vs. Wake Forest, 1981
Season: 6.16 (630-3881) in 1950

FEWEST OFFENSIVE TURNOVERS
Game: 0 vs. many (Last vs. Duke, 1995)
Season: 8 in 1940
Per Game: 0.89 (8 in 9 games), 1940

TOUCHDOWNS
Game: 12 vs. Wake Forest, 1981
Season: 48 in 1950
Per Game: 4.8 (48 in 10 games), 1950

RUSHING TOUCHDOWNS
Game: 11 vs. Presbyterian, 1948
Season: 39 in 1978
Per Game: 3.5 (35 in 10 games), 1950

PASSING TOUCHDOWNS
Game: 4 vs. Auburn, 1947
Season: 17 in 1984
Per Game: 1.55 (17 in 11 games), 1984

TOUCHDOWNS BY RETURN
Game: 2 vs. Georgia Tech, 1987 (1 punt, 1 kickoff); 2 vs. Long Beach State, 1990 (1 kickoff, 1 interception); 2 vs. Citadel, 1954 (1 interception, 1 blocked punt); 2 vs. Maryland, 1970 (1 punt, 1 interception)
Season: 7 in 1990 (4 by interceptions, 2 kickoffs, 1 fumble)
Per Game: 0.58 (7 in 12 games), 1990

POINTS
Game: 122 vs. Guilford, 1901; 94 vs. Furman, 1915; 82 vs. Wake Forest, 1981
Season: 368 in 1978, 1989
Per Game: 32.9 (329 in 10 games), 1950

FIELD GOALS
Game: 5 vs. N.C. State, 1991; at Maryland, 1992; at N. Carolina, 1994
Season: 23 in 1980
Per Game: 2.09 (23 in 11 games) in 1980

FIELD GOAL ATTEMPTS
Game: 6 vs. Georgia, 1983; vs N.C. State, 1991; at Maryland, 1992
Season: 32 in 1988
Per Game: 2.72 (30 in 11 games), 1980

PUNTS

Game: 17 vs. South Carolina, 1943
Season: 91 in 1939
Per Game: 10.0 (90 in 9 games), 1945

PUNTING YARDS

Game: 504 vs. Tulane, 1939
Season: 3731 in 1939
Per Game: 373.1 (3731 in 10 games), 1939

PUNTING AVERAGE

Game: (min 3 att): 56.6 (3-170) vs Wake Forest, 1986
Season: 43.98 (56-2463) in 1984

PUNT RETURNS

Game: 11 vs. George Washigton, 1941; Georgia Tech, 1987
Season: 53 in 1945, 1987
Per Game: 5.77 (52 in 9 games), 1941

PUNT RETURN YARDS

Game: 227 vs. Georgia Tech, 1987
Season: 720 in 1987
Per Game: 64.8 (584 in 9 games), 1938

KICKOFF RETURNS

Game: 10 vs. Georgia Tech, 1944
Season: 57 in 1970, 1946
Per Game: 6.33 (57 in 9 games), 1946

KICKOFF RETURN YARDS

Game: 198 vs. Florida, 1952; at Maryland, 1992
Season: 1187 in 1970
Per Game: 107.9 (1187 in 11 games), 1970

PENALTIES

Game: 18 vs. Duke, 1983
Season: 104 in 1987
Per Game: 8.67 (104 in 12 games), 1987

PENALTY YARDAGE

Game: 180 vs. Furman, 1964
Season: 938 in 1987
Per Game: 69.9 (839 in 12 games), 1987

TIME OF POSSESSION

Game: 42:58 vs. North Carolina, 1992
Season: 410:57 (12 games), 1989
Per Game: 34:15 (410:57 in 12 games), 1989

THIRD DOWN CONVERSION %

Game: 1.000 (12-12) vs. Wake Forest, 1981
Season: .516 (99-192), 1978

FIRST DOWNS

Game: 35 vs. Wake Forest, 1981
Season/Game: 22.75 (273 in 12 games), 1978
Season: 273, 1978

FIRST DOWNS RUSHING

Game: 27 vs. Presbyterian, 1957; Wake Forest 1981
Season: 192 in 1978
Per Game: 16.0 (192 in 12 games), 1978

FIRST DOWNS PASSING

Game: 17 vs. North Carolina, 1965
Season: 89 in 1969
Per Game: 8.9 (89 in 10 games), 1969

TEAM DEFENSIVE RECORDS

FEWEST RUSHING YARDS ALLOWED

Game: -21 vs. Furman, 1941
Season: 733 in 1991
Per Game: 61.1 in 1991

FEWEST RUSHING YARDS/ATTEMPT

Game: -1.48 vs. Furman, 1941
Season: 1.82 (402-733) in 1991

FEWEST RUSHING ATTEMPTS

Game: 14 vs. Presbyterian, 1941
Season: 334 in 1941
Per Game: 33.4 (334 in 10 games), 1941

FEWEST PASS ATTEMPTS ALLOWED

Game: 0 vs. many teams
Seasons: 105 in 1938
Per Game: 10.9 (109 in 10 games), 1939

FEWEST PASS COMPLETIONS

Game: 0 vs. many teams (Last time vs. Rice, 1959)
Season: 32 in 1939
Per Game: 3.2 (32 in 10 games), 1939

FEWEST PASSING YARDS

Game: 0 vs. many teams (Last time vs. Rice, 1959)
Season: 449 in 1939

INTERCEPTIONS

Game: 6 vs. South Carolina, 1971; 6 vs. N.C. State, 1995
Season: 25 in 1951
Per Game: 2.50 (25 in 10 games), 1951

INTERCEPTION RETURN YARDS

Game: 143 (4 int) vs. Maryland, 1970
Season: 361 in 1951
Per Game: 36.1 in 1951 (10 games)

SACKS

Game: 10 vs. Maryland, 1979; vs. Duke, 1992
Season: 46 (279 yards) in 1992
Per Game: 4.18 (46 in 11 games), 1992

PASSES BROKEN UP

Game: 18 vs. The Citadel, 1986
Season: 96 in 1989
Per Game: 8.0 (96 in 12 games), 1989

RECOVERED FUMBLES

Game: 6 vs. Duke, 1965
Season: 21 in 1956
Per Game: 1.91 (21 in 11 games), 1956

FEWEST FIRST DOWNS

Game: 0 vs. The Citadel, 1948
Season: 80 in 1939
Per Game: 8.0 in 1939

TACKLES FOR LOSS

Game: 19 vs. N.C. State, 1987
Season: 119 (for 492 yards) in 1991
Per Game: 9.91 (119 in 12 games) in 1991

TURNOVERS FORCED

Game: 9 vs. Georgia, 1981
Season: 41 in 1981
Per Game: 3.42 (41 in 12 games), 1981

LOWEST TOTAL PLAYS

Game: 29 vs. Furman, 1939
Season: 462 in 1943
Per Game: 52.0 (468 in 9 games), 1940

LOWEST TOTAL OFFENSE

Game: -12 vs. Furman, 1948
Season: 1575 in 1939
Per Game: 157.5 in 1939

LOWEST TOTAL OFFENSE/PLAY

Game:-0.34 vs. Furman, 1948
Season: 3.03 in 1939

INDIVIDUAL OFFENSIVE RECORDS

RUSHES

Game: 36, Jim Shirley vs. N.C. State, 1951; Ray
    Yauger vs. Wake Forest, 1969
Season: 238, Raymond Priester, 1995
Career: 600, Buddy Gore, 1966-68

CAREER TOTAL CARRIES

RK	Name	Years	Yds	Y/A	Car.
1.	Buddy Gore	1966-68	2571	4.29	600
2.	Kenny Flowers	1983-86	2914	4.94	590
3.	Ray Yauger	1968-70	2439	4.39	555
4.	Steve Fuller	1975-78	1737	3.20	535
5.	Terry Allen	1987-89	2778	5.31	523
6.	Rodney Blunt	1989-93	2173	4.28	508
7.	Lester Brown	1976-79	2228	4.45	505
8.	Ken Callicutt	1973-77	2256	4.59	492
9.	Chuck McSwain	1979-82	2320	4.80	483
10.	Stacey Driver	1982-85	2292	4.82	476
11.	Fred Cone	1948-50	2172	4.66	466
12.	Cliff Austin	1978-82	2139	5.06	423
13.	Charlie Timmons	1939-41	1545	3.72	415
14.	Rodney Blunt	1989-92	1857	4.52	411
15.	Joel Wells	1954-56	1937	5.06	383

CONSECUTIVE ATTEMPTS

Game: 8, Stacey Driver vs. Wake Forest, 1983

RUSHING YARDS

Game: 263, Raymond Priester vs. Duke, 1995
Season: 1322, Raymond Priester, 1995
Career: 2914, Kenny Flowers, 1983-86

CAREER RUSHING YARDAGE

Rk	Name	Years	TC	Avg	TD	Yards
1.	Kenny Flowers	1983-86	590	4.94	26	2914
2.	Terry Allen	1987-89	523	5.31	28	2778
3.	Buddy Gore	1966-68	600	4.29	15	2571
4.	Ray Yauger	1968-70	555	4.39	16	2439
5.	Chuck McSwain	1979-82	483	4.80	23	2320
6.	Stacey Driver	1982-85	476	4.82	15	2293
7.	Ken Callicutt	1973-77	492	4.59	11	2256
8.	Lester Brown	1976-79	505	4.45	31	2228
9.	Rodney Blunt	1989-93	508	4.28	13	2173
10.	Fred Cone	1948-50	466	4.66	30	2172
11.	Terrence Flagler	1982-86	379	5.70	17	2162
12.	Cliff Austin	1978-82	423	5.06	27	2139
13.	Joel Wells	1954-56	383	5.06	16	1937
14.	Ray Mathews	1947-50	331	5.70	20	1886
15.	Ronald Williams	1990-92	326	5.60	13	1824

RUSHING YARDS PER GAME

Season: 110.2 (1322 in 12 games), Raymond Priester,
    1995
Career: 89.6 (2778 in 31 games), Terry Allen, 1987-89

YARDS PER ATTEMPT

Game: 30.4 (5-152), Ken Moore vs. The Citadel, 1954
Season: (Min. 300 Yards) 7.4, Billy Hair (71-525), 1950
Career: (Min. 1,000 Yards) 5.922 (194-1149) by
    Jackie Calvert, 1948-50

RUSHING TOUCHDOWNS

Game: 5, Maxcey Welch vs. Newberry, 1930; Stumpy
    Banks vs. Furman, 1917
Season: 17, Lester Brown, 1978
Career: 31, Lester Brown, 1976-79

CAREER RUSHING TOUCHDOWNS

Rk	Name	Years	Att	Yds	TD
1.	Lester Brown	1976-79	505	2228	31
2.	Fred Cone	1948-50	466	2172	30
3.	Terry Allen	1987-89	523	2778	28
4.	Cliff Austin	1978-82	423	2139	27
5.	Kenny Flowers	1983-86	590	2914	26
6.	Chuck McSwain	1979-82	483	2320	23
7.	Tracy Johnson	1985-88	377	1579	23
8.	Steve Fuller	1975-78	535	1737	22
9.	Ray Mathews	1947-50	331	1886	20
10.	Emory Smith	1993-95	278	1244	19

ALL-PURPOSE RUNNING YARDS

Game: 274, Terrence Flagler vs. Wake Forest, 1986,
    (209 Rushing, 65 Receiving)
Season: 1446, Terrence Flagler, 1986 (1258 rushing,
    188 receiving)
Career: 3273, Buddy Gore, 1966-68 (2571 rushing,
    65 receiving, 637 kickoff returns)

PASS ATTEMPTS

Half: 46, Rodney Williams vs. N.C. State (2nd), 1987
Game: 55, Patrick Sapp vs. Maryland, 1992
Season: 267, Tommy Kendrick, 1970
Career: 717, Rodney Williams, 1985-88

PASS ATTEMPTS PER GAME

Season: 24.3, Tommy Kendrick, 1970 (267 in 11
    games)
Career: 20.1, Tommy Kendrick, 1969-71 (644 in 32
    games)

PASS COMPLETIONS

Game: 25 Tommy Kendrick vs. Florida St., 1970; 25
    Patrick Sapp vs. Maryland, 1992
Season: 133, Tommy Kendrick, 1970
Career: 333, Rodney Williams, 1985-88

COMPLETIONS PER GAME

Season: 12.1, Tommy Kendrick, 1970 (133 in 11
    games)
Career: 9.5, Tommy Kendrick, 1969-71 (303 in 32
    games)

COMPLETION PERCENTAGE

Game: (Min. 9 Comp.) 1.000 Steve Fuller (9-9) vs. The Citadel, 1978
Game: (Min 10 Comp.) .800, Mike Eppley (12-15) vs. Virginia, 1983
Game: (Min 15 Comp.) .689, Homer Jordan (20-29) vs. Maryland, 1981
Season: (Min 100 Att..) .596, Mike Eppley (99-166), 1983
Career: (Min 150 Att.) .567, Chris Morroco (89-157), 1986-89

CAREER PASS COMPLETIONS

Rk	Name	Years	Att	Yds	Cmp
1.	Rodney Williams	1985-88	717	4647	333
2.	Tommy Kendrick	1969-71	644	3893	303
3.	Steve Fuller	1975-78	554	4359	287
4.	DeChane Cameron	1988-91	470	3300	257
5.	Mike Eppley	1980-84	449	3354	252
6.	Homer Jordan	1979-82	479	3643	250
7.	Jimmy Addison	1965-67	393	2616	202
8.	Nealon Greene	1994-95	296	2061	167
9.	Patrick Sapp	1992-94	365	2278	165
10.	Ken Pengitore	1971-73	356	2412	154
11.	Harvey White	1957-59	289	2103	145
12.	Don King	1952-54	318	2077	134
13.	Jim Parker	1961-63	282	1895	126
14.	Bobby Gage	1945-48	278	2448	123
15.	Billy Hair	1950-52	295	1885	116

PASSES HAD INTERCEPTED

Game: 5, Don King vs. Auburn, 1953
Season: 20, Tommy Kendrick, 1969
Career: 42, Tommy Kendrick, 1969-71

LOWEST INTERCEPTION PERCENTAGE

Season: (Min. 75 Att.) 1.06%, Nealon Greene, 1994 (1 in 94 att.)
Career: (Min. 100 Att.) 2.55 %, Chris Morocco, 1986-89 (4 in 157 att.)

CONSECUTIVE PASSES WITHOUT INTERCEPTION

At Start of Career: 92, Nealon Greene, 1994
Season: 122, Rodney Williams, 1988

MOST GAMES WON AS STARTING QUARTERBACK

Season: 12, Homer Jordan, 1981
Career: 32, Rodney Williams, 1985-88 (32-10-2)

BEST WINNING PER. AS STARTING QUARTERBACK

Season: 1.000 (12-0), Homer Jordan, 1981
Career: (Min. 15 Games) .813, DeChane Cameron (19-4-1), 1988-91

CONSECUTIVE GAMES STARTED AT QUARTERBACK

Career: 32 by Tommy Kendrick, 1969-71

GAMES STARTED AT QUARTERBACK

Career: 44, Rodney Williams, 1985-88

YARDS PASSING

Game: 323, Thomas Ray vs. North Carolina, 1965
Season: 1655, Steve Fuller, 1977
Career: 4647, Rodney Williams, 1985-88

CAREER PASSING YARDAGE

Rk	Name	Years	Att	Cmp	Pct	Yards
1.	Rodney Williams	1985-88	717	333	.464	4647
2.	Steve Fuller	1975-78	554	287	.518	4359
3.	Tommy Kendrick	1969-71	644	303	.470	3893
4.	Homer Jordan	1979-82	479	250	.522	3643
5.	Mike Eppley	1980-84	449	252	.561	3354
6.	DeChane Cameron	1988-91	470	257	.547	3300
7.	Jimmy Addison	1965-67	393	202	.514	2616
8.	Bobby Gage	1945-48	278	123	.442	2448
9.	Ken Pengitore	1971-73	356	154	.433	2412
10.	Patrick Sapp	1992-94	365	165	.452	2278
11.	Harvey White	1957-59	289	145	.502	2103
12.	Don King	1952-54	318	134	.421	2077
13.	Nealon Greene	1994-95	296	167	.564	2061
14.	Jim Parker	1961-63	282	126	.447	1895
15.	Billy Hair	1950-52	295	116	.393	1885

YARDS PER GAME PASSING

Season: 149.1, Jimmy Addison, 1966
Career: 121.6, Tommy Kendrick, 1969-71

YARDS PER COMPLETION

Game: (Min. 8 Comp.) 28.0, Tommy Kendrick (9 for 252 yards) vs. Virginia, 1971
Season: (Min. 45 Comp.) 21.3, Bobby Gage (47 for 1002 yards), 1947
Career: (Min. 100 Comp.) 19.9, Bobby Gage (123 for 2448 yards), 1945-48

YARDS PER ATTEMPT

Game: (Min. 8 Att.) 22.0, Bobby Gage (11 for 245) vs. Furman, 1947
Season: (Min. 75 Att.) 9.19 , Bobby Gage (115 for 1002), 1947
Career: (Min. 100 Att.) 8.81, Bobby Gage (278 for 2448 yards), 1945-48

TOUCHDOWN PASSES

Game: 4, Bobby Gage vs. Auburn, 1947
Season: 14, Mike Eppley, 1984
Career: 28, Mike Eppley, 1980-84

Rk	Name	Years	ATT	INT	TD
1.	Mike Eppley	1980-84	449	26	28
2.	Tommy Kendrick	1969-71	644	42	24
	Bobby Gage	1945-48	278	27	24
4.	Steve Fuller	1975-78	554	21	22
5.	Harvey White	1967-59	289	12	18
6.	Jimmy Addison	1965-67	393	27	16
7.	Rodney Williams	1985-88	717	27	16
8.	Homer Jordan	1979-82	479	27	15
9.	Billy Hair	1950-52	295	28	15
10.	Don King	1952-54	318	37	14

Rk	Name	Years	ATT	INT	TD
11.	DeChane Cameron	1988-91	470	15	13
12.	Mark Fellers	1972-74	124	7	12
13.	Ray Matthews	1947-50	118	9	11
	Nealon Greene	1994-95	296	9	11
15.	Ken Pengitore	1971-73	356	18	11

RECEPTIONS

Game: 11, Phil Rogers vs. North Carolina, 1965
Season: 58, Jerry Butler, 1978
Career: 162, Terry Smith, 1990-93

CAREER RECEPTION LEADERS

Rk	Name, Pos	Years	Yds	Avg	TD	Rec
1.	Terry Smith, WR	1990-93	2681	16.5	15	162
2.	Perry Tuttle, WR	1978-81	2534	16.9	17	150
3.	Jerry Butler, WR	1975-78	2223	16.0	11	139
4.	Phil Rogers, WR	1965-67	1469	13.9	5	106
5.	John McMakin, TE	1969-71	1255	13.5	12	93
6.	Terrance Roulhac, WR	1983-86	1487	16.2	16	92
7.	Glenn Smith, TE	1949-51	1576	17.9	18	88
8.	Ray Williams, WR	1983-86	1290	15.0	6	86
9.	Gary Cooper, WR	1985-89	1592	20.2	11	79
10.	Keith Jennings, WR	1985-88	1117	14.3	2	78
11.	Antwuan Wyatt, WR	1993-95	972	12.8	6	76
12.	Charlie Waters, WR	1967-69	1196	17.1	4	68
13.	Jerry Gaillard, WR	1978-81	831	12.6	1	66
14.	Bennie Cunningham, TE	1972-75	1044	16.31	10	64
15.	Joey Walters, WR	1974-76	963	16.32	6	59

CAREER RECEPTION YARDAGE

Rk	Name, Pos	Years	Rec	Yds
1.	Terry Smith, WR	1990-93	162	2681
2.	Perry Tuttle, WR	1978-81	150	2534
3.	Jerry Butler, WR	1975-78	139	2223
4.	Gary Cooper, WR	1985-89	79	1592
5.	Glenn Smith, TE	1949-51	88	1576
6.	Terrence Roulhac, WR	1983-86	92	1487
7.	Phil Rogers, WR	1965-67	106	1469
8.	Ray Williams, WR	1983-86	86	1290
9.	John McMakin, WR	1969-71	92	1255
10.	Charlie Waters, WR	1967-69	68	1166
11.	Keith Jennings, WR	1985-88	78	1117
12.	Bennie Cunningham, TE	1972-75	69	1044
13.	Antwuan Wyatt, WR	1993-95	76	972
14.	Joey Walters, WR	1974-76	59	963
15.	Frank Magwood, WR	1979-82	51	920

CAREER YARDS PER RECEPTION

Rk	Name, Pos	Years	Rec.	Yds	Y/Rec
1.	Joe Blalock, TE	1939-41	38	773	20.34
2.	Gary Cooper, FLK	1985-89	79	1592	20.15
3.	Frank Magwood, WR	1979-82	51	920	18.04
4.	Glenn Smith, TE	1949-51	88	1516	17.91
5.	Eddis Freeman, TE	1943-46	37	655	17.70
6.	Dwight Clark, WR	1975-78	33	571	17.30
7.	Bill Mathis, TB	1957-59	35	602	17.20
8.	Charlie Waters, WR	1967-69	68	1166	17.15
9.	Perry Tuttle, WR	1978-81	150	2534	16.89
10.	Tony Horne, WR	1994-95	30	504	16.80
11.	Terry Smith, WR	1990-93	162	2681	16.55
12.	Wayne Bell, TE	1964-66	54	883	16.35
13.	Joey Walters, WR	1974-76	59	963	16.32
14.	Bennie Cunningham, TE	1972-75	64	1044	16.31
15.	Terrance Roulhac, WR	1983-86	92	1487	16.16

RECEIVING YARDS

Game: 163, Jerry Butler vs. Georgia Tech, 1977
Season: 915, Perry Tuttle, 1980
Career: 2681, Terry Smith, 1990-93

RECEIVING YARDS PER GAME

Season: 83.1, Perry Tuttle, 1980
Career: 58.3, Terry Smith, 1990-93

YARDS PER RECEPTION

Game: (Min. 5 rec.) 32.6, Jerry Butler (5-163) vs.
Georgia Tech, 1977
Season: (Min. 10 rec.) 32.1, Gary Cooper (13-417) in
1988
Season: (Min. 20 rec.) 22.6, Glenn Smith (22-498) in
1950
Career: (Min. 35 rec.) 20.34, Joe Blalock (38-773),
1939-41

TOUCHDOWN PASSES CAUGHT

Game: 3, Dreher Gaskin vs. Auburn, 1953
Season: 8, Perry Tuttle, 1981 and Terrance Roulhac,
1984
Career: 18, Glenn Smith, 1949-51

CAREER TOUCHDOWN RECEPTIONS

Rk	Name, Pos	Years	TD
1.	Glenn Smith, TE	1949-51	18
2.	Perry Tuttle, WR	1978-81	17
3.	Terrance Roulhac, WR	1983-86	16
4.	Terry Smith, WR	1990-93	15
5.	John McMakin, TE	1969-71	12
6.	Jerry Butler, WR	1975-78	11
7.	Joe Blalock, TE	1939-41	11
	Gary Cooper, WR	1985-89	11
9.	Bennie Cunningham, TE	1972-75	10

RECEPTIONS BY A RUNNING BACK

Game: 7 (for 31 yards) by Dick Bukowsky vs. Florida
State, 1970
Season: 21, Ray Yauger, 1969
Career: 45, Ray Yauger, 1968-70

RECEPTIONS BY A TIGHT END

Game: 9, John McMakin vs. Florida State, 1970
Season: 40, John McMakin, 1970
Career: 93, John McMakin, 1969-71

CONSECUTIVE GAMES CATCHING A PASS

Career: 35, Jerry Butler, 1975-78, Caught at least 1
pass in all games in 1976, 1977 and 1978.

OFFENSIVE PLAYS

Game: 64, Patrick Sapp vs. Maryland, 1992
Season: 383, Steve Fuller, 1977
Career: 1089, Steve Fuller, 1975-78

TOTAL OFFENSE YARDS

Game: 374, Bobby Gage vs. Auburn, 1947
Season: 2164, Steve Fuller, 1978
Career: 6096, Steve Fuller, 1975-78

CAREER TOTAL OFFENSE

Rk	Name	Years	Plays	Rush	Pass	Total
1.	Steve Fuller	1975-78	1089	1737	4359	6096
2.	Rodney Williams	1985-88	1024	863	4647	5510
3.	Homer Jordan	1979-82	859	971	3643	4614
4.	DeChane Cameron	1988-91	765	926	3300	4226
5.	Bobby Gage	1945-48	594	1309	2448	3757
6.	Mike Eppley	1980-84	614	398	3354	3752
7.	Billy Hair	1950-52	616	1579	1885	3464
8.	Tommy Kendrick	1969-71	794	-484	3893	3409
9.	Ken Pengitore	1971-73	703	898	2412	3310
10.	Kenny Flowers	1983-86	590	2914	0	2914
11.	Terry Allen	1987-89	525	2778	66	2844
12.	Ray Mathews	1947-50	449	1886	907	2793
13.	Jimmy Addison	1965-67	472	172	2616	2788
14.	Don King	1952-54	574	684	2077	2761
15.	Nealon Greene	1994-95	456	531	2061	2592
	Harvey White	1957-59	483	489	2103	2592

TOTAL OFFENSE PER GAME

Season: 180.3, Steve Fuller, 1978
Career: 141.7, Steve Fuller, 1975-78

YARDS PER PLAY

Game: 12.0, Billy Hair vs. Duquesne, 1950 (24 plays,
104 rush, 185 pass for 289)
Season: 8.1, Jackie Calvert, 1950 (157 plays, 714
rush, 557 pass for 1271)
Career: 6.32, Bobby Gage, 1945-48 (594 plays, 1309
rush, 2448 pass for 3757)

CAREER SCORING

Rk	Name	Years	TD	PAT	FGA	TPS
1.	Nelson Welch, PK	1991-94	0	85-92	72-102	301
2.	Obed Ariri, PK	1977-80	0	99-103	63-97	288
3.	Chris Gardocki, PK	1988-90	0	72-72	63-89	261
4.	David Treadwell, PK	1985-87	0	92-93	47-66	233
5.	Bob Paulling, PK	1979-83	0	107-109	23-41	209
6.	Lester Brown, RB	1976-79	32			192
7.	Fred Cone, RB	1948-50	31	3-4		189
8.	Ray Mathews, RB	1947-50	28			168
	Terry Allen, RB	1987-89	28			168
	Kenny Flowers, RB	1983-86	28			168
11.	Cliff Austin, RB	1978-82	27			162
12.	Ray Yauger, RB	1968-70	23	2		140
13.	Donald Igwebuike, PK	1981-84		41-41	32-43	139
14.	Chuck McSwain, RB	1979-82	23			138
	Tracy Johnson, RB	1985-88	23			138

POINTS

Game: 33, Maxcey Welch vs. Newberry, 1930
Season: 107, Chris Gardocki, 1989
Career: 301, Nelson Welch, 1991-94

POINTS PER GAME

Season: 10.2, Fred Cone (92 in 9 games), 1950
Career: 7.25, Chris Gardocki (261 in 36 games), 1988-90

TOUCHDOWNS

Game: 5, Stumpy Banks vs. Furman , 1917 (all-rushing), Maxcey Welch vs. Newberry, 1930 (all rushing)
Season: 17, Lester Brown, 1978 (all rushing)
Career: 32, Lester Brown, 1976-79 (31 rush, 1 receiving)

TOUCHDOWNS RUN AND PASS

Game: 5, Maxcey Welch vs. Newberry, 1930; Bobby Gage vs. Auburn, 1947; Stumpy Banks vs. Furman, 1917
Season: 19, Mark Fellers, 1974
Career: 44, Steve Fuller, 1975-78

LONGEST SCORING LATERAL

Game: 65 yards, Don Willis to Shad Bryant vs. George Washington, 1938

LONGEST FUMBLE RETURN

Non-Scoring: 83 yards, Tim Childers vs. W. Carolina, 1982
Scoring: 91 yards, Michael Barber vs. UTC, 1992

EXTRA POINTS MADE

Game: 11 (of 11), W.C. Forsythe vs. Bingham, 1898; 9 (of 10), Tommy Chandler vs. Presbyterian, 1949 (modern record)
Season: 44, (of 46), Obed Ariri, 1978
Career: 107 (of 109), Bob Paulling, 1979-81-82-83

EXTRA POINTS ATTEMPTED

Game: 11, W.C. Forsythe vs. Bingham, 1898
Season: 47, Charles Radcliffe, 1950
Career: 109, Bob Paulling, 1979-81-82-83

EXTRA POINT PERCENTAGE

Season: 1.000, (41-41) Donald Igwebuike, 1984; 1.000 (32-32) Bob Paulling, 1982; 1.000 (34-34) David Treadwell, 1986; (25-25) David Treadwell, 1985; 1.000 (41-41), Chris Gardocki, 1989; 1.000 (30-30), Chris Gardocki, 1990; Nelson Welch (14-14), 1994
Career: 1.000 (43-43), Donald Igwebuike, 1981-84; (72-72) Chris Gardocki, 1988-90

CONSECUTIVE EXTRA POINTS

72, Chris Gardocki (1 in 1988, all 41 in 1989, 30 in 1990)
70, Bob Paulling (Last 3 in 1981, all 32 in 1982, and first 35 of 1983)
63, David Treadwell (all 25 in 1985, all 34 in 1986, first 4 of 1987)

FIELD GOALS ATTEMPTED

Game: 6, Chris Gardocki vs. Georgia Tech, 1990; 6, Nelson Welch vs. N.C. State, 1991, vs. Maryland, 1992
Season: 32, Chris Gardocki, 1988
Career: 102, Nelson Welch, 1991-94

FIELD GOALS MADE

Game: 5, Nelson Welch vs. N.C. State, 1991, vs. Maryland, 1992, vs. No. Carolina, 1994
Season: 23, Obed Ariri, 1980
Career: 72, Nelson Welch, 1991-94

FIELD GOAL PERCENTAGE

Game: 1.000 (5-5) Nelson Welch vs. North Carolina, 1994
Season: .941, Donald Igwebuike (16-17), 1984
Career: .829, Bob Paulling (34-41), 1979-81-82-83

KICK-SCORING POINTS

Game: 17, Nelson Welch vs. N.C. State, 1991 (5 FGs, 2 PATs)
Season: 107, Chris Gardocki, 1989
Career: 301, Nelson Welch, 1991-94

MOST FIELD GOALS 40 YARDS OR MORE

Game: 3, Bob Paulling (46, 43, 46) vs. North Carolina, 1982; 3, Nelson Welch (42,46, 41) vs. N. C. State, 1991
Season: 10, Chris Gardocki (10-14), 1989
Career: 23, Chris Gardocki (23-39), 1988-90

MOST FIELD GOALS 50 YARDS OR MORE

Game: 1 by many
Season: 2, by Donald Igwebuike, 1984; 2, by Chris Gardocki, 1988; 2, by Nelson Welch, 1992
Career: 5, by Chris Gardocki, 1988-90; 5, by Donald Igwebuike, 1981-84

HIGHEST PERCENTAGE FIELD GOALS, 40 YARDS OR MORE

Game: (Min. 3 Made), 1.000 (3-3) by Bob Paulling vs. UNC, 1982
Season: (Min. 10 Made), .818 (9-11) by Nelson Welch, 1992
Season: (Min. 8 Made), 1.000 (8-8) by Donald Igwebuike, 1984
Career: (Min. 10 Made), .609 (14-23) by Donald Igwebuike, 1981-84

PUNTS

Game: 13, Marion Butler vs. Wake Forest, 1942
Season: 81, David Sims, 1979
Career: 197, David Sims, 1977-80

PUNTING AVERAGE

Game: (Min. 3 punts) 55.3 Dale Hatcher (3 for 166) vs. Kentucky, 1982
Season: (Min. 25 punts) 44.48, Chris Gardocki (58-2580), 1990
Career: (Min. 50 punts) 43.48, Chris Gardocki (151-6566), 1988-90

CAREER PUNTING AVERAGE LEADERS

Rk	Name	Years	Att	Yds	Avg
1.	Chris Gardocki	1988-90	151	6566	43.48
2.	Dale Hatcher	1981-84	191	8191	42.99
3.	Banks McFadden	1937-39	94	3967	42.20
4.	David Sims	1977-80	197	8126	41.25
5.	Mitch Tyner	1973-74	127	5201	40.95
6.	Jack Anderson	1968-70	56	2276	40.64
7.	Chris McInally	1993-95	73	2946	40.36
8.	Andy Newell	1984-85	59	2378	40.31
9.	Nelson Welch	1991-94	180	7084	39.36
10.	Eddie Werntz	1960-62	135	5292	39.20

PUNT RETURNS

Game: 10, Shad Bryant vs. Furman, 1939
Season: 34, Billy Davis, 1981
Career: 88, Marion Butler, 1941-42-43-45

PUNT RETURN YARDAGE

Game: 167, Don Kelley on 4 returns vs. Maryland, 1970
Season: 487, Shad Bryant on 27 returns, 1938
Career: 779, Shad Bryant, 1937-39

CAREER PUNT RETURN YARDAGE

Rk	Name	Years	No	Avg	TD	Yds
1.	Shad Bryant	1937-39	65	12.0	1	779
2.	Donnell Woolford	1985-88	78	9.6	2	754
3.	James Lott	1986-89	71	9.6	0	683
4.	Don Kelley	1969-71	56	11.3	2	632
5.	Willie Jordan	1975-78	54	10.5	0	569
6.	Billy Davis	1980-83	87	6.4	0	555
7.	Darnell Stephens	1991-93	44	10.5	1	463
8.	Steak Lawton	1934-36	26	17.5	2	456
9.	Richie Luzzi	1966-68	56	7.9	1	441
10.	Bobby Gage	1945-48	39	11.3	1	439
11.	Jackie Calvert	1948-50	33	13.2	0	433
12.	Robert O'Neal	1989-92	45	9.1	0	410
13.	Hugh Mauldin	1963-65	32	10.5	0	336
	George Usry	1957-59	35	9.6	0	336
15.	Frank Liberatore	1964-67	29	11.2	2	325

AVERAGE PUNT RETURN

Game: (Min. 2 Ret.) 51.0 (102 on 2), Richie Luzzi vs. Georgia, 1968
Season: (Min. 10 Att) 16.9 Bobby Gage (12-203), 1948
Career: (Min. 20 Att.): 17.5 Streak Lawton (26-456), 1934-36

KICKOFF RETURNS

Game: 7, John Shields vs. Alabama, 1969
Season: 29, Andre Humphrey, 1993
Career: 66, Ray Williams, 1983-86

KICKOFF RETURN YARDAGE

Game: 174, David Thomas on 5 returns vs. Ga. Tech, 1972
Season: 663, Andre Humphrey, 1993
Career: 1373, Andre Humphrey, on 62 returns, 1992-95

CAREER KICKOFF RETURN YARDAGE

Rk	Name	Years	No	Avg	TD	Yds
1.	Andre Humphrey	1992-95	68	21.9	0	1486
2.	Ray Williams	1983-86	66	20.5	0	1350
3.	Terrence Roulhac	1983-86	42	26.4	0	1108
4.	Warren Ratchford	1974-78	44	22.0	0	848
5.	Joe Henderson	1987-89	30	27.6	1	802
6.	William Scott	1974-75	36	20.1	0	723
7.	John Shields	1968-69	30	21.6	0	647
8.	Buddy Gore	1966-68	26	24.5	0	637
9.	Willie Jordan	1975-78	29	21.0	0	610
10.	Doug Thomas	1987-90	23	25.3	2	582
11.	Jacky Jackson	1965-67	27	21.4	0	578
12.	Steve Griffin	1982-86	27	21.4	0	577
13.	Bob Bosler	1970-72	29	19.6	0	568
14.	Larry Ryans	1989-92	26	20.5	0	532
15.	David Thomas	1972	23	22.7	0	522

KICKOFF RETURN FOR TOUCHDOWN

Game: 1 by five players. Last- Doug Thomas vs. Maryland 1990
Season: 2, Doug Thomas, 1990
Career: 2 Doug Thomas, 1987-90

AVERAGE KICKOFF RETURN

Game: (Min. 2 ret.) 60.0, Terrance Roulhac (120 on 2), 1986
Season: (Min 10 ret.) 33.0, Terrance Roulhac (17-561), 1986
Career: (Min. 20 ret.) 26.7, Joe Henderson (30-802), 1987-89

INDIVIDUAL DEFENSIVE RECORDS

(Since 1976)

TOTAL TACKLES

Game: 24, by Jeff Davis vs. North Carolina (1980)
Season: 175, by Jeff Davis (1981)
Career: 515, by Bubba Brown (1976-79)

GAME TACKLE LEADERS

No	Name	Opponent	Year
24	Jeff Davis, LB	North Carolina	1980
22	Jeff Davis, LB	Maryland	1980
22	Bubba Brown, LB	Ohio State	1978
22	Bubba Brown, LB	N.C. State	1979
21	Henry Walls, LB	Georgia Tech	1985
21	Willie Anderson, MG	South Carolina	1974
20	Jeff Davis, LB	Tulane	1981
20	Henry Walls, LB	Boston College	1983
20	Tim Jones, LB	Duke	1994

SEASON TACKLE LEADERS

Rk	Name	Season	No
1.	Jeff Davis, LB	1981	175
2.	Bubba Brown, LB	1978	170
3.	Jeff Davis, LB	1980	160
4.	Henry Walls, LB	1985	153
5.	Bubba Brown, LB	1979	150
	Anthony Simmons, LB	1995	150
7.	Keith Williams, LB	1985	138
8.	Randy Scott, LB	1978	134
9.	Randy Scott, LB	1977	133
10.	Jeff Davis, LB	1979	123

CAREER TACKLE LEADERS

Rk	Player Pos	Years	No
1.	Bubba Brown, LB	1976-79	515
2.	Jeff Davis, LB	1978-81	469
3.	Ed McDaniel, LB	1988-91	389
4.	Randy Scott, LB	1975-78	382
5.	Tim Jones, LB	1991-94	338
6.	Henry Walls, LB	1983-85	316
7.	Jim Stuckey, DT	1976-79	314
8.	Doug Brewster, LB	1987-90	312
9.	Terry Kinard, FS	1978-82	294
10.	Terence Mack, DE	1983-86	285
11.	Levon Kirkland, OLB	1988-91	273
12.	William Perry, MG	1981-84	261
13.	Keith Williams, LB	1983-85	259
14.	Brentson Buckner, DT	1990-93	253
15.	Robert O'Neal, FS	1989-92	252

SEASON TACKLES FOR LOSS LEADERS

Rk	Name	Season	No
1.	William Perry, MG	1984	27
	Rob Bodine, MG	1991	27
3.	Michael Dean Perry, DT	1987	24
4.	Jim Stuckey, DT	1979	20
5.	Jeff Bryant, DT	1981	19
6.	Randy Scott, LB	1977	18
	Chester McGlockton, DT	1991	18
	Brentson Buckner, DT	1992	18
9.	Archie Reese, DT	1977	16
	Steve Durham, DT	1979	16

CAREER TACKLES FOR LOSS LEADERS

Rk	Name	Years	No
1.	Michael Dean Perry, DT	1984-87	61
2.	William Perry, MG	1981-84	60
3.	Rob Bodine, MG	1989-91	48
4.	Brentson Buckner, DT	1990-93	46
5.	Randy Scott, LB	1975-78	43
6.	Levon Kirkland, OLB	1988-91	40
7.	Chester McGlockton, DT	1989-91	39
8.	Jim Stuckey, DT	1976-79	36
	Wayne Simmons, OLB	1989-92	36
10.	Ed McDaniel, ILB	1988-91	30
11.	Ashley Sheppard, OLB	1989-92	29
12.	Jeff Bryant, DT	1978-81	28
13.	Vance Hammond, DT	1987-90	27
14.	James Robinson, DT	1979-83	25
15.	Steve Berlin, DT	1981-85	24
	Mark Drag, MG	1985-88	24

INTERCEPTIONS

Quarter: 3, Brian Dawkins vs. Duke, 1995
Game: 3, Kit Jackson vs. Wake Forest, 1965; 3, by
Leomont Evans vs. N.C. State, 1995; 3, by Brian
Dawkins vs. Duke, 1995
Season: 8, Robert O'Neal, 1989
Career: 17, Terry Kinard, 1978-82

CAREER INTERCEPTIONS

Rk	Name, Pos	Years	Yds	Avg	TD	Int
1.	Terry Kinard, FS	1978-82	147	8.6	0	17
2.	Fred Knoebel, DB	1950-52	122	8.1	0	15
3.	Eddie Geathers, CB	1977-80	114	9.5	0	12
	Robert O'Neal, FS	1989-92	119	9.9	0	12
5.	Pete Cook, CB	1950-52	129	11.7	0	11
	Brian Dawkins, SS	1992-95	101	9.2	1	11
7.	Ray Mathews, DB	1947-50	131	13.1	0	10
	Dexter Davis, CB	1988-90	27	2.7	1	10
	Bobby Gage, DB	1945-48	97	9.7	0	10
	Steve Ryans, FS	1975-78	107	10.7	0	10
	Rex Varn, FS	1976-79	275	27.5	2	10
	Donnell Woolford, CB	1985-88	26	2.6	0	10
13.	Dennis Smith, DB	1973-75	102	11.3	1	9
	Ben Anderson, DB	1970-72	76	8.4	0	9
	Peter Ford, CB	1993-95	72	9.0	0	9

INTERCEPTION RETURN YARDAGE

Game: 102, Don Kelley on 1 return vs. Duke, 1970
Season: 156, Don Kelley on 3 interceptions, 1970
Career: 275, Rex Varn on 10 interceptions, 1976-79

AVERAGE INTERCEPTION RETURN

Game: (Min. 2) 50.5, Willie Underwood (2-101) vs.
South Carolina, 1980
Season: (Min. 3) 52.0, Don Kelley (3-156), 1970
Career: (Min. 5) 27.5, Rex Varn (10-275) 1976-79

INTERCEPTION RETURNS FOR TOUCHDOWN

Game: 1 by Many
Season: 3 by Arlington Nunn, 1990
Career: 3 by Arlington Nunn, 1987-90

INTERCEPTIONS BY A LINEBACKER

Game: 2, Johnny Rembert vs. W. Carolina, 1982
Season: 6, Johnny Rembert, 1982
Career: 8, Johnny Rembert, 1981-82

PASSES BROKEN UP

Game: 5, Perry Williams vs. VPI (1985)
Season: 15, Ty Davis (1984); Ty Davis (1984); Delton Hall (1985); Donnell Woolford (1987, 1988)
Career: 44, by Donnell Woolford (1985-88)

SACKS

Game: 3, Jim Stuckey vs. W. Forest, Maryland (1979); Steve Durham vs. Maryland (1979); Michael Dean Perry vs. N.C. State (1984); Michael Dean Perry vs. Virginia Tech (1987); Chester McGlockton vs. South Carolina (1990); Brentson Buckner vs. North Carolina (1992); Wardell Rouse vs. Maryland (1993)
Season: 10, by Jim Stuckey (1979); William Perry (1984); Michael Dean Perry (1987)
Career: 28, Michael Dean Perry (1984-87)

FUMBLE RECOVERIES

Games: 2, Randy Scott vs. Duke (1978); Jim Scott vs. Boston College (1983); Henry Walls vs. Duke (1985); Gene Beasley vs. Furman (1988); Levon Kirkland vs. Georgia Tech (1989); Tyron Mouzon vs. South Carolina (1989)
Season: 4, Jeff Davis (1981); William Devane (1983)
Career: 8, Jeff Davis (1977-81)

INTERCEPTIONS

Game: 3, Kit Jackson vs. Wake Forest (1965); Leomont Evans vs. NC State (1995); Brian Dawkins vs. Duke (1995)
Season: 8, by Robert O'Neal (1989)
Career: 17, by Terry Kinard (1978-82)

INTERCEPTION RETURN YARDS

Game: 101 (2 int.), by Willie Underwood vs. S. Carolina (1980)
Season: 156 (3 int.), by Don Kelley (1970)
Career: 275 (10 int.), by Rex Varn (1976-79)

TAKEAWAYS

Game: 3 (3 int.), Kit Jackson vs. Wake Forest (1965); 3 (3 int.), Leomont Evans vs. NC State (1995); 3 (3 int.), Brian Dawkins vs. Duke (1995); 3 (1 int., 2 FR), Randy Scott vs. Duke (1978); 3 (2 int.,1 FR), Andre Carter vs. Virginia (1994)
Season: 9 (8 int., 1 FR), Robert O'Neal (1989)
Career: 19 (17 int., 2 FR), Terry Kinard (1978-92)

TIGERS IN THE NFL

A *Allen, Terry, TB (1989) — 1991-1994 Minnesota Vikings; 1995-present Washington Redskins

Ariri, Obed, PK (1980) — 1983 Washington Federals (USFL); 1984 Tampa Bay Buccaneers; 1987 Washington Redskins

Austin, Cliff, TB (1982) — 1983-1984 New Orleans Saints; 1984-86 Atlanta Falcons; 1987 Tampa Bay Bucs

B Baldwin, Bob, Back (1964) — 1966-67 Baltimore Colts

Barber, Mike, LB (1994) — 1995-present Seattle Seahawks

Barnes, Gary, OE (1961) -1962-63 Green Bay Packers; 1963 Dallas Cowboys; 1964 Chicago Bears; 1966-67 Atlanta Falcons (first player signed and scored first points by a Falcon)

Benish, Dan, DT (1982) — 1983-86 Atlanta Falcons; 1987-88 Washington Redskins; 1987 Super Bowl Champions

Bostic, Jeff, C (1979) — 1980-1993 Washington Redskins; 1982, 1987 and 1991 Super Bowl Champions

Bostic, Joe, OG (1978) — 1979-88 St. Louis Cardinals. 1979 — All Rookie Team

Boyer, Shelton, WR (1985) — 1987 Miami Dolphins (replacement player)

Brewster, Doug, LB (1990) — 1991 Saskatchewan Roughriders (CFL); 1993 Winnepeg Blue Bombers (CFL)

Brooks, Jonathan, LB (1978) — 1979 Detroit Lions; 1980 Atlanta Falcons; 1983-84 Philadelphia Stars (USFL); 1984 USFL Champions

Brown, Lester, TB (1979) — 1980-81 Saskatchewan Roughriders (CFL); 1983 Montreal Concordes (CFL); 1984-85 Toronto Argonauts (CFL); 1986 Winnipeg Blue Bombers (CFL)

Bryant, Jeff, DT (1981) — 1982-93 Seattle Seahawks, First Round Draft Choice, sixth player chosen

*Buckner, Brentson, DT (1993) — 1994-Present Pittsburgh Steelers, played in 1996 Super Bowl

Butler, Jerry, WR (1978) — 1979-87 Buffalo Bills; AFC Offensive Rookie-of-the-Year; First round draft choice, fifth player chosen

C Cagle, John, DT-LB-G (1968) — 1969 Boston Patriots

Callicut, Ken, TB (1977) — 1978-1982 Detroit Lions

Cameron, DeChane, QB (1991) — 1992 Edmonton Eskimos (CFL)

Chuy, Don, OG (1962) — 1963-68 Los Angeles Rams; 1969 Philadelphia Eagles

Clark, Brian, OG (1981) — 1982 Denver Broncos

Clark, Dwight, WR (1978) — 1979-87 San Francisco 49ers; led NFC in receiving, 1981-82; Super Bowl Champion, 1981 and 1984; NFL Pro Bowl, 1982-83

Cline, Doug, LB (1959) — 1960-66 Houston Oilers; 1966 San Diego Chargers

Coley, James, TE (1988) — TE, 1990-91, 1992 Chicago Bears; 1991 Indianapois Colts

Cone, Fred, Back-PK (1950) — 1951-57 Green Bay Packers; 1960 Dallas Cowboys; 1955 NFL Field Goal leader

Cooper, Gary, WR (1989) — 1991 Montreal Machine (WLAF)

Cordileone, Lou, DE-DT-OG (1959) — 1960 New York Giants; 1961 San Francisco 49ers; 1962 Los Angeles Rams; 1962-63 Pittsburgh Steelers; 1967-68 New Orleans Saints; First round draft choice

Cunningham, Bennie, TE (1975) — 1976-85 Pittsburgh Steelers; First round draft choice; 28th player chosen; 1978 and 1979 Super Bowl Champion

D Daigneault, Doug, Back (1959) — 1960-63 Ottawa RoughRiders (CFL); 1964-65 Winnipeg Blue Bombers (CFL)

Danforth, Kenny, SS (1985) — 1987 L.A. Raiders (replacement player)

Davis, Billy, LB (1983) — 1984 St. Louis Cardinals

*Davis, Dexter, CB (1990) — 1991-1992 Phoenix Cardinals; 1993-Present L.A. Rams

Davis, Jeff, LB (1981) — 1982-87 Tampa Bay Buccaneers; Captain of Tampa Bay 1984-87

Davis, Ty, CB (1984) — 1985-86 New York Giants; injured reserve entire 1986 season with Super Bowl Champions; 1987 Detroit Lions

Diggs, Bubba, TE (1981) — 1983 Washington Federals (USFL)

Dolce, Chris, OG (1979) — 1983 Washington Federals (USFL)

Driver, Stacy, TB (1985) — 1987 Cleveland Browns (replacement player)

Dukes, Mike, LB (1958) — 1960-63 Houston Oilers; 1964-65 Boston Patriots; 1965 New York Jets

Dunn, K.D., TE (1984) — 1985 Tampa Bay Buccaneers; 1987 Washington Redskins; 1988 New York Jets; 1991 Montreal Machine (WLAF)

Durham, Steve, DE (1980) — 1982 Baltimore Colts

E Eppes, Roy, DB (1977) — 1983 Tampa Bay Bandits (USFL); 1984 Arizona Wranglers (USFL)

F Farr, James, OG (1983) — 1984 Washington Federals (USFL); 1985 Orlando Renegades (USFL)

Flagler, Terrence, TB (1986) — 1987-89 San Francisco 49ers; 1990 Dallas Cowboys; 1990-91 Phoenix Cardinals; 1987 first-round pick; 25th player chosen; 1988-89 Super Bowl Champion

Flowers, Kenny, TB (1986) — 1987, 89 Atlanta Falcons

Fritts, George, OT (1941) — 1945 Philadelphia Eagles

Fuller, Steve, QB (1978) — 1979-83 Kansas City Chiefs; 1983 Los Angeles Rams; 1984-87 Chicago Bears; 1988 San Diego Chargers; First round draft choice; 23rd player chosen; 1985 Super Bowl Champion

G Gage, Bobby, TB (1948) — 1949-50 Pittsburgh Steelers; First round draft choice

*Gardocki, Chris, P-PK (1990) — 1991-94 Chicago Bears; 1995-present Indianapolis Colts

Geter, Eric, DB (1992) — 1994 — Las Vegas Posse (CFL)

Griffin, Steve, TB (1986) — 1987 Atlanta Falcons

H Hall, Delton, CB (1986) — 1987-91 Pittsburgh Steelers; 1992-93 San Diego Chargers; 1987 NFL All-Rookie Team

Hall, Hollis, DB (1981) — 1983 Arizona Wranglers (USFL); 1984 Houston Gamblers (USFL)

Hammond, Vance, DT (1990) — 1994 Sacramento Goldminers (CFL)

Hatcher, Dale, P (1984) — 1985-89, 91 Los Angeles Rams; 1993 Miami Dolphins; 1985 All-Pro; 1985 All-Rookie; 1985 Pro Bowl Team; first kicker chosen in 1985 draft

Harrell, Ricky, C (1972) — 1973 New York Jets

Harris, Rudy, FB (1992) — 1993-94 Tampa Bay Bucs

Hayes, Rudy, LB (1958) — 1959-60, 1962 Pittsburgh Steelers

Headen, Andy, LB (1982) — 1983-88 New York Giants; 1986 Super Bowl Champions

Hefner, Larry, LB (1971) — 1972-75 Green Bay Packers

*Henderson, Jerome, CB (1990) — 1991-1993 New England Patriots; 1993-94 Buffalo Bills; 1994 Super Bowl; 1995 — present Philadelphia Eagles

Hendley, Dick, QB (1950) — 1951 Pittsburgh Steelers

Hudson, Bill, DT (1956) — 1957-60 Montreal Alouettes (CFL); 1961-62 San Diego Chargers; 1963 Boston Patriots; Pro Bowl 1962

Hudson, Bob, DE-LB-DB (1950) — 1951-52 New

York Giants; 1953-55, 1957-58 Philadelphia Eagles; 1959 Washington Redskins; 1960 Dallas Texans; 1960-61 Denver Broncos

I Igwebuike, Donald, PK (1984) — 1985-89 Tampa Bay Buccaneers; 1990 Minnesota Vikings; 1994 Baltimore (CFL)

Inabinet, Clarence, OG (1935) — 1936 Rochester Tigers

J Jenkins, Ralph, C (1946) — 1947 Pittsburgh Steelers

*Jennings, Keith, WR (1988) — 1989 Dallas Cowboys; 1991 Montreal Machine; 1991-present Chicago Bears

Johnson, John, OLB (1990) — 1991-93 San Francisco 49ers; 1994 Cincinnati Bengals; 1995 New Orleans Saints

*Johnson, Tracy, FB (1988) — 1989 Houston Oilers; 1990-91 Atlanta Falcons; 1992-95 Seattle Seahawks

Jordan, Homer, QB (1982) — 1983-85 Saskatchewan Roughriders (CFL); 1985 Ottawa Roughriders (CFL); 1986 Winnepeg Blue Bombers (CFL); 1987 Cleveland Browns (replacement player)

K Kenney, Steve, OT (1978) — 1979-86 Philadelphia Eagles; 1986-87 Detroit Lions

Kinard, Terry, DB (1982) -1983-89 New York Giants; 1990 Houston Oilers; First-round choice, 10th player chosen; 1983 All-Rookie team; 1986 Super Bowl Champions; 1988 Pro Bowl

*Kirkland, Levon, OLB (1991) — 1992-present Pittsburgh Steelers; played in 1996 Super Bowl

L Latimer, Al, DB (1978) — 1979 Philadelphia Eagles; 1980 San Francisco 49ers; 1981 Winnipeg Blue Bombers (CFL); 1982-84 Detroit Lions

M Mack, Kevin, RB (1983) — 1984 Los AngelesExpress (USFL); 1985-93 Cleveland Browns; 1985 and 1987 Pro Bowl, 1985 All-Rookie Team

Mack, Terence, TE (1986) — 1987 St. Louis Cardinals

Mass, Wayne, T (1967) — 1968-70 Chicago Bears; 1971 Miami Dolphins; 1972 New England Patriots; 1972 Philadelphia Eagles

Mathews, Ray, END (1950) — 1951-59 Pittsburgh Steelers; 1960 Dallas Cowboys; 1961 Calgary Stampeders; 1952, 1953, 1955 NFL Pro Bowl

Mathis, Bill, RB (1959) — 1960-62 New York Titans; 1963-69 New York Jets; 1968 Super Bowl Champion; 1961 All-Pro; AFL Pro Bowl 1961, 63

McCall, Jeff, FB-TE (1982) — 1983 Los Angeles Raiders; 1983 Super Bowl Champion

McCanless, Jim, OG (1958) — 1960 Houston Oilers

McCullough, Richard, DT (1988) — 1989-90 Denver Broncos

*McDaniel, Ed, ILB (1991) — 1992-present Minnesota Vikings

McFadden, Banks, Back (1939) — 1940 Brooklyn Dodgers

*McGlockton, Chester, DT (1991) — 1992-present Oakland Raiders; 1994, '95 All-Pro; 1994, '95 Pro Bowl

McMakin, John, TE (1971) — 1972-74 Pittsburgh Steelers; 1975 Detroit Lions; 1976 Seattle Seahawks; 1974 Super Bowl Champion

McSwain, Chuck, RB (1982) — 1983-84 Dallas Cowboys; 1987 New England Patriots

McSwain, Rod, DB (1983) — 1984-90 New England Patriots

Milton, Eldridge, LB (1985) — 1987 Chicago Bears (replacement player)

Moore, Otis, DT (1989) — 1991-92 Birmingham Fire

Mulligan, Wayne, C (1969) — 1969-73 St. Louis

Cardinals; 1974- 75 New York Jets

O Olson, Harold, OT (1959) — 1960-62 Buffalo Bills; 1963-64 Denver Broncos; 1962 All-Pro

Olszewski, Harry, OG (1967) — 1969-70 Montreal Alouettes

O'Neal, Robert, FS (1992) — 1993-95 Indianapolis Colts

P Pagliei, Joe, Back (1955) — 1956 Calgary Stampeders; 1959 Philadelphia Eagles; 1960 New York Titans

Patton, Bob, OT (1951) — 1952 New York Giants

Peeples, Ken, OG (1974) — 1975 Winnipeg Blue Bombers

*Perry, Michael Dean, DT (1987) — 1988-94 Cleveland Browns; 1995 — present Denver Broncos; 1988 All-Rookie Team; 1989, 1990, 1991, 1993 All-Pro; 1989, 1990, 1991, 1993, 1994 Pro Bowl

*Perry, William, MG-FB (1984) — 1985-1992 Chicago Bears; 1993-94 Philadelphia Eagles; 1985 Super Bowl Champion, 1985 All-Rookie Team, 1985 First Round Pick, 22nd Player Chosen; 1996 — London Monarchs

Pleasant, Reggie, CB (1984) — 1985 Atlanta; 1986-94 Toronto Argonauts; 1988, 1990, 1991 All-Division; 1991 Grey Cup Champion

Poole, Bob, END (1963) — 1964-65 San Francisco 49ers; 1966-67 Houston Oilers

Potts, Robert, Tackle (1919) — 1926 Frankford Yellow Jackets

R Reese, Archie, DE (1977) — 1978-81 San Francisco 49ers; 1981 Super Bowl Champion; 1982-83 Los Angeles Raiders; 1983 Super Bowl Champion; 1984 Pittsburgh Maulers (USFL)

Reeves, Marion, TB (1973) — 1974 Philadelphia Eagles; 1975-76 Winnipeg Blue Bombers

Rembert, Johnny, LB (1982) — 1983-92, New England Patriots; 1988 All-Pro; 1988 Pro Bowl

Riggs, Jim, TE (1986) — 1987-1992 Cincinnati Bengals, 1993 Washington Redskins

Robinson, James, DT (1983) — 1984-85 Los Angeles Express (USFL)

Rome, Stan, WR (1975) — 1979-82 Kansas City Chiefs; 1983 Washington Federals (USFL)

*Rouse, Wardell, OLB (1994) — 1995-present Tampa Bay Bucs

Ryans, Larry, WR (1992) — 1993 Detroit Lions

S Scott, Jim, DL (1983) — 1985 Orlando Renegades

Scott, Randy, LB (1978) — 1980 Winnipeg Blue Bombers; 1980 Calgary Stampeders

*Sheppard, Ashley, OLB (1992) — 1993-95 Minnesota Vikings; 1995 Jacksonville Jaguars; 1995 Los Angeles Rams

*Simmons, Wayne, OLB (1992) — 1993-present Green Bay Packers; 1993 All-Rookie Team

Sims, Marvin, FB (1979) — 1980-81 Baltimore Colts

Smith, Richard, DB (1988) — 1991 Raleigh-Durham Skyhawks

Smith, Ronnie, LB (1977) — 1980 Saskatchewan Roughriders

*Stephens, Darnell, OLB (1995) — 1995-present Tampa Bay Bucs

Stuckey, Jim, DT, (1979) — 1980-86 San Francisco 49ers; 1986 New York Jets; 1987 San Diego Chargers; First round draft choice, 20th player chosen; 1981 and 1984 Super Bowl Champion

Swift, Bob, FB-C-G (1963) — 1964-65 British Columbia Lions; 1966-70 Toronto Argonauts; 1971-78 Winnipeg Blue Bombers; All-Pro 1972, 74

T Testerman, Don, RB (1975) — 1976-78 Seattle Seahawks; 1979 Washington Redskins; 1980 Miami Dolphins

Thomas, Doug, WR (1990) — 1991-93 Seattle Seahawks

Thompson, Dave, C-OG-T (1970) — 1971-73 Detroit Lions; 1974-75 New Orleans Saints

Thorsland, Oscar, End (1962) — 1963 Ottawa Rough Riders

Timmons, Charlie, BACK (1941) — 1946 Brooklyn Dodgers

Treadwell, David, PK (1987) — 1989-1992 Denver Broncos; 1993-94 New York Giants; 1989 Pro Bowl; 1989 All-Rookie Team

Tinsley, Sid, TB (1944) — 1945 Pittsburgh Steelers

*Trapp, James, DB (1992) — 1993 — present Oakland Raiders

Triplett, Danny, LB (1982) — 1984 Washington Federals

Tuten, Rich, DL (1978) — 1980 Ottawa Rough Riders

Tuttle, Perry, WR (1981) — 1982-83 Buffalo Bills; 1984 Tampa Bay Buccaneers; 1984 Atlanta Falcons; 1986-91 Winnipeg Blue Bombers; 1987 All-CFL; 1990 Grey Cup Champion; First round NFL Draft pick, 19th player chosen

W Walls, Henry, LB (1985) — 1987 New York Jets (replacement player); 1991 Montreal Machine

Walters, Joey, WR-DB (1976) — 1977 Winnipeg Blue Bombers; 1977-78, 1980-82 Saskatchewan Roughriders; 1979 British Columbia Lions; 1983-84 Washington Federals (USFL); 1985 Orlando Renegades (USFL); 1987 Houston Oilers; 1982 All-CFL; 1982 Leading pass receiver in CFL; set CFL pass receiving record in 1982

Washington, Jay, RB (1973) — 1974-79 Winnipeg Bombers; 1980 Saskatchewan Roughriders; 1976 CFL Rushing Leader

Waters, Charlie, CB (1969) — 1970-78, 80-81 Dallas Cowboys; 1971, 1977 Super Bowl Champion; 1977, 1978 All-Pro; 1976, 1977, 1978 Pro Bowl; selected to all-time Cowboys team

Wells, Joel, Back (1956) — 1957-60 Montreal Alouettes; 1961 New York Giants

White, Harvey, QB (1959) — 1960 Boston Patriots; first player ever signed by Patriots

*Whitley, Curtis, C (1991) — 1992-94 San Diego Chargers; played in 1995 Super Bowl; 1995 — present Carolina Panthers; 1995 All-Pro by Sports Illustrated

Williams, Keith, LB (1986) — 1987 Los Angeles Raiders (replacement player)

Williams, Perry, CB (1986) — 1987 New England Patriots (replacement player)

Williams, Ray, WR (1986) — 1987 Cleveland Browns (replacement player)

*Witherspoon, Derrick, RB (1993) — 1994 Shreveport Pirates; 1995 — present Phildelphia Eagles

*Woolford, Donnell, CB (1988) — 1989-present Chicago Bears; 1993 Pro Bowl

Worthy, Fred, END (1983 track) — 1984 Oakland Invaders

* Denotes active players; Note -- All Super Bowl years are seasons, not year Super Bowl was played.

HONORS

NATIONAL FOOTBALL FOUNDATION HALL OF FAME

These men have received the highest honor the game of football accords in their selection to the Hall of Fame, which is located in South Bend, IN.

COACH
Jess Neely, Coach 1931-39 (Inducted, 1971)
John Heisman, Coach 1900-1903 (Inducted, 1954)
Frank Howard, Coach 1940-69 (Inducted, 1989)

PLAYER
Banks McFadden, back 1939 (Inducted, 1959)

CITIZENS SAVINGS ATHLETIC FOUNDATION HALL OF FAME

Clemson representatives have received recognition from the Citizen Savings Foundation (formerly the Helms Athletic Foundation) which is located in Los Angeles, CA.

Athletic Director — Frank Howard, 1941-1971 (Elected 1979)
Coach — Frank Howard, 1940-69 (Elected 1973)
Player — Banks McFadden, Back 1937-38-39 (Elected 1969)
Sports Information Director — Bob Bradley, 1954-89 (Elected 1972); Joe Sherman, 1934-47 (Elected 1980)
Athletic Trainer — Herman McGee, 1934-80 (Elected 1981); Fred Hoover, 1958-present (Elected 1982)

SOUTH CAROLINA ATHLETIC HALL OF FAME

Frank Howard, 1972; Banks McFadden, 1972; Fred Cone, 1973; Joel Wells, 1974; Bill Mathis, 1977; Bobby Gage, 1978; Bill A. Hudson, Bob Hudson, Bob Sharpe, 1979; Charlie Waters, 1980; Danny Ford, 1982; Dwight Clark, 1986; Tom Barton, 1987; Harry Olszewski, 1990; Steve Fuller, 1991; Mac Folger, 1993; Bennie Cunningham 1993; Bob Jones, 1993; Jim Stuckey, 1995
Deceased Members: Joe Blalock, B.C. Inabinet, Jess Neely, Rock Norman, John Heisman

ACC PLAYER OF THE YEAR

Presented annually by the Atlantic Coast Sports Writers Association to the outstanding player in the conference for that season.
1967   Buddy Gore, TB
1977   Steve Fuller, QB
1978   Steve Fuller, QB
1981   Jeff Davis, LB
1984   William Perry, MG
1987   Michael Dean Perry, DT

ACC COACH OF THE YEAR

Presented annually by the Atlantic Coast Sports Writers Association to the outstanding coach in the conference for that season.
1958   Frank Howard
1966   Frank Howard
1974   Red Parker
1977   Charley Pell
1978   Charley Pell
1981   Danny Ford
1983   Danny Ford (UPI)

NATIONAL AWARD FINALISTS

1983   William Perry   Outland (Final 10)
1984   William Perry   Lombardi (Final 4)
1987   Michael Dean Perry   Outland (Final 3)
1988   Donnell Woolford   Thorpe (Final 16)
1990   Levon Kirkland   Butkus (Final 5)

1991   Levon Kirkland   Butkus (Final 12)
       Ed McDaniel   Butkus (Final 4)
       Robert O'Neal   Thorpe (Final 20)

ALL-ACC

1953   Dreher Gaskin (2), E; Don King (2), B
1954   Clyde White, T; Don King (2), B; Scott Jackson (2), E
1955   Joel Wells, TB
1956   John Grdijan (2), G; Dalton Rivers (2), E; Charlie Bussey (2), QB; Joel Wells, TB
1957   John Grdijan (2), G; Harvey White, QB; Ray Masneri (2), E
1958   Ray Masneri (2), E; Bill Thomas (2), C; Jim Padgett, T; Harvey White (2), B
1959   Gary Barnes, E; Doug Cline, FB; Lou Cordileone (2), T; Bill Mathis, HB; Harold Olson, T; Paul Snyder (2), C
1960   Lowndes Shingler, QB; Dave Lynn (2), G; Bill McGuirt (2), B
1961   Tommy King, E
1962   Don Chuy, T
1963   Ted Bunton (2), C; Billy Weaver, G; Pat Crain, FB; Lou Fogle (2), E; Jack Aaron (2), T
1965   Butch Sursavage, DE; Johnny Boyette, OT; Bill Hecht, LB; Hugh Mauldin, TB
1966   Jimmy Addison, QB; Wayne Mass, OT; Harry Olszewski, OG; Wayne Page, DB; Butch Sursavage, DE
1967   Jim Catoe, LB; Ronnie Ducworth, DE; Buddy Gore, TB; Frank Liberatore, DB; Wayne Mass, OT; Harry Olszewski, OG
1968   Joe Lhotsky, OT; Buddy Gore, TB; Ronnie Ducworth, DE; John Cagle, DT; Jimmy Catoe, LB
1969   Charlie Waters, OE; Ray Yauger, TB; Ivan Southerland, E
1970   Dave Thompson, OG; Don Kelley, DB
1971   Wayne Baker, DE; Larry Hefner, LB; John McMakin, TE
1972   Frank Wirth, DT
1973   Ken Pengitore, QB; Peanut Martin, DB; Ken Peeples, OT
1974   Willie Anderson, MG; Bennie Cunningham, TE; Jim Ness, DB; Ken Peeples, OT
1975   Bennie Cunningham, TE
1977   Joe Bostic, OG; Jonathan Brooks, DE; Lacy Brumley, OT; Jerry Butler, SE; Steve Fuller, QB; Steve Ryan, DB; Randy Scott, LB
1978   Joe Bostic, OG; Jonathan Brooks, DE; Bubba Brown, LB; Lester Brown, TB; Jerry Butler, SE; Steve Fuller, QB; Steve Kenney, OT; Steve Ryan, DB; Randy Scott, LB; Jim Stuckey, DT
1979   Jeff Bostic, OG; Bubba Brown, LB; Steve Durham, DT; David Sims, P; Jim Stuckey, DT; Rex Varn, DB
1980   Obed Ariri, PK; Perry Tuttle, FLK
1981   Dan Benish, DT; Tony Berryhill, C; Jeff Bryant, DT; Jeff Davis, LB; Homer Jordan, QB; Terry Kinard, FS; Perry Tuttle, FLK
1982   Cliff Austin, TB; Andy Headen, DE; Terry Kinard, FS; Frank Magwood, WR (AP); Bob Paulling, PK (AP); William Perry, MG; Johnny Rembert, LB
1983   James Farr, OG; Rod McSwain, DB; Bob Paulling, PK; James Robinson, DT; Edgar Pickett, DE; William Perry, MG; Henry Walls,

LB (AP); K.D. Dunn, TE
1984 Mike Eppley, QB (AP); Dale Hatcher, P; Donald Igwebuike, PK; William Perry, MG; Steve Reese, OG; Terrance Roulhac, WR; Ronald Watson, DB
1985 Steve Berlin, DT; Kenny Flowers, TB; Steve Reese, OG; Jim Riggs, TE
1986 Jim Riggs, TE; John Phillips, OG; Terrence Flagler, TB; Terence Mack, DE; Michael Dean Perry, DT; Delton Hall, CB
1987 Terry Allen, TB; Jeff Nunamacher, OT; Tony Stephens, MG; David Treadwell, PK; Michael Dean Perry, DT; John Phillips, OG; Donnell Woolford, CB
1988 Jeff Nunamacher, OT; Terry Allen, TB; Mark Drag, MG; Donnell Woolford, CB; Jesse Hatcher, OLB (2nd, AP); James Lott, FS (2nd, AP); Chris Gardocki, P (2nd, AP); Rich. McCullough, DT (2nd, AP)
1989 Vance Hammond, DT; Doug Brewster, LB; Stacy Long, OT; Chris Gardocki, PK-P; Levon Kirkland, OLB (UPI); Doug Brewster, LB; Dexter Davis, CB (UPI, 2nd AP); Robert O'Neal, FS (AP); Hank Phillips, C (UPI); James Lott, FS; Jeb Flesch, OG (2nd, AP); John Johnson, OLB (2nd, AP); Otis Moore, DT (UPI)
1990 Chris Gardocki, P-PK; Eric Harmon, OG; Stacy Long, OT; Ronald Williams, TB; Levon Kirkland, OLB; Vance Hammond, DT; Dexter Davis, CB; Jeb Flesch, OG (2nd); John Johnson, OLB (2nd); Doug Brewster, LB (2nd); Ed McDaniel, LB (2nd)
1991 Rob Bodine, MG ; Mike Brown, C; Jeb Flesch, OG; Levon Kirkland, OLB; Ed McDaniel, LB; Chester McGlockton, DT; Robert O'Neal, FS; Terry Smith, WR; Nelson Welch, PK; Ronald Williams, TB (2nd); Bruce Bratton, OT (2nd)
1992 Stacy Seegars, OG; Nelson Welch, PK (2nd); Brentson Buckner, DT (2nd); Ashley Sheppard, OLB (2nd); Robert O'Neal, FS (2nd)
1993 Brentson Buckner, DT; Stacy Seegars, OG; Brian Dawkins, SS (2nd); Andre Humphrey, CB (2nd); Tim Jones, LB (2nd); Nelson Welch, PK (2nd)
1994 Tim Jones, LB; Brian Dawkins, SS (2nd); Marvin Cross, DT (2nd); Wardell Rouse, OLB (2nd); Nelson Welch, PK (2nd)
1995 Brian Dawkins, SS; Anthony Simmons, LB; Lamarick Simpson, DT; Will Young, OG; Raymond Priester, TB (2nd); Dwayne Morgan, OT (2nd); Jeff Sauve, PK (2nd); Leomont Evans, FS (2nd)

ALL-SOUTHERN CONFERENCE (1902-1953)

1902 Hope Sadler, E; John Maxwell, QB
1903 Vet Sitton, E; O.L. Derrick, G; John Maxwell, QB; Jock Hanvey, FB
1904 O.L. Derrick, T
1905 O.L. Derrick, T; Fritz Furtick, HB
1913 W. A. Schiletter, T
1917 Mutt Gee, C
1919 L.M. Lightsey, G; R.C. Potts, G; Stumpy Banks, B
1920 L.M. Lightsey, G
1922 L.M. Lightsey, T
1928 O.K. Pressley, C
1929 Goat McMillan, TB
1935 Tom Brown, T; Clarence Inabinet, G
1937 Charlie Woods, C; Bob Bailey, B
1938 Gus Goins, E; Don Willis, B

1939 Joe Blalock, E; George Fritts, T; Banks McFadden, B; Shad Bryant, B
1940 Joe Blalock, E; George Fritts, T; Charlie Timmons, B
1941 Joe Blalock, E; George Fritts, T; Charlie Timmons, B
1942 Chip Clark, E
1944 Ralph Jenkins, C
1945 Ralph Jenkins, C; Bob Turner, T
1948 Frank Gillespie, G; Bobby Gage, B
1949 Ray Mathews, B
1950 Glenn Smith; Fred Cone, B
1951 Glenn Smith, E; Billy Hair, B
1952 Billy Hair, B

ALL-SOUTH CONFERENCE

1937 Charlie Woods, C; Don Willis, B
1938 Gus Goins, E; Don Willis, B
1939 George Fritts, T; Bob Sharpe, C
1939 Banks McFadden, B
1948 Bobby Gage, B
1950 Wyndie Wyndham, LB; Bob Patton, T
1952 Tom Barton, G

ALL-SOUTH ATLANTIC CONFERENCE

1930 Red Fordham, C
1934 Randy Hinson, B
1935 Clarence Inabinet, G
1935 Bob Jones, E
1936 Mac Folger, B

ACADEMIC ALL-AMERICAN

1956 Charlie Bussey, QB
1957 Harvey White, QB
1959 Lou Cordileone, OT
1971 Don Kelley, DB
1971 Ben Anderson, DB
1977 Steve Fuller, QB
1978 Steve Fuller, qB
1984 Mike Eppley, QB
1991 Bruce Bratten, OT
1994 Ed Glenn, TE
1995 Andye McCrorey, LB

(Breakdown by Team of Clemson's All-America selections)

Year	Name	AP	UPI	FC	FW	WC	SN	FN	Other
1928	O.K. Pressley	—	—	—	—	—	—	—	Heisman (3), NEA (3)
1939	Banks McFadden	1	—	1	1	—	—	—	Colliers (1), NEA (1)
1940	Joe Blalock	—	2	—	—	—	—	—	Hearst (1)
1941	Joe Blalock	—	2	—	1	—	—	1	Central Press (1)
1945	Ralph Jenkins	3	—	—	—	—	—	—	INS (1)
1948	Bobby Gage	—	—	—	—	—	—	—	INS (1)
1950	Jackie Calvert	2	—	—	—	—	—	—	
1952	Tom Barton	—	2	—	—	—	—	—	
1955	Joel Wells	—	3	—	—	—	—	—	
1959	Lou Cordileone	1	—	—	—	1	—	—	
1966	Wayne Mass	—	2	—	—	—	—	—	Dell Sports (1)
1967	Harry Olszewski	2	1	1	1	1	2	—	
1970	Dave Thompson	—	2	—	—	—	—	—	NEA (1)
1974	Bennie Cunningham	1	1	1	—	—	—	—	
1975	Bennie Cunningham	—	—	—	—	—	1	—	Time (1)
1977	Joe Bostic	3	—	—	1	—	—	3	
1978	Joe Bostic	2	2	—	—	—	—	1	
	Jerry Butler	1	—	—	—	1	—	—	NEA (2)
	Steve Fuller	3	—	—	—	—	—	—	
1979	Jim Stuckey	1	1	—	1	—	1	—	
1980	Obed Ariri	—	—	—	—	—	—	—	NEA (2)
1981	Jeff Davis	2	1	1	1	1	—	1	
	Terry Kinard	1	—	—	1	—	—	—	NEA (1)
	Perry Tuttle	—	—	—	—	—	1	2	
	Jeff Bryant	—	—	—	—	—	—	2	
1982	Terry Kinard	1	1	1	1	1	1	1	
	William Perry	3	—	—	—	—	—	—	
	Johnny Rembert	3	—	—	—	—	—	—	
	Lee Nanney	—	2	—	—	—	—	—	
1983	William Perry	3	1	—	—	1	—	2	
	James Robinson	—	—	—	—	—	2	—	
	James Farr	3	—	—	—	—	—	—	
1984	William Perry	3	1	—	—	1	—	1	
	Dale Hatcher	—	—	—	—	—	2	—	
	Donald Igwebuike	3	—	—	—	—	—	—	
1985	Steve Reese	—	—	—	—	—	—	2	
1986	Terrence Flagler	3	—	—	1	—	—	3	
	John Phillips	—	1	—	—	—	2	2	
1987	Michael Dean Perry	—	2	—	1	—	2	2	
	John Phillips	2	—	—	—	—	—	3	
	David Treadwell	1	1	1	—	1	1	1	
	Donnell Woolford	3	—	1	—	—	2	—	
1988	Donnell Woolford	—	1	1	1	1	1	2	
1989	Stacy Long	3	—	—	—	—	1	—	
	Chris Gardocki	3	—	—	—	—	—	—	
1990	Stacy Long	1	1	1	—	1	1	—	
	Chris Gardocki	2	2	—	—	—	—	3	
	Levon Kirkland	2	2	—	—	—	—	3	
1991	Jeb Flesch	1	1	—	—	1	2	1	
	Levon Kirkland	—	2	1	—	1	1	2	SH (1)
	Rob Bodine	2	—	—	1	—	2	—	CP (2)
	Ed McDaniel	3	—	—	—	—	—	—	CP (1)
1992	Stacy Seegars	2	2	—	—	—	—	3	
	Nelson Welch	3	—	*—	—	—	—	—	
1993	Stacy Seegars	1	2	—	—	1	1	1	CP (2)
1995	Brian Dawkins	2	—	—	—	—	2	—	
	Anthony Simmons	3	—	—	—	—	—	—	

Note: AP — Associated Press; UPI — United Press International; FC — Football Coaches; FW — Football Writers; WC — Walter Camp; SN — Sporting News; FN — Football News; NEA — Newspaper Enterprise of America; SH — Scripps-Howard; CP — College & Pro Football Weekly; INS — International News Service

LETTERMEN

*Deceased

A Aaron, Jack, 1961-62-63; *Abell, Frank, 1931-32; Abney, Terrence, 1992; Abrams, Jimmy, 1966-67; *Adams, J.P., 1914-15-16; Abreu, Ed, 1978; Adams, Rod, 1991; Addison, Jimmy, 1965-66-67 (Capt.); *Adkins, Gary, 1976-77-78-79; Alexander, Gary, 1973-74-75; Alford, Hugh, 1945; *Alford, J.L., 1916; Aliffi, Vic, 1961-63; *Allen, Banks, 1906-07; Allen, Michael, 1995; Allen, Terry, 1987-88-89; Allen, Thad, 1974-75-76-77; Alley, Kendall, 1981-82-83; *Allison, J.W. "Switzer," 1917-18-19-20; Ammons, Billy, 1966-67-68 (Capt.); Anderson, Ben, 1970-71-72; Anderson, Jack, 1968-69-70; *Anderson, Joe, 1960-61-62; Anderson, Randy, 1985-86-87; Anderson, Sam, 1958-59-60; Anderson, Tony, 1970-71-72; Anderson, Willie -1972-73-74 (Co Capt.); Andreas, Karl, 1971-72-73; Andreo, Ron, 1959-60-61 (Capt.); Ankuta, Neuf, 1954-55; Anthony, Vernie, 1981-82; Ard, Wendall, 1943-44; Ariri, Obed, 1977-78-79-80; Armstrong, F.E. "Boo," 1918 (Acting Capt.)-1919-1920 (Capt.); *Armstrong, Hoyt, 1921; Armstrong, Junior, 1930; Armstrong, Lon, 1959-60-61; Arrington, Vandell, 1981-82-83; Arthur, Gary, 1966-67-68; Asbill, Henry, 1927-28-29; Austin, Cliff, 1978-80-81-82; *Austin, P.B. "Plowboy," 1925-26; Avery, Wingo, 1953-54-55 (Alt. Capt.).

B *Bailes, J.P., 1919-20-21; *Bailes, W.B., 1922; Bailey, Bob, 1936-37-38; Bailey, Greg, 1987; Bailey, Rick, 1982-83-84; Bak, Jeff, 1985-86-87-88; Baker, Archie, 1950-51-52; Baker, Wayne, 1969-70-71; Baldwin, Bob, 1964; Baldwin, Mike, 1974; Balles, Joe, 1961-63; Banasiewicz, Brent, 1995; *Banks, B.C. "Stumpy," 1915-16-17-18 (Capt.) 19 (Capt.); Barbary, Bill, 1955-57; Barber, Mike, 1991-92-93-94; Barfield, Don, 1964-65-66; Barnes, Gary, 1959-60-61; Barnette, Jimmy, 1968-69; *Barnwell, T.G, 1902; Barter, Lynn, 1971-72; Bartlet, J.H., 1917; Barton, Paul, 1994; Barton, Tom, 1950-51-52; Basich, Rick, 1980; *Bates, Joe A. "Warhose" -1909-10-11; *Bates, J. Mc, 1918; Bauman, Charlie, 1977-78-79-80; Beasley, Gene, 1985-86-87-88; Beasley, Kenny, 1985; Bell, Jimmy, 1962-63-64 (Alt. Capt.); Bell, Randy, 1967; Bell, Larry, 1969-70; Bell, Wayne, 1964-65-66; Bell, William, 1988; *Bellows, C.A., 1900; Belton, Mitch, 1988-89-90; Bench, Elmer, 1994-95; Bengel, Gordy, 1971-72-73; Benish, Dan, 1979-80-81-82; Berlin, Steve, 1983-84-85 (Capt.); Berry, Mike, 1989; Berry, Joe "Net," 1934-35-36 (Capt.); Berryhill, Tony, 1979-80-81; Bethea, Fitzhugh, 1983; Bethea, Frank, 1973-74-75; Beville, Scott, 1988-89-90; *Bissell, Paul L., 1909-10-11 (Capt.); Black, Carl, 1936-38-39 (Alt. Capt.); Black, Manuel, 1934-35-36 (Alt. Capt.); Black, Tommy, 1961; Black, Wendall, 1959-60-61; Blackwelder, Tim, 1975; Blackwell, Joe, 1963-64; *Blain, J.M., 1896; Blakeney, Rock, 1930; *Blalock, Joe, 1939-40-41; Blanton, Bo, 1979-80; *Blease, J. W., 1898-1900; Blessing, Jim, 1939-40; Blinsky, Nick, 1993; Blunt, Rodney, 1990-91-92-93; Bodine, Rob, 1989-90-91 (Capt.); Bolin, Doug, 1991; Bollinger, Rich, 1976; Bolubasz, John, 1971-72-73; Boozer, Tom, 1972-73-74; Bosler, Bob, 1970-71-72; Bost, Ed, 1959-60-61; Bostic, Jeff, 1977-78-79; Bostic, Joe, 1975-76-77-78; Bounds, David, 1981; Bowen, Joe, 1953-55; Bowick, Ray, 1958; Bowlan, Roland, 1973-74; Bowles, H. Julian, 1923-24-25; Bowles, M.G. "Monk," 1929-30-31; Bowman, Nick, 1979-80-81; Boyer, Shelton, 1983-84-85; Boyette, Johnny, 1962-64-65 (Capt.); *Boykin, Bolivar, 1909; *Box, Carlon, 1984; Bradford, Eric, 1995; *Bradley, L.T. "Prep," 1925; *Brady, Kevin, 1984-85; *Brandon, T. B., 1914-15-16; Brantley, Craig, 1973-74-75; Branton, Joey, 1965-66-67; Bratton, Bruce, 1988-89-90-91; Bray, Cliff, 1976-77-78; Breedlove, Billy, 1956; *Breedon, Joe, 1901; Brewster, Doug, 1987-88-89-90; Brickley, Glenn, 1985; Brisacher, Art, 1971-72-73; Brisendine, Rod, 1946; *Bristol, W. H., 1912-13-14; *Britt, Ben, 1910-11-12

(Capt.); *Britt, D.C. "Toots," 1907-09; *Britt, S.L., 1910; Broadwater, Crosby, 1986-87; Brodie, Bunny, 1948-49; *Brock, W. T., 1896-97 (Capt.); Brooks, Jonathan, 1975-76-77-78; Broomfield, Donald, 1995; Brown, Dave, 1962; Brown, Gary, 1979-80-81-82; *Brown, H.W., 1916; Brown, Ken, 1980-81-83-84; Brown, Lester, 1976-77-78-79; Brown, Lockie, 1981; Brown, Marlon "Bubba," 1976-77-78-79 (Capt.); Brown, Mike, 1989-90-91; Brown, Norris, 1989-90-91-92; Brown, Ray, 1979-81-82-83; Brown, Ricky, 1971-72-73; Brown, Roy, 1980-81-82-83; *Brown, Tom I., 1933-34-35; *Browne, G. H. "Skeet," 1913; Browning, Sebo, 1984; Brumley, Lacy, 1974-75-76-77; Brunson, Jack, 1948-49-50; Brunson, Lawrence, 1984-85; Bruorton, H. B., 1954-55-56; *Bryant, Bill, 1935-36-37; Bryant, Dwayne, 1990-91-92; Bryant, Jeff, 1978-79-80-81; Bryant, Joe, 1950-51-52; *Bryant, Shad, 1937-38-39; Buckner, Brentson, 1990-91-92-93; Buckner, Mike, 1971-72-73 (Capt.); Buford, William, 1992; Bukowsky, Dick, 1969-70-71; Bullard, Wilbur, 1983; Bulman, Matt, 1994; Bundren, Jim, 1994-95; Bunton, Donnie, 1955-56-57; Bunton, Ted, 1962-63-64 (Capt.); Burbick, Bruce, 1967; Burgess, Robert, 1973-74; Burgner, Grady, 1967-68-69; Burley, Rion, 1993; *Burnett, George, 1966-67-68; Burnette, Derek, 1992-93; Burton, C.C., 1921-22; Burton, Dave, 1965; Burton, Richard, 1984; Buscher, L.E., 1934-36; Bush, Jack, 1955-56-57; Bussey, Charlie -1954-55-56(Capt.); Bussie, Arthur, 1990-91; Bustle, Rickey, 1974-75-76; Butcher, Brian, 1980-81-82; Butler, Butch, 1941-42-43-45; Butler, Jerry, 1976-77-78; Butler, Matt, 1995; Butler, Richard, 1982-83-84; Buttermore, Curt, 1972-73-74; Butz, Sam, 1945; *Byers, Monty, 1942; *Byrd, Gary, 1950-51-52.

C *Cagle, Bully, 1940-41-42; Cagle, John, 1966-67-68; Cagle, Mavis, 1944-45-46-47; Cain, Harold, 1974-75-76; Cain, Jack, 1978-79-80; Cain, Sammy, 1967-68-69; Caldwell, Charlie, 1969-70; Caldwell, Mark, 1980; Calhoun, Darren, 1990-91-92-93; Callahan, Sonny, 1971; Callicutt, Ken, 1973-74-75-77; Calvert, Forrest, 1950-53; Calvert, Jackie, 1948-49-50; *Calvert, Jim, 1949-50; Cameron, DeChane, 1989-90-91 (Capt.); *Camp, Bill, 1904; Campbell, Blake, 1988; Candler, Steedley, 1967; Cann, George, 1920-21; *Cannon, C.L., 1907; *Cannon, W. M., 1915; Caplan, Stu, 1964-65; Caputo, Paul, 1990-91-92; Carothers, Rocky, 1948-49-50; Carr, Michael, 1989; Carson, Gene, 1948-49; *Carson, Jules L. "Doc" -1910-11-12-13; Carson, Lynn, 1973-75; Carter, Andre, 1993-94-95; *Carter, Bert, 1906; Carter, Henry, 1984-86-87-88; Carter, Oscar, 1969-70; Case, Johnny, 1961-62-63; Cassady, Sonny, 1968-69-70; Cassidy, Richard, 1992; Cathcart, Joe, 1933; Catoe, Jimmy, 1966-67-68 (Capt.); Cauble, Charlie, 1969; *Caughman, F. Porter, 1907; *Caughman, Kenny, 1911-12-13; Chamberlain, Force, 1970-71-72; Chandler, Tommy, 1949; Charpia, Rusty, 1986-87-88; Chappelear, Glenn, 1984; Chappell, Henry, 1943; Chappell, James, 1995; Charleston, Pat, 1983-84-85; Chatlin, Rabbit, 1957-58-59; Chavous, Raymond -1985-86-87-88; Cheatham, Andy, 1982-83-84; Cheek, Randy, 1980-81; Childers, Stan, 1971; Childers, Tim, 1981-82-83; Childers, Tracy, 1962-63 (Capt.); Childers, Wilson, 1965-66-67; *Childress, John, 1948-49-50; Childress, O.J., 1995; Chipley, Bill, 1940-41; *Chovan, Phil, 1938; *Chreitzberg, C. K., 1898; *Chreitzberg, A.M., 1896; Chuy, Don, 1961-62; Ciniero, Geoff, 1985-86; Clamp, John, 1991; Clanton, Ray, 1945-46-47-48; *Clardy, Warren, 1904; Clark, Brian, 1979-80-81 ; Clark, Chip, 1942-45-46 (Capt.); Clark, Dwight, 1975-76-77-78; *Clark, W.C., 1906-07; Clayton, David, 1984; Cleveland, Olin, 1945-46; Clifford, Chris -1975-76; Clifford, Mark, 1979; *Cline, Doug, 1957-58-59; Cobb, Joe, 1989; Cobb, Maret, 1972-73-74; *Cochran, J.T. "Boots," 1908-09-10; Cockfield, Barry, 1966; Coffey, Bob, 1974-75; *Cogburn, H.L., 1903; *Colbert, W.C.

"Pinky," 1919-20-21; Coleman, Bob, 1959-60-61; *Coleman, Dan, 1937-38-40; Coleman, Jim, 1954-55-56; *Coles, Marion "Pony," 1910-11-12; *Coles, Strick, 1906-07-08 (Capt.); Coley, James, 1985-86-87-88; Collins, James, 1995; Collins, Jason, 1994; *Collins, Joe, 1928; Compton, Gary, 1958-59; Cone, Fred, 1948-49-50 (Capt.); *Connelly, Bill, 1909-10; *Cook, Pete, 1950-51-52; Cooper, Gary, 1986-87-88-89; Cooper, Jay, 1964-65-66; Cooper, Richard, 1963-64; Cordileone, Lou, 1957-58-59; Cornell, Mike, 1973-74-75; Coursey, Tom, 1949; Cox, Carol, 1945-47-48-49; Cox, Cary, 1946-47 (Capt.); Cox, Ed, 1949; Cox, Jack, 1948-49; *Cox, M.E., 1914-15; Cox, Walter, Sr., 1938-39; Cox, Walter, Jr., 1961-62-63; *Cox, Wyatt, 1957-58; Craig, Arthur, 1965-55-67; Craig, Bob, 1966-68-69; *Craig, Johnson, 1931-32; *Craig, Marion "Hawk," 1940-41-42 (Alt. Capt.); Crain, Pat, 1962-63-64; Crain, Willis, 1954; Crawford, Barclay, 1950-51-52; Crawford, Craig, 1983-84; Crawford, Eddie, 1974; Crite, Brendon, 1980-81-82; Crolley, Ronnie, 1959-60-61; Crooks, Kenya, 1994-95; Cropp, Willie, 1966-68; Cross, Marvin, 1992-93-94; *Crout, Sammy, 1958-59; Croxton, Bill, 1933-34-35; Cruce, Jeff, 1983-84; *Crumbie, Alton, 1944-45; Cunningham, Bennie, 1973-74-75 (Co-Capt.); Cunningham, James, 1975; *Cummings, Pony, 1932-33-34; Currie, Rudy, 1995; Curry, Carlos, 1992-93-94-95; Curtis, Ralph, 1946; Curtis, Rodney, 1985; Cuttino, H.B. "Hop," 1925-26.

D Daigneault, Doug, 1958-59; *Dailey, B.T., 1915; Daniel, Ralph, 1969-70-71; Danforth, Kenny, 1983-84-85; Dantzler, Ellis, 1963-64-65; Davis, Billy, 1980-81-82-83; Davis, Chip, 1986-87-88-89; Davis, David, 1988-89-90-91; Davis, Dexter, 1988-89-90; Davis, Footsie, 1930-31-32; Davis, Guy, 1926-27-28; Davis, Hal, 1962-63-64; Davis, Heide, 1970-71-72; Davis, Jason, 1990-91-92-93; Davis, Jeff, 1978-79-80-81 (Capt.); Davis, Jerry, 1972-73; Davis, Jud, 1944-45-47-48; Davis, Orlando, 1995; *Davis, St. Clair, 1928; Davis, Tyrone, 1982-83-84; Davidson, L.S., 1925-26; Dawkins, Brian, 1992-93-94-95; Dawson, Eric, 1985; Day, Dean, 1981; Deanhardt, Luke, 1946-47-48-49; Deanhardt, Luke, Jr., 1971; DeBardelaben, Bob, 1958-59; Decock, Bruce, 1971-72-73; *DeCosta, E.J. "Beef," 1901-02; *Deitz, Frank, 1939-40; Deluliis, Frank, 1985-86-87-88; *DeLoach, Billy, 1949; Demery, Pete, 1981; Demps, Reggie, 1989-90; DePew, Bill, 1968-69; *Derrick, O.L. "Puss" -1903-05-06; Derriso, Steve, 1990-91-92-93; DeSimone, Dick, 1954-56-57; DeSue, Tony, 1993-94-95; Devane, William, 1980-81-82-83; *Dickson, Laury, 1905; Diggs, Bubba, 1978-79-81-82; Dillard, Bill, 1932-33-34; DiMucci, Dan, 1949-50-51; Dingle, Adrian, 1995; Dixon, Bruce, 1989; Dixon, Terrance, 1992; Dolce, Chris, 1978-79; Donaldson, Richard, 1982-83-84; Dorn, Jim, 1969-70-71; *Dotterer, E.G. "Gilly," 1922-23; Dotherow, Fudge, 1962; *Douthit, Claude "Pug," 1898-99-1900-01 (Capt.); Downs, Anthony, 1994-95; Dozier, Ted, 1931-32-33; Drag, Mark, 1985-86-87-88; Driver, Stacey, 1982-83-84-85; *Duckett, Graves, 1916; *Duckworth, Joe, 1898-89-1900; Ducworth, C.H., 1974; Ducworth, George, 1968-69-70; Ducworth, Ronnie -1966-67-68 (Capt.); Ducworth, Thomas, 1973; Dukes, Mike, 1956-57-58; Duley, Tom, 1965; Dumas, Charlie, 1962-63-64; Duncan, John, 1984; *Dunlap, Tom, 1919-20; Dunn, K.D., 1981-82-83-84; Dunnican, Kelton, 1994-95; Durham, Steve, 1977-78-79-80; Dyer, Clint, 1945-46-48; *Dyess, Jimmy, 1929.

E Earle, James, 1984-85-86-87; *Earle, J.C., 1900; Easton, Lance, 1991-92; Eaves, Robin, 1990; Eberhart, Terry, 1958; Edwards, Antwan, 1995; Eidson, Wesley, 1967-68; Eley, Thomas, 1975; Ellenburg, Charlie, 1966-67; Ellis, Joe, 1981-83-84; *Ellison, Gill, 1904-05; Elvington, B.B., 1968-69-70 (Capt.); Emanuel, Emmett -1910-21-22 (Capt.); *Emerson, Jack, 1947; Engel, Karl, 1962; English, Tom, 1968; Enzor, Scott, 1985-86; Eppes, Roy, 1976-77; Eppley, Mike, 1982-83-84 (Capt.); *Epps, M.H. "Pepper," 1910; Esgro, Greg,

1984; *Eskew, H.L. "Bud" -1925-26-27 (Capt.); Ethridge, Brooks, 1970; Ethridge, Don, 1969-70-71; Evans, Charlie, 1962; Evans, Leomont, 1992-93-94-95; Eyler, Rick, 1968-70; *Ezell, J.F. "Sam," 1909-10; *Ezell, R. B. "Doc," 1912.

F Fabers, Leon, 1972-73; Facciolo, Mike, 1964-65-66 (Capt.); Farnham, Dave, 1969-70-71; Farr, James, 1980-81-82-83 (Capt.); Fellers, Mark-1972-73-74 (Co. Capt.); Fellers, Stan, 1932-33-34; Few, Bill, 1955-56-57; Fewell, J. A. "Jake," 1924-25; Fewster, Butch, 1990-91-92; Fields, Stacy, 1987-88-89-90; *Finklea, Gary, 1923-24-25 (Capt.); *Finley, States Right G., 1916-17; Fisher, Brad, 1979-80-81; Fitzpatrick, Pat, 1978; Flagler, Terrence, 1982-84-85-86 (Capt.); *Flathman, Gene, 1936; *Fleming, F, 1907-08; Fleming, J.M. "Fatty," 1925; *Fleming, Vic, 1930-31; Fleming, W.H., 1929-30; Flesch, Jeb, 1988-89-90-91; Fletcher, Rodney, 1988-89; Flowers, Kenny 1983-84-85-86; *Floyd, George, 1939-40; Fogle, Lou, 1961-62-63; *Folger, Mac, 1934-35-36; Ford, Andy, 1993-94-95; Ford, Peter, 1993-94-95; *Fordham, Red, 1930-31 (Capt.); Forney, Warren, 1991-92-94-95; Foster, Jon, 1988; *Forsythe, J.A. "PeeWee," 1901-02-03; *Forsythe, W.C., 1898-99-1900-01; Fortner, Jeff, 1991-92; Fox, Angelo, 1987-88; Franklin, Chris, 1993-94; *Franklin, Harry, 1941-42; *Freeman, Eddis, 1943-44-45-46; *Frew, W.L. "Red," 1918; Frierson, Bob, 1982; *Fritts, George, 1939-40-41; Fuller, Steve, 1975-76-77 (Capt.)-78 (Capt.); Fulmer, John, 1967-68-69; Funderburk, Mike, 1968; *Furtick, Fritz, 1903-04-05-06 (Capt.).

G Gage, Bobby, 1945-46-47-48; Gaillard, Jerry, 1978-79-80-81; Gainer, Chick, 1943-46-47-48; Galloway, G.G., 1972-73-74-75; Galuska, Pete, 1969-70-71; *Gandy, A.P. "Hop," 1909-11-12-13 (Capt.); *Gantt, W.A., 1905; *Gantt, Jonnie, 1902; Gardocki, Chris, 1988-89-90; Garick, Richard, 1966-67-68; *Garrison, Bill, 1902-03; *Garrison, C.C., 1923; Garrison, Gene, 1953; Gaskin, Dreher, 1950-51-53 (Co-Capt.); Gasque, Mike, 1980-81; *Gassaway, Jim, 1928-29; Gaston, Clark, 1961-62-63; *Gaston, R.T., 1905-06-07; Geathers, Eddie, 1978-79-80; *Gee, C.F. "Little Mutt," 1912-13-14; *Gee, J.G. "Mutt," 1914-15-16-17; Gehret, Guy, 1972-73-74; Gemas, Kevin, 1983-84; Gennerich, Gary, 1970-71-72; *Gentry, Charlie, 1896-97-98; Gentry, Frank, 1950-51-52; *George, A.P., 1899-1900; George, Buck, 1951-52-53-54 (Capt.); Gerald, Henry, 1965; Gerrald, Steve, 1988; Geter, Eric, 1989-90-91-92; *Gettys, E.F. "Red," 1918-19-20-21; Gibbs, Steve, 1974-76-77-78; Gibson, Cameron, 1988; Gibson, Tyrone, 1989-91-92; Gillespie, Bill, 1943; *Gillespie, Dick, 1948-50; Gillespie, Frank, 1946-47-48; *Gilmer, Grover G., 1917-19-20-21; *Gilmer, Frank, 1908-09-10; Gilstrap, Clay, 1986-87; Gilstrap, Earl, 1970-71; Gilstrap, Rick, 1969-70-71; Glaze, Coleman, 1960-61-62; Glenn, Ed, 1993-94; Glenn, Joe, 1979-80-81-82; Gobble, Robert, 1958; Godfrey, Steve, 1976-77 (Capt.); Goehring, Jim, 1976-77; Goff, Johnnie Mac, 1968; Goggins, Harold, 1975-76-77-78; *Goins, Gus, 1936-37-38; Goldberg, Bob, 1977-78; *Gooding, R.F. "Fatty," 1904; Goodloe, John, 1977; Goudelock, David, 1990-91; Gordon, Chuck, 1976; Gore, Buddy, 1966-67-68; Goss, Dennis, 1971-72; Graham, Bernie, 1950-51; *Graham, George, 1944; Granger, Ty, 1985-86-87-88; Gravely, Mike, 1974; *Gray, Bill, 1911; Gray, Ricky, 1980; Grdijan, John-1955-56-57 (Co-Capt.); *Green, Harry, 1901-02; Green, Mervin, 1988; Greene, Earle, 1955-56; Greene, Gerry, 1991; Greene, Johnny, 1955; Greene, Nealon, 1994-95; Greenwalt, Stan, 1973; Gresham, Metz, 1929; Gressette, Larry, 1951-52-53 (Co-Capt.); Gressette, Nathan, 1951-52-53 (Co-Capt.); Grier, Marrio, 1992-93; Griffin, Steve, 1982-84-85- 86; Griffith, Frank, 1954-55; Grigsby, Billy Luke, 1948-49-50; Grimes, Tyler, 1986-87-88; Gue, Tommy, 1959-60-61; Gues, Henry, 1992-93-94-95; *Gunnells, Bill, 1928-29; Gunnells, Dan, 1965-66-67; Guy, Ruben, 1932.

H Haddock, Lee, 1970-71; Hagen, Arthur, 1944; Haglan, J.D., 1976-77-78; Hair, Billy, 1950-51-52 (Co-Capt.); *Hair, J.C., 1924-26-27; *Hall, Bill, 1938-39-40 (Alt. Capt.); Hall, Delton, 1983-84-85-86; Hall, Hollis, 1979-80-81; Hall, Howard, 1989-90-91-92; Hall, Lamont, 1994-95; Hall, Les, 1989-90-91-92; *Hall, R.M. "Fatty," 1926-27-28; Hall, Wade, 1960-63; *Hamer, Ray, 1939-40-41; *Hamilton, R.G., 1896 (Capt.); *Hammett, L.O., 1918; Hammond, Brian, 1985; Hammond, Vance, 1987-88-89-90; *Hane, J.K., 1924-25-28; Haney, Don, 1993; Hankins, Kelvin, 1989-90-91; Hankinson, Crimmins, 1953-54; *Hankle, Witt H., 1908-09-10 (Capt.); Hansford, Ogden, 1974-75-78; *Hanvey, Ernest, 1913; *Hanvey, George, 1897-98; *Hanvey, Jock T., 1896-97-1902-03; *Hardin, L.G., 1916; Harman, Dean, 1991; Harmon, Eric, 1987-88-89-90; *Harmon, H.M. "Duck," 1914-15-16; *Harmon, S.E. "Pat," 1922-23-24; Harper, J.C., 1985-86-87-88; Harps, Wayne, 1986-87-88-89; Harrell, Ricky, 1970-71-72; *Harris, H.S. "Lazy Bill," 1914-15-16; Harris, John, 1990-91-92; *Harris, L.D., 1919; Harris, Reggie, 1986-87-88; Harris, Rudy, 1990-91-92; Hart, Chris, 1989; *Hart, Willard L. "Bub," 1916-17; Harvey, B.C. "Chubby," 1925-26 (Capt.); *Harvey, Randy, 1967-68; *Harvey, S.A. "Speck," 1922; Harvey, Travis, 1993-95; Harvin, Lionell, 1929-30-31; *Harvley, Clyde, 1931; Hatcher, Dale, 1981-82-83-84; Hatcher, Jesse, 1987-88; Hauser, Tad, 1980; Hausgen, Ed, 1992-93-94-95; *Hayden, C.J., 1911; Hayes, Rudy, 1956-57-58 (Alt. Capt.); Haynes, Joey, 1987; Haynes, Norman, 1985-86-87; Headen, Andy, 1979-80-81-82; Hecht, Bill, 1963-64-65 (Capt.); *Heffner, L.B., 1920; Hefner, Larry, 1969-70-71 (Capt.); Heilig, Don, 1959; *Heinemann, John-1931-32-33 (Capt.); Hemphill, James, 1993; *Hendee, H.M. "Tick," 1925-26; Henderson, Jerome, 1987-88-89-90; Henderson, Joe, 1987-88-89; Hendley, Dick, 1946-48-49-50; Hendley, Richard, 1980-81-82; *Hendricks, L.L., 1896-97; Heniford, Mark, 1974-75-76-77; Heniford, Todd, 1984; *Henley, Cliff, 1934-35; Henry, Dale, 1969-70-71; Herlong, Doug, 1948-51; *Herlong, Henry, 1930; Hewitt, Andre, 1993; Hicks, Harry, 1954; Hicks, Ken, 1972; Hill, Jerome, 1974-75; Hilderbrand, Nolten, 1953; Hinson, Randy, 1933-34-35; Hinton, Marcus, 1992-93-94-95; *Holland, Joe, 1904 (Capt.); Holland, Lawson, 1974; Holloman, Duke, 1983-84; *Holohan, R. F. "Butch," 1921-22-23 (Capt.) -24; Homonoff, Edward, 1973-74; Hood, Greg, 1992-93; Hook, Charlie, 1965-66-68; *Hook, Fred, 1931-32; Hooper, Ricardo, 1986-87-88; Hope, Leon, 1973-74-75; Hooper, Ricardo, 1986-87-88; Hopkins, Stan, 1971-72; Horne, Charlie, 1956-57-58; Horne, Tony, 1994-95; Horton, Tate, 1933-34-35; Hostetler, Hoss, 1964-66-67; Hough, James, 1945; Howard, Jimmy, 1961-62-63; Howell, Trey, 1988; Hubert, Pooley, 1950-53; Hudson, Alex, 1980-82-83; Hudson, Bill, 1954-55-56; Hudson, Billy, 1976-77-78; Hudson, Bob, 1947-48-49-50; Hudson, J.C., 1950-51-52; Hughes, Wade, 1971-72 (Capt.); Humphrey, Andre, 1992-93-94-95; Hunt, Revonne, 1951; Hunter, Bill, 1942-46-47; Hunter, Brian, 1992; Hunter, Hamp, 1953-54-55; *Hunter, N.M. "Buster," 1899-1900-01; Huntley, Chuck, 1970-73; Hutchins, Roger, 1991-92; *Hydrick, Onan, 1908-09; Hynes, Dave, 1960-61-62.

I Igwebuike, Donald, 1981-82-83-84; *Inabinet, B.C., 1953-54-55; *Inabinet, Clarence J., 1933-34-35; Inge, Mark, 1986-87-88; Ingle, Reid, 1982-83-84; Ingram, Keith, 1987; Inman, Don, 1984; Isaacs, Mike, 1983-84-85.

J Jackson, Jack, 1969; Jackson, Jacky, 1965-66-67; Jackson, Jackie Lee, 1966-67-68; Jackson, Kenzil, 1989-90-91-92; Jackson, Kit, 1965-66-67; Jackson, M.E., 1921; Jackson, Robert, 1993-94-95; Jackson, Scott, 1952-53-54 (Capt.); *Jackson, S.L. "Stonewall" -1922-23-24; Jackson, Wister, 1938-39; James, Charlie, 1988-89; *James, M.B. "Jimmy," 1911-12-13-14; Jameson, Hugh, 1939-40-41; Jansen, John, 1984-85-86; Jaynes, Danny, 1976-77; Jehlen, George, 1974-75-76; Jenkins,

James, 1994; *Jenkins, Ralph, 1943-44 (Capt.) 45 (Capt.); 46 (Alt. Capt.); *Jennings, A.T., 1914; Jennings, Keith, 1985-86-87-88; *Jeter, J.P., 1913; Jetton, Neal, 1973-74-75 (Co. Capt.); Johnson, A.J., 1984-85; Johnson, Bobby, 1970-71-72; Johnson, John, 1987-88-89-90; Johnson, Ricky, 1963-64-65; Johnson, Tracy, 1985, 86-87-88; Jollay, Mike, 1985-86; Jolley, Bobby, 1951; *Jones, Bob, 1928-29-30; Jones, Bob, 1972-73; Jones, Chris, 1995; Jones, Jimmy, 1949; Jones, Tim, 1991-92-93-94; Jordan, Homer, 1980-81-82 (Capt.); Jordan, Leonard, 1941; Jordan, Whitey, 1955-56-57; Jordan, Willie, 1975-76-77-78; Joye, David, 1990-91; Justus, Johnny, 1928-29-30 (Capt.).

K *Kaigler, Ben, 1902; *Kaigler, J.G., 1898-99-1900; Kaltenback, Leon, 1955-56-57 (Co-Capt.); Kane, Mark, 1953-54 (Capt.); *Kangeter, Jonnie, 1910-11-12; Katana, Ted, 1965-66; *Kay, L.R., 1917-19; *Keasler, A.L. "Gus," 1904-05; *Keel, J.W. "Rastus," 1906; Keller, Morris, 1959; Kelley, Don, 1969-70-71; Kelley, Freddy, 1965-66-67; Kelley, Steve, 1973; Kempson, Otis, 1950-51-52; Kendrick, Tommy, 1969-70-71; Kennedy, Frank, 1950-51; Kennedy, Tony, 1988-89-90-91; Kenney, Steve, 1976-77-78; Kesack, Gary, 1974-75-76; Keys, Larry, 1965-66-67; *Keyserling, H.L. "Golden," 1920; Kier, Brian, 1974-76-77; Killen, Pat, 1959; Kinard, Terry, 1979-80-81-82 (Capt.); King, Anthony, 1976-77-78; King, Buddy, 1970-71-72 (Capt.); King, Don, 1952-53-54-55 (Capt.); King, Jack, 1968-69; King, Jimmy, 1959-60-61; *King, L.O., 1901-02; King, Tommy, 1959-60-61; *Kinsler, J.H., 1900; Kirkconnell, Ben, 1932; Kirkland, Levon, 1988-89-90-91 (Capt.); *Kissam, Roddy, 1933-34-35; Kitchens, Ronnie, 1967-68-69; Knight, Herman, 1949-51; *Klugh, W.W., 1925-26; Knoebel, Fred, 1950-51- 52; Knott, Hal, 1959; Kormanicki, Dave, 1968-69; Kreis, Kevin, 1976; Kubu, Jon, 1989; Kunz, Michael, 1994.

L *Lachicotte, G.E. "Boo," 1910; Laird, Kevin, 1995; Lam, Elmo, 1960-61-62 (Capt.); *Lambert, John, 1931; LaMontagne, Joe, 1951-52-53; Lancaster, Chris, 1985-86-87-88; Landry, Mark, 1994-95; Langford, Charlie, 1979; Langston, J.L., 1920; Lanzendoen, Jim, 1973; Laraway, Walt, 1953-54-55; Latimer, Al, 1978; *Latimer, Bill, 1906; *Lawrence, Bert, 1902; Lawrence, Floyd, 1956; Lawrence, Reggie, 1988-89-90; Lawson, Larry, 1970; Lawton, Streak, 1935-36; Lawton, Winston, 1969; Learn, Randy, 1979-80-81-82; LeBel, David, 1973-74-75; *Lee, A.C. "Bun," 1907; Lee, Mark, 1974-75; Lee, Harry, 1934-35; LeJeune, Brent, 1991-92-93; Leonard, Hal, 1946-47; Leverman, Gerald, 1945; *Lewis, Alex P., 1911-12-13; *Lewis, Gus, 1900-01; *Lewis, Harold, 1935-36-37 (Capt.); *Lewis, J. B., 1898-99-1900; Lewis, Merritt, 1932-33-34; Lewis, Stacy, 1989-90; Lewis, Zane, 1995; Lewter, Steve, 1969-70-71; Lhotsky, Joe, 1966-67-68; Liberatore, Frank, 1964-66-67(Capt.); *Lightsey, F.B. "Bull," 1922-24-25; *Lightsey, L.M. "Yen," 1917-18-19-20; Lindsey, Otis, 1981-82; Link, A.C., 1926; *Littlejohn, C.E. "Mule," 1913-14-15; *Locklair, Ed "Pop," 1941; Locklair, Mike, 1966-67-68; Locurcio, Todd, 1993; Logan, Jimmy, 1966; *Logan, J.R., 1912-13; Long, Evans, 1930; Long, Stacy, 1986-88-89-90; Lott, Billy, 1977-78-79 (Capt.); Lott, James, 1986-87-88-89; Lovelace, Chris, 1993; Lowman, P.I. "Pi," 1918-19; Lundeen, Danny, 1970-71; Luzzi, Richie, 1966-67-68; *Lykes, Powell, 1905-06; *Lynah, Jim, 1900-01; Lynch, Chuck, 1991; Lynn, Dave, 1958-59-60 (Capt.); Lytton, Jeff, 1983-84-85.

Mc McBride, Dan, 1973; McCall, Jeff, 1979-80-81-82; McCanless, Jim, 1955-56-58; McCarley, Bob, 1927-28-29; McCauley, Jim, 1949; McCleon, Dexter, 1993-94-95; McClure, Bruce, 1963-64-65; *McConnell, H.S., 1914-15; *McConnell, R.E., 1925-26; McConnell, S.W., 1934-35-36; *McConnell, T.S., 1934-35-36; McCory, Bob, 1944; McCown, Fred, 1942; McCown, Slick, 1933-34; McCown, T.M., 1918; McCrorey, Andye, 1992-93-94-95; McCullough, Richard, 1985-86-87-88; McCurty, Damon, 1979; McDaniel, Ed, 1988-89-90-91;

McDowell, Garry, 1974-75; McElmurray, Mac, 1964-65-66; McElveen, Norwood, 1939-40-41; McFadden, Banks, 1937-38-39; *McFadden, R.D., 1908; *McFadden, R.H. "Doc," 1906-07; McFadden, Wesley, 1985-87-88-89 (Capt.); McGee, Edgar, 1965-66-67; *McGill, C.A., 1925; McGlockton, Chester, 1989-90-91; McGlone, T.F., 1926; McGuirt, Bill, 1960-61; McInally, Chris, 1993-95; *McIver, Rick, 1904-05; McKenney, Pat, 1985-86; McKenzie, Damonte, 1995; McKenzie, W.W., 1918; *McKeown, J.A., 1903; McLane, Riley, 1966-67; McLaurin, Jewell, 1969-70; *McLaurin, J.N., 1904-05-06-07 (Capt.); McLees, Jimmy, 1990-91; McLellan, Bill, 1953-54; McLellan, Cliff, 1981; *McLendon, Ed, 1939; McLendon, Lem, 1955; McMahan, Dave, 1969-70; McMakin, John, 1969-70-71 (Capt.); *McMillan, Goat, 1928-29; McMillan, Raiford, 1926-27-28; *McMillan, W.L. "Red," 1913-14-15; McSwain, Chuck, 1979-80-81-82; McSwain, Rod, 1980-81-82-83.

M Mack, Terence, 1983-84-85-86 (Capt.); Mack, Kevin, 1980-81-82-83; Mader, Eric, 1989-90; *Magee, Watson, 1936-37-38; *Magill, Dick, 1927-28-29; *Magill, W.K. "Rummy," 1913-14-15 (Capt.); Magwood, Frank, 1980-81-82; *Major, C.S. "Dopey," 1913-14-15-16 (Capt.); Maness, Ed "Chippy," 1938-39-40; Mann, Wes, 1983-84-85; Mannella, Dave, 1979; Manos, Pete, 1949-50-51; Marazza, Dick, 1954-55-56; Mariable, Dorian, 1986-87-88-89; Marion, Phil, 1964-65-66; Marler, Malcolm, 1973-74-75-76 (Co- Capt.); *Marshall, L.E., 1926; Martin, Bob, 1946-47-48 (Co-Capt.); Martin, Carl, 1981-82; *Martin, J.M., 1909-10-11; Martin, Khang, 1993; Martin, Peanut, 1972-73-75; *Martin, W.N., 1925-27; Masneri, Ray, 1956-57-58; Mass, Wayne, 1965-66-67; Massaro, Cary, 1980-81-82; Massengill, Wells, 1972; Mathews, Mike, 1971; Mathews, Ray, 1947-48-49-50; Mathews, Tony, 1973-74; *Mathis, A.J., 1898; Mathis, Bill, 1957-58-59; *Matthews, Bill, 1915-16; Matthews, Mack, 1960-62-63; Mattos, Tommy, 1952-53-54; Mauldin, Hugh, 1963-64-65; Mauney, Tony, 1988-89-90-91; *Maxwell, Jeff, 1896-97; *Maxwell, John, 1902-03; Mayberry, Bob, 1979-80-81-82; Mayer, Charlie, 1969-70-71; Meadowcroft, Charlie, 1963-64-65; Meadows, Dwayne, 1984-85-86; Medlin, Rick, 1967-68-69; Meeks, Chuck, 1982; *Mellette, F.M., 1911; *Melton, L.H. "Doc," 1923-24; Michael, Benny, 1966-67-68; *Midkiff, Bob, 1926; Miller, Bill, 1962; Miller, Billy, 1943; *Miller, Bob, 1931-32 (Capt.); Miller, H.E., 1937-38; *Miller, Jack, 1944-47-48; Miller, Jim, 1948; Miller, Ron, 1958; Mills, Jeff, 1974-75; Milton, Eldridge, 1981-83-84-85; Milton, Fred, 1968-69-70; *Mimms, Charlie, 1946; Moncrief, Richard, 1990-91-92-93 (Capt.); Monledous, Zag, 1927-28; Mooneyham, Jack, 1949-50-51; Montone, Neil, 1947; Moore, Gene, 1947-48-49 (Capt.); Moore, Ken, 1952-53-54; Moore, Otis, 1986-87-88-89 (Capt.); Moore, Ted, 1964; Moorer, John, 1945-46-47 (Alt- Capt.); *Moorer, Tom, 1938-39; Morgan, Bobby, 1958-59; Morgan, Dwayne, 1994-95; Morgan, Lewis, 1946; Morocco, Chris, 1986-87-88-89; Morris, David, 1973; Morrison, Pete, 1961; Moss, Charlie, 1930-31-32; Mouzon, Tyron, 1988-89-90-91; *Mulherin, Eddie, 1928; Mullen, Ray, 1965-66; Mulligan,Wayne, 1966-67-68; *Mullins, H.D. "Horse," 1923-24; Murray, Al, 1972-73-74; Murray, John, 1978; Myrick, Rocky, 1979.

N Nanney, Lee, 1978-79-80 (Co-Capt.) 81 (Co-Capt.); Nelson, Bryce, 1992-93; Ness, Jim, 1972-73-74 (Co-Capt.); Neville, J.L., 1943; Newell, Andy, 1985; Newell, Mike, 1969-70; Nimitz, H.J. "Foots," 1916; Nix, Eric, 1984-85-86; Noelte, Dave, 1982; Nunamacher, Jeff, 1985-86-87-88; Nunn, Arlington, 1987-88-89-90.

O O'Brien, Chuck, 1987-88-90-91; O'Cain, Mike, 1974-75-76 (Co-Capt.); O'Dell, Billy, 1953-54-55; *O'Dell, John H., 1918-19; *O'Dell, Wayne, 1941; *Odom, W.F., 1908; Ogle, Chris, 1989-90; Ohan, Chinedu, 1987-88; *O'Kurowski, Whitey, 1937-38-39; Olson, Dave, 1958-59-60; Olson, Harold, 1957-58-59;

Olszewski, Harry, 1965-66-67; *O'Neal, Belton "Speck," 1920; O'Neal, Brad, 1969-70; O'Neal, Robert, 1989-90-91-92 (Capt.); Orban, Turk, 1936; Osborne, Ronnie, 1959-60-61; Otorubio, Adubarie, 1985; *Owens, J.C. "Susie," 1919-20; Owens, Mark, 1993.

P *Padgett, F.M., 1918; *Padgett, G.D., 1931; Padgett, Jim, 1957-58; *Padgett, O.D., 1928-29 (Capt.); Padgett, Wade, 1939-40-41; Page, Wayne, 1965-66; Pagliei, Joe, 1953-54-55; Palmer, Cary, 1989; *Palmer, E.D. "Frog," 1925; Palmer, Johnny, 1963-64-65; Paredes, Bob, 1951-54; Parete, Anthony, 1981-82-83-84; *Parker, Ace, 1940-41; *Parker, Harry L., 1912-13; Parker, Jim, 1962-63 (Alt. Capt.); Pasley, Jim, 1939-40; Pate, Milton, 1951-52; Patrick, Chris, 1932; *Patterson, Gene, 1931-32; *Patton, Bob, 1949-50-51 (Capt.); Paulling, Bob, 1979-81-82-83; Pavilack, Harry, 1959-60-61; Payne, Booty, 1940-41; Payne, Jim, 1956-57-58; *Payne, Joe, 1937-38-39 (Capt.); Payne, Oliver, 1936-37; Pearce, Frank, 1963-64-65; Pearce, Roy, 1939-40; Pearman, Dan, 1985-86; *Pearman, Fred, 1899-1900-01; Pearson, Ken, 1937-38-39; Peeler, Coby, 1993-94; Peeples, Ken, 1972-73-74 (Co-Capt.); Pegues, Lamont, 1994-95; *Pegues, E.S., 1899; Pengitore, Ken, 1971-72-73 (Capt.); *Pennington, Clyde, 1935; Pennington, Curtis, 1936-37-38 (Alt. Capt.); *Perry, Bill, 1911; *Perry, L. "Tom," 1911; Perry, Michael Dean, 1984-85-86-87 (Capt.); *Perry, Tracy, 1976-77-78-79; Perry, William, 1981-82-83-84 (Capt.); Petoskey, Ted, 1963-64; Phillips, Erik, 1992; Phillips, Hank, 1986-87-88-89; Phillips, Harley, 1943-44; Phillips, Jim, 1945; Phillips, John, 1984-85-86-87 (Capt.); Pickett, Edgar, 1980-81-82-83; Pierce, Hal, 1940-41- 42; Pilot, Joe, 1958; *Pinckney, E.H., 1909; *Pitts, Lewis, 1927-28; Plantin, Tony, 1994-95; Pleasant, Reggie, 1982-83-84; Poe, Billy, 1944-45-46; *Pollitzer, H.R. "Polly," 1902; Poole, Bob, 1961-62-63; *Poole, R.F. "Sarg," 1915-16; Pope, Brad, 1994-95; Pope, Jamie, 1979; Portas, Lou, 1964-65; Postell, Holland, 1995; *Potts, R.C. "Daddy " 1917-18-19; Poulos, John, 1944-47-48-49; *Pressley, E. H. "Buck," 1912-13; Pressley, O.K., 1926-27-28 (Capt.); *Pressley, Harlan, 1927; Price, John, 1970-71-72; Price, L.C., 1925; Priester, Buck, 1930-31; Priester, Buck, 1953-54-55; Priester, Raymond, 1994-95; Prince, Phil, 1944-46-47-48 (Co Capt.); Pringle, Harom, 1992-93; *Pritchett, Jess, 1937; Pruett, Chip, 1978-79; *Pruitt, June, 1945-46; *Proctor, Landrum, 1930-31; Puckett, David, 1988-89-90; Pusey, Mike, 1975; Putnam, Trevor, 1993-94-95.

Q Quarles, Jimmy, 1951-52; Quick, Rodney, 1983-84-85; Quinn, Dewey, 1945-46; Quesenbury, Sonny, 1957-58.

R Raber, Brian, 1983-84-85-86; *Radcliff, Charles, 1950-51-52; Radford, Kevin, 1980; Ramtahal, Eldred, 1992; *Randle, E.L. "Cat," 1913-14-15; *Randle, M.B. "Little Cat," 1918-19-20; Randolph, Bernard, 1993-95; Rankin, Gary, 1963-64; Rash, Dustin, 1993; Ratchford, Warren, 1974-76-77-78; Ray, Thomas, 1963-64-65; Rayburn, Lee, 1966-67-68; *Reams, T. Jack, 1918-22; Reed, David, 1978-79; Reese, Archie, 1974-75-76-77; Reese, Steve, 1982-83-84-85 (Capt.); Reeves, Marion, 1971-72-73; Reeves, Matt, 1992-93-94-95; Rembert, Johnny, 1981-82; *Reynolds, Clifford M. "Pete," 1926; Reynolds, Jim 1945-47-48-49; Rhinehart, Jim, 1955; Rhodes, Jim, 1971-72; Richard, Al, 1989-90-91-92; Richardson, Chuckle, 1980-82-83-84; Richardson, Cotton, 1943-44; *Richardson, Joe, 1940; Richardson, Mark, 1980-81-82; Riddle, Leonard, 1943; Ridgley, Thad, 1992-93; *Riggs, A.F., 1897-98-99; Riggs, Jim, 1983-84-85-86; Riggs, Matt, 1985-86-87; *Rion, Aubrey, 1939-40; Rivers, Dalton, 1955-56; Robbins, Butch, 1963-64; *Robbs, C.M., 1907-08-09 (Capt.); *Robinson, Charlie, 1922-23-24(Capt.); *Robinson, E.D., 1934; Robinson, James, 1979-80-82-83 (Capt.); *Robinson, Joe, 1927; Rodgers, George, 1950-51-52 (Co-Capt.); Rogers, Bill, 1943-46; Rogers, Billy G., 1944-46; Rogers, Floyd, 1965-66 (Capt.); *Rogers,

Johnny, 1929; *Rogers, Phil, 1965-66-67; Rogers, Rodney, 1961-62; Rogers, Shot, 1955-56; Rollins, Bubba, 1978; Rome, Stan, 1975; *Roper, T.H. "Pug," 1918-19; Rose, Anthony, 1979-80-81; Rose, Chuck, 1978-79-80; Ross, Don, 1952-53-54; Ross, Jack, 1942-46-47; *Rothell, Claude, 1941-42; Roulhac, Terrance, 1983-84-85-86; Rountree, Glenn, 1994-95; Rouse, Wardell, 1993-94; Rowell, Spivey, 1944; Roy, Wallace, 1923-24-25; Ruffner, Bo, 1965-66-67; Ruffner, Jim, 1964; Rushton, Gil, 1945-48-49-50; Russell, J.A., 1943; Russell, Jimmy, 1976; Rutledge, Bill, 1943; Ryans, Larry, 1989-90-91-92; Ryan, Steve, 1977-78.

S *Sadler, Hope, 1902 (Capt.), 03 (Capt.); Salisbury, Tom, 1943-44-47-48; Salley, Grady, 1928-29-30; Samnik, Mike, 1990-91; *Sams, Hal, 1916; *Sanders, Al, 1935-36-37; Sanders, Smiley, 1971-72-73; Sandifer, Red, 1940-41; Sanford, Chuck, 1983-84-85; Sapp, Patrick, 1992-93-94-95; Sasser, David, 1971-72-73; Saunders, Bo, 1945-46; Sauve, Jeff, 1991-92-94-95; Scheibel, Tim, 1994; *Schilletter, W.A. "Shorty ," 1911-12-13-14 (Capt.); *Schneck, J.R., 1918-19; Schonhar, Todd, 1985-86; *Schroder, F.E., 1912; Scott, Jim, 1981-82-83; Scott, Randy, 1975-76 (Co-Capt.) 1977, 1978 (Capt.); Scott, Shane, 1989-90-91; Scott, William, 1974-75; Scrudato, Ron, 1959-60-61; Sealy, Sonny, 1982; Sease, Jody, 1984-85; Sease, Tommy, 1955-56; Seay, Pitts, 1943; Seegars, Stacy, 1990-91-92-93; Seigler, Eddie, 1970-71-72; *Segars, Al, 1937; *Segars, Kent, 1936; Sellers, Joe, 1963-65; Setzekorn, Ken, 1984-85; Seyle, Rusty, 1986-87-88; Sharpe, Bill, 1964; Sharpe, Bob, 1938-39-40 (Capt.); Sharpe, Bob Jr., 1975-76; *Sharpe, F.J., 1931; Shaw, Milt, 1994; *Shealy, A.S. "Shack," 1896-97-98 (Capt.), 99; Shealy, Pat, 1971-72; Shell, Bob, 1970-72-73; Sheppard, Ashley, 1989-90-91-92 (Capt.); Shields, John, 1968-69; *Shingler, Lowndes 1958-59-60 (Co-Capt.); Shirley, Jim, 1950-51-52; Shish, Paul, 1969; *Shockley, J.A., 1922; Shore, Henry, 1933-34-35 (Capt.); Shown, Jack, 1952-53; Shuford, Don, 1934-35-36; *Siegel, Reuben, 1929-30-31; Seipe, Jeff, 1970-71-72; Silver, Dennis, 1974; Simmons, Anthony, 1995; *Simmons, T.D. "Shag," 1919; Simmons, Ralph, 1937; Simmons, Wayne, 1989-90-91-92 (Capt.); Simpson, Don, 1943; Simpson, LaMarick, 1992-93-94-95; Simpson, Tyrone, 1989-90-93; Sims, David, 1977-78-79-80; Sims, Marvin, 1977-78-79; *Sitton, Vet, 1902-03; Sizer, Danny, 1988-89-90; Skiffey, Jim, 1962; Smalls, Andy, 1950-52-53; Smart, Bill, 1944; Smith, Bill, 1977-78-79-81; Smith, Dennis, 1973-74-75 (Co- Capt.); Smith, Emory, 1993-94-95; Smith, Glenn, 1949-50-51; Smith, Gregg, 1976; Smith, Harold, 1959; Smith, Jack, 1958-59; Smith, Joey, 1979- 80; Smith, Lynn, 1979; Smith, Matt, 1977-78-79; Smith, Randy, 1965; Smith, Richard, 1985-86-97-88; Smith, Ronnie, 1974-75-76-77; Smith, Sterling, 1949-50; Smith, Terry, 1990-91-92-93; Smith, Thorny, 1968; Smith, Willie, 1954-55-57; *Snead, W.F. "Bill," 1901; *Snowden, Moon, 1927; Snyder, Paul, 1957-58-59 (Co-Capt.); Solomon, Louis, 1992-93-94-95; Soloman, Homer, 1930; Soowal, Jeff, 1976-77-78; Southerland, Ivan, 1967-68-69 (Capt.); *Sowell, Frank, 1930; Sox, Greg, 1986; *Spearman, Jack, 1920-21 (Capt.); Spector, Robbie, 1988-89-90; Speros, Jim -1980; Spiers, Bill, 1986; Spooner, Bob, 1955-56-57; Spry, David, 1983-85-86-87; Squires, Tappey, 1969; Stacey, Jack, 1942; Stanford, Calloway, 1940; Stephens, Darnell, 1991-92-93-94; Stephens, Tony, 1986-87; Stevens, Alex, 1932-33-34; *Stevens, R.G., 1909; *Stewart, J.D., 1924; Stewart, Watt, 1944; Stocks, Jeff, 1971-72-73; Stockstill, Jeff, 1980-81-82; Stone, Don, 1973; Stough, Tim, 1973-74-75-76; Strayer, Phil, 1969; Stribling, J.W., 1913-14-15; *Strother, Frank, 1923; Stuckey, Jim, 1976-77-78-79; Sublette, Dick, 1948; *Suggs, H.L., 1914-15; *Sullivan, Frank, 1897-98-99; Sultis, Jim, 1945-46-47; *Summers, J.C. "Chuck," 1905-06; Sursavage, Butch, 1965-66-67; Sursavage, Jim, 1968-69-70 (Capt.); Suttle, Jeff, 1980-81-82-83; Sutton, George, 1962; *Sweatte, Johnny, 1941;

*Swetenburg, J.R., 1920-21; Swift, Bob, 1963; Swing, Dale, 1982-83-84; Swofford, Bob, 1927-28-29; *Swygert, George, 1896-97.

T Talley, J.H., 1926; Taylor, Bruce, 1990; Taylor, Jeff, 1989; *Taylor, Jerry, 1961-62; Taylor, J.W., 1943; Taylor, Vince, 1986-87-88-89; Temples, Jamison, 1992; *Tennant, A.B. "Dutch," 1921-22-23-24; Testerman, Don, 1974-75; *Thackston, L.P., 1917-18-19; Thomas, Bill, 1956-57-58 (Capt.); Thomas, David, 1972; Thomas, Doug, 1987-88-89-90; Thomas, Franklin, 1992-93; Thomason, Johnny, 1955; Thompson, Dave, 1968-69-70; *Thompson, Doug, 1955; *Thompson, J.W., 1916; Thompson, Marion, 1950-51-52; Thompson, Oscar, 1946-47-48; Thornton, Mark, 1978-79; *Thornton, R.E., 1918; Thorsland, Oscar, 1960-61-62; Thurman, Cardell, 1992; Tice, Johnny, 1954; *Tillman, Henry, 1902; Tillotson, Brian, 1994; Timmerman, W.P. "Pap," 1926-27; *Timmons, Charlie, 1939-40-41; Tinsley, Sid, 1940-41-44 (Alt. Capt.); Tisdale, Charlie, 1938-39-40; Todd, Moe, 1969; Tolley, Charlie, 1967-69 (Capt.); *Tomkins, F.G., 1896; Tomkins, James, 1966-67-68; Trapp, James, 1989-90-91-92; Trayham, Arden, 1943; Treadwell, David, 1985-86-87; *Trembley, Jimmy, 1969; Trexler, Bru, 1937-39; Trimble, Jamie, 1994-95; Triplett, Danny, 1979-80-81-82; *Trobaugh, Allen, 1938; *Trobaugh, Earl, 1938; Troy, Mike, 1963-64; Trumpore, Arthur, 1943; *Troutman, John, 1933-34-35; Tucker, Richard, 1988; *Turbeville, A.C., 1912; Turbeville, Horace, 1956; Turner, Bo, 1945-46; *Turner, H.M. "Tuck," 1907; *Turnipseed, Rhett, 1922; Turpin, Bucky, 1966-67; Tuten, Rich, 1976-77-78; Tuttle, Perry, 1978-79-80-81 (Capt.); Tyler, O.J., 1974-76; Tyner, Mitch, 1973-74.

U Underwood, Willie, 1977-78-79-80 (Capt.); Usher, Lewis, 1991-92-93-94; Usry, George, 1957-58-59.

V *Valentine, Jack, 1926; Varn, Guy, 1983; Varn, Rex, 1976-77-78; Vaughan, Mark, 1985; *Veronee, Jack, 1959-60-61; *Vogel, R.T., 1896-97.

W Wade, Connie, 1966-67; Wade, Don, 1950-51-52; *Wade, Grady, 1920; Wade, Mike, 1981; Wagner, Larry, 1958; Waldrep, Joe, 1964-65; Waldrep, Perry, 1967; Walker, Duane, 1984-85-86-87; Walker, Henry, 1946-47; *Walker, John E., 1923-24-25; *Walker, Norman, 1897-98-99 (Capt.); 1900 (Capt.); *Walker, R.H., 1909-10; *Wall, J.E., 1926; Wall, Pete, 1953-55; Wallace, Nelson, 1973-74-75-76; Walls, Henry, 1983-84-85; Walters, Henry, 1970-71; Walters, Joey, 1974-75-76 (Co-Capt.); Ward, Billy, 1962-63-64; Ward, Damond, 1995; Ward, Jimmy, 1950-51-52; Ware, Billy, 1966-67-68; *Warr, Elza, 1926-27; *Warren, George, 1906-07; Washington, Jay, 1972-73; Waters, Charlie, 1967-68-69; Watson, Ben, 1969-70; *Watson, Charles, 1933-34; Watson, John, 1985; Watson, "Speedy," 1994-95; Watson, Ronald, 1981-82-83-84; Watts, Waldo, 1969-70; Weaver, Billy, 1962-63; *Webb, Clare "Tanny," 1911-12-13-14; Webb, Gary, 1976-77-78; *Webb, H.B., 1922; Webb, Hugh, 1940; Webb, Jack, 1957-58; *Webb, Mike, 1904; Webb, Travers, 1973-75-76-77; Weddington, Rick, 1976-77; Weeks, Jimmy, 1975-76-77; Weeks, Scott, 1981; Welchel, Ken, 1976-77; *Welch, Maxcey, 1930; Welch, Nelson, 1991-92-93-94; Wells, Jeff, 1980-82-83-84; Wells, Jim, 1976-77; Wells, Jimmy, 1951-52-53; Wells, Joel, 1954-55-56 (Alt. Capt.); Werner, Chuck, 1966-68-69; Werntz, Eddie, 1960-61-62; *Werts, Rufus, 1931-32; Wertz, J.B., 1922-23; Wessinger, Ron, 1989; West, Calvin, 1959-60-61; West, Fernandez, 1988-89; West, Ron, 1978; White, Clyde, 1952-53-54 (Capt.); White, Harvey, 1957-58-59 (Co-Capt.); *White, J.D., 1896; White, Raymond, 1994-95; *White, W.P., 1908-09; Whitley, Curtis, 1988-90-91; Whitmire, Jim, 1943-46-47-48; Whitten, Red, 1952-53-54; *Wiehl, E.M., 1916; Wiggins, Don, 1969-70; Wiggs, Milton, 1945; *Wild, Ormond, 1953; *Wiles, Bill, 1935-36-37; *Wilhite, F. T. "Rusty," 1921; Williams, Bobby, 1947-48-49; *Williams, Bratton, 1923-24; Williams, Braxton, 1982-83; Williams, Brett, 1993-94-95; *Williams, Jack, 1920-21-22; Williams, Jerome, 1986-89; Williams,

Keith, 1983-84-85; *Williams, M.H., 1917-19; *Williams, Pat, 1985-86-87-88; Williams, Paul, 1978; Williams, Perry, 1983-84-85-86; Williams, Ray, 1983-84-85-86; Williams, Rodney, 1985-86-87-88 (Capt.); Williams, Ronald, 1990-91-92; Williams, Scott, 1981-82-83-84; *Williams, Tommie, 1904; Williams, Tommy, 1953-54; Williams, Toney, 1976-77-78; Williams, Undre, 1994-95; Williamson, Jimmy, 1972-74-75 (Co-Capt.); Willimon, Gene, 1932-33; Wills, Albert, 1950; *Willis, Don, 1936-37-38; Wilson, C. C. "Red," 1921-22-23-24; Wilson, C. Mond, 1994-95; Wilson, Jim, 1959; Wilson, Mac, 1969-70-71; Wilson, Pierre -1990-91-92-93; Wilson, Ralph, 1944; *Windham, E. E., 1907; Windham, Kermit, 1936; Wingo, Bill, 1973-74-75-76; Winslow, Charles, 1992-93-94-95; Wirth, Frank, 1969-71-72 (Capt.); Wise, Frank, 1972-73-74-75; *Withers, George, 1950-51-52; Witherspoon, Derrick, 1990-91-92-93; *Witsell, F.L. "Fish," 1915-16-17 (Capt.); Wood,

Benji, 1994; Woodruff, Foggy, 1928-29-30; *Woods, Charlie, 1936-37-38 (Capt.); *Woods, Footsie, 1941-45; Woods, Joe, 1995; *Woods, Smith, 1903; *Woodward, Henry, 1932-33-34; Wya (Capt.); *Woodward, H.M. "Jake," 1900-09-10; Woolford, Donnell, 1985-86-87-88 (Capt.); *Wray, A.F. "Bull," 1921-22; Wray, Jack, 1924-25; Wright, Charlie, 1940-41-42 (Capt.); Wright, Tom, 1940-41; Wrightenberry, Earl, 1950-51-52; Wurst, Jim, 1980-81-82; Wyatt, Antwuan, 1993-94-95; Wyatt, Charlie -1952-53; Wyatt, Rick, 1977-78-79; *Wyndham, Wyndy, 1948-49-50; Wynn, Stephon, 1991-93-94; Wyse, Fred, 1935-36-37.

Y *Yarborough, Mule -1929-30; Yarbrough, Al, 1933-34-35; Yauger, Ray, 1968-69-70; Yeomans, Ken, 1980; Young, Eric, 1977-78-79; Young, Will, 1993-94-95; Yow, Ken, 1983.

Z Zager, Emil, 1958; *Zeigler, F.M., 1920-21-22; Zeiler, David, 1994.

TRIVIA ANSWERS

1. Bob Smith in 1954.
2. Ralph Jenkins (1943-44-45) and Randy Scott (1976-77-78).
3. The Tigers defeated Furman 14-6 on October 31, 1896.
4. Charlie Timmons scored a second quarter TD to give Clemson a 6-3 win over Boston College in the 1940 Cotton Bowl.
5. Tiger quarterback Harvey White prior to the 1960 season.
6. Don Kelley and John McMakin.
7. Minnesota defeated the Tigers 20-13 in the 1985 Independence Bowl.
8. Arkansas.
9. Seven (1948, 1978, 1981, 1987, 1988, 1989, 1990).
10. Tommy Kendrick and Rodney Williams.
11. Alabama defeated the Tigers 74-7 in 1931.
12. The Sugar Bowl on January 1, 1959, and The Bluebonnet Bowl on December 19, 1959.
13. A. B. Shealy coached Clemson to a 3-3-1 record in 1904 and was the captain of the 1898 team that was 3-1.
14. Harvey White led both in 1957.
15. Buddy Gore had 1,045 yards in 1967.
16. Nelson Welch in 1991 and 1992.
17. Southern Cal who defeated the Tigers 30-0 in 1966.
18. Guard Harry Olszewski.
19. Don Willis in 1938 by the New York Giants.
20. Banks McFadden with the Brooklyn Dodgers in 1940.
21. Patrick Sapp threw 55 passes against Maryland in 1992.
22. DeChane Cameron scored on a 62-yard run against California in the 1992 Citrus Bowl.
23. Bill Mathis with the New York Jets in Super Bowl III (1969).
24. Phil Rogers caught 11 passes against North Carolina in 1965.
25. Levon Kirkland.
26. Jeff Bryant (1981), Jim Riggs (1985-86), Rob Bodine (1990-91).
27. 1966 when Clemson defeated Duke 9-6 on ABC-TV.
28. Richie Luzzi.
29. Don Wade.
30. Steve Satterfield.
31. Maryland has 10 wins.

32. Gary Barnes.
33. The Tigers have defeated South Carolina 55 times.
34. Lou Cordileone in 1959.
35. South Carolina tied the Tigers 14-14 on Big Thursday.
36. Sterling Smith.
37. Fred Cone ('49 Gator and '51 Orange), Cliff Austin ('78 Gator and '82 Orange), Terry Allen ('88 Citrus and '89 Citrus), Joe Henderson ('88 Citrus and '89 Gator).
38. Chester McGlockton both caused and recovered the fumble.
39. Miami, Fla., in the 1951 Orange Bowl and the 1952 Gator Bowl.
40. Harvey White (1957-58-59), Lowndes Shingler (1958-59-60), Joe Anderson (1960-61-62).
41. Lester Brown scored 102 in 1979 and Chris Gardocki 107 in 1989.
42. Tailback Jacky Jackson.
43. Ed Bost.
44. Dwight Clark of the San Francisco 49ers.
45. Bennie Cunningham in 1976.
46. Lou Cordileone.
47. Charlie Waters.
48. B. C. "Stumpy" Banks lettered in 1915-16-17-18-19, serving as team captain in 1918-19, and coached backs in 1920-21.
49. Clemson defeated Missouri 34-0 on September 30, 1950.
50. Fullback Doug Cline.
51. Jeff Davis.
52. John McMakin caught 40 in 1970.
53. Rick Stockstill whose younger brother Jeff was a Tiger wide receiver in 1980-81-82.
54. Offensive Guard Eric Harmon started 47 games in 1987-88-89-90.
55. Tackle Dick Marazza in 1955.
56. Don King.
57. Terrence Flagler had 1,258 yards in 1986.
58. Cliff Austin had 260 yards against Duke in 1982.
59. Steve Fuller.
60. Obed Ariri and Chris Gardocki shared the old record with 63.
61. Chris Gardocki with 72.
62. Glenn Smith with 18.
63. Fred Knoebel.
64. Dale Hatcher in 1981-82-83-84.
65. Mike Eppley in 1983.
66. Jerry Butler in 1978 and Perry Tuttle in 1980.